The Crooked Stick

WEAPONS IN HISTORY

The
Crooked
Stick

A History of the Longbow

Hugh D. H. Soar

WESTHOLME
Yardley

All rights reserved under International and Pan-American Copyright
Conventions.
Published by Westholme Publishing, LLC, Eight Harvey Avenue, Yardley,
Pennsylvania 19067.

10 9 8 7 6 5 4 3 2 1
First Printing

ISBN 1-59416-002-3

www.westholmepublishing.com

Printed in Canada on acid-free paper.

In memory of Muriel Gladys Soar (1900–1937), whose dreams I have strived to realize.

Contents

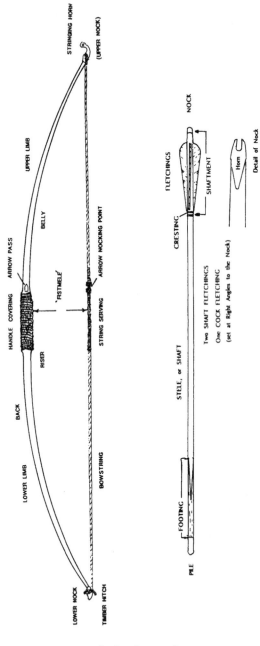

Parts of a longbow and arrow

Introduction

England were but a fling,
But for the crooked stick and the gray goose wing.—Old adage

This is the story of that crooked stick: a euphemistic title for the most ancient and charismatic of standoff weapons—the traditional English war bow. Sculpted from slow-grown forest yew, it was the medieval master of Continental battlefields. Its companion arrow was the English battle shaft, slim and deadly, feathered from the gray goose wing.

Why crooked? This reflects the irregular contours of the yew tree from which it is fashioned. Though a gnarled tree, it is one preferred above all others by bow makers throughout the ages. It is a name evocative of nature's shape. But why yew? What is the special quality possessed by the genus *Taxus*? Why did early humans favor it when other woods were closer at hand and easier to work? To answer that, we must understand the nature of the weapon.

A bow relies upon two necessary features for its power: the qualities of tension and compression. These come from the essential springiness of the timber used in bow construction, which gives it the ability to keep its original shape. This, in a word, is its elasticity. All woods possess these properties to some degree, but yew is the king of the forest. Not all of its many variants are suitable (there are over 170 yew cultivars), but the European *Taxus baccata* and the North American *Taxus brevifolia* fit the bowyer's needs. Although notoriously difficult to work because of its often tortuous grain, yew has an elasticity superior to all other timber; and from prehistory until modern times, it was used by choice where it could be obtained.

The traditional recreational longbow, dismissed by some technophiles as the stick bow, is formed of two limbs, the lower of which is shorter than the upper to balance the arcs of force, with a handle section from which each limb tapers evenly to its tip. At these tips are grooves into which the bowstring fits; often, although not always, these grooves are cut into a protective sheath of horn that is commonly called the nock. The word comes from the Dutch and was used originally to describe that end of a yardarm on a sailing vessel where it slotted against the mast.[1]

The bow maker shapes the limbs so that in cross section they resemble a D. The curved part of the D we call the belly, and the flat part is known as the back. The belly faces toward the archer when the bow is to be shot. Cross sections may also be elliptical, triangular, or rectangular depending upon the function of the bow or even the whim of the maker. We will meet them all in the course of this book.

With the bow comes its essential component: the bowstring, which is formed with an upper loop and a lower tail secured by a timber hitch. In prehistoric times, this string would have been fashioned of plaited grass, woven tree bast, or sinew; later, of hemp or retted nettle; later still, as things evolved, of linen thread or silk. Central whipping, or serving, on the bowstring offered protection from the wear of arrow notches.

And what of the arrow? The flint-tipped hunting shaft of early humans became the armor-piercing English battle shaft—the "gray goose wing" of history—fletched with strong goose feathers to serve the mighty English war bow. For peaceful pleasure, there was the target arrow, fletched with peacock or turkey feathers for butt, clout, or roving. Shafts, or steles, were often footed with tougher wood for strength; their string notches, or nocks, fashioned of horn or cut directly into the wood and strengthened by a horn wedge, or nockpiece. Beneath the nock, upon the shaftment, three feathers were glued and bound, each set at 120 degrees to the other, with the cock feather directly below the nock.[2] Below these, a mark, or cresting, would be set to identify the owner. Each arrow had its purpose; we will meet them all. But there is much to be told, so let us begin.

We can have no idea of how, or indeed why, the principle of shooting with a bow was first discovered and then used. We may surmise however. Did it begin with a throwing stick and a fletched dart—the Mexican native's atlatl? That is certainly a possibility. Was it an adaptation of a fishing pole? Perhaps. Or again, could it have been a development from a static animal trap? Who can say? It is enough that its roots lie deeply embedded in the past, and there perforce we must let them lie.

Fancy may run riot here untouched by either fact or, indeed, artifact, for nothing survives to provide us with a clue. However, evidence for bow use is suggested by early rock drawings.[3] These show animals driven toward a group of archers who are busily engaged in their culling; and what seems probable is that by the late Stone Age, a simple bow for this purpose had emerged in common use.

Humans had discovered that by converting muscular potential to kinetic energy, one could influence the order of things. This was partly for the better, for hunting with bow and arrow was both efficient of power and effective of purpose; but it was also partly for the worse, since with this new standoff weapon would come a revolution in warfare and from it, with awesome certainty, would come the intercontinental ballistic missile. Within this book will be found dimension and technical detail side by side with accounts of the longbow's purpose and use through the ages.

We move on. The Bronze Age may seem to lack examples of the usage of the bow, perhaps for socioeconomic reasons, as civilizations and religious beliefs with their implied stability became more sophisticated. The succeeding Iron Age, however, with its great migrations has provided bounty in plenty. From Oberflacht in Germany have come weapons with curiously deep handles used by the Alammanic peoples, while Nydam, a site in southern Sweden, has provided fine examples of war bows and arrows that were the forerunners of the Saxon's hunting bow.

While the Saxons used their weapon for hunting and personal protection, it seems to have played little part in warfare. Their military ethic required reliance upon the shield wall and personal combat to decide battles. Only occasionally do the Saxon bowmen emerge from the shadows and just as silently slip away. Not so their Norman enemy. The battle of Hastings on England's south coast in 1066 saw the clash of two disparate military ideologies.[4] The combination of the standoff capability of massed archery and the arrow storm used tactically in support of cavalry on that October day ultimately proved successful against the dogged Saxon defensive shield wall. The presence of archery as a decisive tactical force in future set-piece battles had been assured.

Although, as we believe, the bow was developed primarily for hunting purposes, it is in its role as a weapon of war that we know it best. Great battles were fought (some lost, but many won), and history was made through its powerful limbs and the stolid determination of those who tamed it. These were individuals of whom one Philip de Commines, who had occasion to meet with them "professionally," wrote, *"Milices redoubtable! La fleur des archiers du monde."*[5]

But for all its warlike vigor, the bow has a gentler side. Few weapons match it for the pleasure it brings in this civil role. Monarch and commoner alike have recognized its power or used it to relax from life's stresses. Notable among English royalty who did so were Henry III, whose statute in 1251 required his citizens to muster with bows and arrows; Edward III and Henry V, who used them to such military effect; and Henry VIII, who, by the excellence of his example, encouraged his subjects to develop their skills with bow and arrow and who inspired the formation of archery societies at which people honed their skills.[6]

Then there was Edward VI, whose careful practice is meticulously noted in his diary.[7] Although the reign of his half-sister, Elizabeth I, saw the decline and finally the demise of the bow as a warrior's weapon, she was taught the pleasure of shooting the bow as a young woman by Roger Ascham, whose 1544 treatise *Toxophilus* remains a vade mecum, a handy reference book, for traditional archers today. Most notable of all perhaps was Charles II, who took pleasure in shooting the longbow while exiled on the Continent; his encouragement of it upon restoration of the monarchy led directly to its revival for recreation.

It is from this revival that today's traditional archery stems. There is a relearning of the old skills as aspirant bowyer and fletcher alike seek to replicate both the recreational weapon and war bow. We have British and American bowmen and women shooting their York, Hereford, and Columbia target rounds at 100, 80, and 60 yards; straining to reach the nine-score clout; or roving over vast heath moors. We have American bow hunters harvesting their prey with simple stick and string. We have English field archers roaming native woods as their ancestors did so many years ago. Each is at one with nature; each takes pleasure from the past.

It is the purpose of this book to draw these strings together and, in so doing, to advertise the pain and the pleasure inherent in shooting the "crooked stick" and the "gray goose wing." Read on and enjoy.

1) *The Early Days*

Matters were not easy for our early ancestors. It was their fate to be at once both predator and prey. At best, this was an unattractive lifestyle and one fraught with inevitable uncertainty and danger; at worst, it was short and brutal. It is no small wonder that the ability to control events from a comparatively safe distance appealed, and a sharpened stick became essential personal furniture for early Homo sapiens. The gift of life or the certainty of death lay quite literally with the pliancy of a length of pointed wood.

Used for hunting, warfare, and personal protection, the spear evolved from a close-range stabbing weapon to one capable of being thrown with accuracy, marking the nascence of a more ordered existence. From this spear, by now armed with flint shards to kill or wound, emerged eventually the arrow—at first itself a throwing weapon fletched with feathers for stability in flight. Following it, perhaps millennia later, came that most sophisticated of all primitive technology, the bow. This was a device of much social significance, since through its accuracy and power, meat might be more readily won, allowing time for activities beyond the hunt as well as providing a potential surplus with which to help the weaker members of the group. In order to understand and appreciate the significance of the longbow as a device, it will be most useful and appropriate to review the history of bows as best we can from the archaeological records, and we will now endeavor to do so.

While the origin of the bow is lost in the mists of time and speculation must inevitably rule, there are cave paintings in Spain and France from Paleolithic times that depict animals wounded seemingly by either arrows or light spears fitted with vanes. From le Mas d'Azil in eastern France comes a picture that might just provide us with clues. Scratched on a piece of bone, it is a picture of a man holding a stick in one hand with the other extended backward. From its appearance the stick may have been intended to represent a bow [1]

There is of course no certainty that these missiles depicted in cave paintings were propelled by a bow, since none is shown, so the throwing stick must therefore remain a strong alternative. However, if the purpose of the paintings was to show those parts of the animal most susceptible to injury—and, we may presume, death—then this suggests precision and some degree of accuracy. Precision points toward control, and an arrow is arguably more accurate than a thrown spear. It is thus conceivable that the drawings may reflect the intended outcome of hunting with bow and arrow. This is a tenuous speculation though, and one that academically at least, we may reluctantly have to abandon. The paintings are enigmatic and suggestive of archery but no more than that. However, before we put them behind us, we should note that they do show one thing clearly: the use of vanes to stabilize flight. Whether or not they made and used the bow, Paleolithic humans in Europe had acquired at least a rudimentary knowledge of aerodynamics. They knew a thing or two, those Paleolithic people did.

By its nature, wood decays. This much is obvious. But by happy chance, during the archaeological excavation of an important and rewarding Mesolithic site at Stellmoor in Schleswig-Holstein, Germany, parts of two bow limbs together with many arrow shafts, some with their stone points still attached, have been found.[2] Although less than 10 inches in length, these fragmentary pieces of pine (*Pinus silvestris*) display a cross section common not only to later prehistoric weapons but also to the D-shaped cross section of the traditional longbow of today. The thickest part of the back (the part of the weapon that faces forward when the bow is drawn up), is flat; and the belly (the part that faces toward the archer), is rounded. As the limb tapers toward its tip, the cross section becomes triangular. It has also been shown that the limbs were not from a light self-sapling but cut deliberately from a comparatively thick log. Whether it came from branch or bole of tree cannot now be determined, but it is notable that even by this early period in time, the splitting of a log to obtain a suitable stave had been both understood and practiced.

This design shows a basic understanding of the theoretical principal of bow making—one accomplished, we may fairly assume, by trial and error. The proportionate distribution of tensile and compressive strength through a cambered section with a broadly equal width-to-depth ratio, a configuration deemed necessary for optimum power—or, to give it a modern title, "cast"— had been accomplished by the shaping of the Stellmoor bow stave.[3]

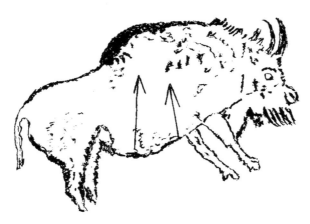

Paleolithic engraving cut into a clay cave floor at Niaux, southeastern France, perhaps indicating places on an animal vulnerable to missiles. After Tucker, *Journal of the Society of Archer Antiquaries* 35, (1992).

The Stellmoor bows are of heartwood alone, the sapwood having been discarded. This detail suggests a lack of appreciation of sapwood's property, since when used along the length of a bow and in conjunction with heartwood, it provides that tensile strength necessary to balance the compressive property of the harder heartwood. While this may be so, the outer sapwood layer of pine—that just beneath the bark—is soft and spongy and quite unsuited to providing tensile strength. The fact that sapwood does not appear in this fashion on prehistoric bows of pine is thus not necessarily an indictment of the maker's skill; it may be merely a proper recognition of the tree's shortcoming and the probable lack of other more suitable material. Pine is not an ideal bow wood; its elasticity is inferior even to elm and particularly so to yew. But later archaeological finds are uniform in the lack of sapwood being used for its tension qualities by ancient bow makers, even in bows made of yew whose sapwood is hard enough to be shaped and can form an important part of the finished bow. It appears that an understanding of the tensile property possessed by sapwood would not become part of general bow making until the latter part of the first millennium AD.

Before leaving Stellmoor, we should say a word about the hundred or more arrows—or more exactly, the pieces of arrow shafting—found at this important archaeological site. Largely made of pine or ash, many are identified as foreshafts. This is an archaeologist's word; let us call them by a fletcher's name. We would say "footings." These footings were shaped to dovetail into the shaft or stele and were the disposable business end of the arrow. If broken by impact, they were replaceable, thus saving the labor of creating a whole new arrow. Some fragments were seemingly near complete however. The longest, at 29 1/2 inches, would match today's arrows and compare with the 31 1/2-inch length of the late medieval English battle shaft.

Moving forward in time, evidence for bow making in the late Mesolithic to early Neolithic period comes from another important European archaeological site, Holmegaard, on the Danish island of Zealand. But here there is an important distinction. While the Stellmoor bows, or the fractions of them that remain, show resemblance to what we are accustomed to call a conventional longbow cross section, those at Holmegaard are of different material and, with a broad-limbed, low width-to-depth ratio, are significantly different in form. Occasionally known as paddle bows from their distinctive shape—and even cataloged occasionally as paddles in the past by archaeologists unversed in bowyery—today we would call them flat bows and add that they were low cambered.[4]

There is a further distinction. Pine was used at Stellmoor, but although this was present at Holmegaard, elm (*Ulmus glabra*)—a recognized bow wood well into historic times and perhaps even used to make the forerunner of the English war bow—was selected in preference by the Holmegaard bow makers. With these distinctive bows were found broken arrow shafts of guelder rose (*Viburnum opulus*)—one a formidable 36 inches in length, missing only its tip—plus several footings. Also reported is a shaft with a thickened blunt head used possibly for taking small game. Such so-called blunts were in common use during later historic times.

The Holmegaard bow was a well-proportioned weapon believed originally to have been 71 inches in length with a markedly inset and shaped handle, which may have once been bound, and broad limbs that taper toward their tips. Although not of conventional high-cambered longbow design, these low-cambered, broad-limbed paddle bows existed simultaneously, suggesting the development of parallel and perhaps even conflicting bow-making traditions in prehistoric times. This variance of design that continued well into the Neolithic era is conveniently exemplified by three specimens found in England's West Country: a paddle bow from Meare Heath, Somerset, and a high-cambered stick bow from nearby Ashcott Heath, each of which carbon date to the mid-third millennium BC, as well as a later high-cambered example recovered from a Somerset peat bog at Edington Burtle that dates from the second millennium BC.[5]

It is appropriate here to look more closely at the construction of each of these three weapons, since they demonstrate a divergence in the understand-

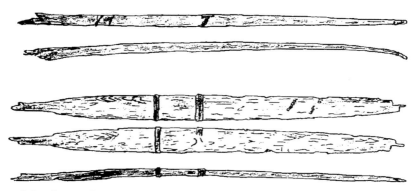

Neolithic bows of yew, carbon dated to 2600 BC, recovered from peat bogs in Aschcott Heath (upper) and Meare Heath (lower). After J. G. D. Clark, "Neolithic Bows from Somerset, England," *Prehistoric Society Proceedings* 29, (1963).

ing of the importance of profile and section; and we'll start by examining the one from Meare Heath, since it exemplifies the early distinction between the paddle and the stick bow, between limbs with high and low width-to-depth ratios. Of the Meare Heath weapon, just one limb and part of the handle measuring about 39 inches remains. The material is yew. Whether this was the upper or the lower limb there is no evidence to say. Assuming that a significant portion of the handle remains and that limbs were symmetrical, the overall length may have been between 71 and 75 inches—a lengthy weapon by any standard. The limb cross section increases from 1 1/8 inches wide at the handle to a maximum of 2 7/8 inches from whence it tapers to the nock groove. A cross section at the handle would show a convex face over a keel, or ridge. One drawn at mid-limb would show opposing convex faces, while toward the limb end, the faces are plano-convex. This is curious and a departure from the norm if one compares it to a longbow form. Observation of the string groove and the incurved handle that faces inward suggests that this weapon was shot with the convex face—normally the belly—facing outward.

The limb end is shaped to take the string groove, while string wear shows it to have been drawn, thereby presumably making it a working weapon. That the owner held it in some esteem we may conclude from its decoration. Two surviving transverse bands of ox-hide leather remain of the original eight or nine, and these were supplemented by thongs—perhaps of leather or sinew—bound in crisscross fashion across the limb. There are cuts on the limb adjacent to the transverse bands, suggesting some unexpected carelessness in the tidying process. Below the nock is evidence for a binding of thin thread, perhaps to support a potentially weakened area or perhaps for additional decoration.

It is certainly an interesting weapon and one that has been replicated several times more or less accurately for experimental purposes. Perhaps the most notable of these, and certainly one that attracted most attention at the time, is that made from 1:1 drawings by Mr. E. C. Lilley of Cambridge University Museum of Archaeology and Ethnology.[6] In 1963, this was shot at a major archery tournament at Dunster in England's West Country by the then-reigning national longbow champion, Mr. H. A. (Bert) Oram. With his third shot, Bert hit the boss at 60 yards to the acclamation, if not the surprise, of his watching fellow bowmen. For the record, Dunster lies just 30 miles from Meare. Here is a bow that even in its present condition, and after almost 5,000 years, still stamps its authority on the world of archery and compels respect both for the bow maker who toiled to produce it and the archer of rank who owned it.

The Ashcott Heath specimen, of which only one limb survives, is also of yew. It is broadly comparable in date to its close neighbor—Meare Heath and Ashcott Heath are contiguous—but has a width-to-depth ratio and a D section broadly conventional to stick bows or longbows. Assuming symmetry of limbs, extrapolation suggests a length of some 62 1/2 inches. The surviving limb tip shows a slight recurve, which may or may not be natural, and a string groove indicates that the belly was held toward the archer. As with other Neolithic bows, although of yew, but for reasons that are not evident today, the sapwood has been removed. Perhaps because sapwood is vulnerable to damage and its tensile properties had yet to be appreciated.[7] Though the Ashcott Heath bow is an essentially functional weapon, unlike its neighbor, it is undecorated.

Somerset is rich in peat, and peat is an excellent preserver of arboreal matter. It is not surprising therefore that a third bow has been recovered from a peat heath at nearby Edington Burtle, and this also has one or two interesting secrets to reveal. It has been carbon dated to around 1320 BC and thus antedates its companions by a millennium. It was originally uncovered over 150 years ago and not finally examined until the beginning of the last century. Although complete, it is severely warped and is believed to have shrunk from its original length; it now measures 59 inches and is thus shorter by some 3 inches than its closest neighbor, the Ashcott Heath example.

Its section is concave-convex, the back of the bow having a concave channel running its length, a feature that will be later noticed in certain modern bows. There is little lateral or longitudinal taper between handle and limb ends. The limb tips are dissimilar, the upper terminating in a knob, or button, and the lower in a tapered rattail end. In comparison with its limbs, the handle section narrows in width from 1 3/4 inches to 1 inch but deepens from 3/4 inch to 1 inch. The yew wood has been carefully worked, and pins and knots, which are potential areas of weakness, have been left proud of the limb, or raised, in the best bowyery traditions. Curiously, however, the limbs are asymmetrical, the lower being some 6 inches longer than the upper, suggesting that if the bow maker intended the weapon to come around in proper compass (to bend in a true arc), the upper was the stiffer part, and the lower was longer to compensate. Alternatively, a fracture of this limb may have resulted in major reworking. From its dimensions, the weapon was seemingly comparatively light in draw weight, which would have been adequate for short-distance hunting and perhaps personal protection.

It is appropriate here to notice prehistoric variations in arrangements for holding the bowstring in place. In both late historic and more particularly modern times, it has been regular practice for limb ends to be protected, usually (although not exclusively) by horn, while accommodating the string in a groove. This was practical in purpose, and they were carefully and sometimes exquisitely carved and shaped. This practice was slow to arrive however; the functionally motivated prehistoric bow maker invariably employed a different method. Sometimes a no-nonsense notch was cut directly into the wood. Today's bowyer would call this a self-nock. Sometimes a shoulder shaped from the limb's tip was made over which a loop or knot could rest. Occasionally neither was employed; a concave indentation on either side of the limb tip could serve to hold the knotted string, or even, as in the Edington Burtle example, a rather basic tapered rattail end could be used.

With the outstanding exception of the Meare Heath bow, which stands alone among its peers for its essentially decorative feature of crisscross banding, and the strange buttonlike excrescence at the upper limb tip of the Edington Burtle example, which may just be a raised pin, of decoration there was none in those early times. While early bows were simple staves and straight of limb, as time passed and knowledge was gained, so profiles changed. The late Dr. Gad Rausing of Sweden, who with Professor J. G. D. Clark of England was eminent in the study of early weapons, identified five distinct bow profiles as follows.

A bow whose stave forms a more-or-less even curve is called a segment-shaped bow. Today we would call it a self-bow that comes around in compass. A bow whose handle and tips, together with a significant part of each limb, are inflexible so that two curves are formed at its extremities is called a doubly convex bow. There is no modern equivalent of this profile. A bow whose limbs are in a straight line and angled toward the body is called an angular bow. There is no modern equivalent of this. A bow whose limbs are swung toward the string is called a doubly concave bow. In its unbraced state, we would say that this bow is duoflexed. A bow whose handle lies behind the plane attained by the back of the limbs of the bow when braced is called a bow with setback, or sunk, handle. We would describe such a bow as recurved, or perhaps colloquially as a Cupid's bow. Of these, just the first two are definable as being of longbow style and profile. The others belong to the East and beyond a passing mention, are no part of this study.[8]

As knowledge developed, sectional variation occurred. A curious example of regional peculiarity comes from some Neolithic stick bows made in the Alpine region of what is now Switzerland. Certain of these are distinguished by a lengthwise concave groove cut into their backs—a peculiarity with no immediately obvious purpose, although one that is found from time to time elsewhere. This feature, which occurs on certain ethnic bows, is briefly discussed by Charles John Longman, coauthor of the *Badminton Library: Archery* and a nineteenth-century archer of consequence, whose collection forms an important part of the Pitt-Rivers Museum of Ethnography in Oxford, England.[9] While not suggesting that this is necessarily the purpose of the groove on prehistoric European weapons, Longman notes the Tongan Islanders practice of carrying an arrow on an unbraced bow, bound in a similar groove. While recognizing the obvious disadvantage of maintaining the integrity of an arrow shaft on a bow that has subsequently become permanently bent, the feature is nevertheless there; it exists, and it would be a foolish person who dismissed a potential purpose out of hand.

A more likely purpose may relate to hunting or even to warfare. A rock painting from the Cueva de la Araña near Valencia, Spain, clearly shows archers hunting animals, probably ibex, with bow drawn and one arrow nocked, while holding another arrow or, in some cases, more than one against the bow limb ready for instant use.[10] A concave back to the bow into which an arrow might fit would avoid it twisting while held by the bow hand and be a helpful aid. A similar painting from Las Dogues, Castellón de la Plaña, also in eastern Spain, depicting two groups of men in combat shows several similarly equipped. It may be that one arrow in the bow and one held in readiness was standard practice for our prehistoric bowmen ancestors. Those concave-backed bows were perhaps a solution to an arrow slipping from the vertical at an inconvenient time. Conversely, a rock painting at nearby Cueva de los Caballos of archers facing a herd of driven animals clearly shows unused arrows lying on the ground, suggesting that there were occasions when this practice was not followed. Nineteenth-century European and Scottish bows constructed with this concave section were intended for specific recreational purposes such as *tir a la perche* or "papingo" shooting and can occasionally be found.

Early Neolithic rock painting. Cueva de la Araña, Valencia, east Spain. It shows bowmen chasing deer. Notice the replacement arrows carried on the bow in readiness.

Discovered recently on Salisbury Plain, not far from the megalithic monument Stonehenge, was the grave of an archer of the early Bronze Age. Among the abundance of grave goods found in this most important of discoveries were 17 flint arrowheads, two stone bracers, and three copper knives. If a bow had been included originally or if the arrowheads had once been fitted to shafts, then sadly, all trace has long been lost. Radiocarbon analysis suggests 2400–2200 BC as the age of the skeletal remains.

Earlier by a thousand years (3200–3300 BC) and slotting neatly into the late Neolithic period are the contents of a remarkable discovery on September 26, 1991, in the Italian Alps of the intact body of a Stone Age man complete with his full complement of archery equipment.[11] Nicknamed "Ötzi" after the Ötztal region in which his remains were found, this obscure Neolithic man whose personal choice in his lifetime was perhaps solitude has, with his lonely death, become the most widely sought and studied exemplar of his age. Here for all now to see is an example of his Neolithic hunting longbow virtually intact, with its string, its arrows of the wayfaring tree (*Viburnum lantana*) held safely in their quiver, and his kit of tools. This represents a veritable goldmine of information for archaeologist and antiquarian archer alike.

Axe marks on the limbs of Ötzi's bow have suggested to some that the weapon was incomplete, since it lacks the smoother finish apparent on other contemporary bows, although a bow does not have to be tidied to be usable. Moreover, careful examination has failed to detect string marks on the limb

Montage of material recovered from the inhumation of a Neolithic archer on Salisbury Plain, Wiltshire, England, including 17 flint arrowheads and two lithic arm guards for protection of the inner forearm. Photo courtesy of Salisbury Museum.

extremities; and while he carried what is believed to have been a string, his weapon was seemingly unstrung. However, in what better way could a lonely practical man spend his day than in fashioning or completing his bow and his arrows? The matter is open to doubt, and we will leave it so. But before departing entirely from the theme, we are uniquely fortunate in knowing something of Stone-Age technology from an unusual source, that of the last survivor of the Yana, or Yahi Indians of southern California.[12] Named "Ishi" ("the strong and straight one"), he has shown us how a Neolithic hunter might have made his arrows.

He would first have selected straight shoots of 3/8-inch diameter from a suitable tree; Ishi used witch (wych) hazel by preference. These he cut to lengths of 32 inches and stripped of bark. He then bound them together and put them aside to dry. When they were dry, he straightened each over hot embers and smoothed them between two grooved sandstones, a tool fully familiar to those excavating Neolithic sites. When they were reduced to 5/16 inch in diameter, Ishi cut them back to 26 inches, binding the thicker end before drilling it to take a foreshaft, or footing. The hole for this he bored using a sharp bone tool held between his toes while revolving the shaft between his palms. No such tool was found in Ötzi's quiver, but then his arrows had no footings. They were self-shafts.

For the footing, Ishi chose mountain mahogany, a hard wood. Cut to 6 inches in length, this was carefully shaped and slotted into the stele. The joint was secured by sinew and set with glue. A groove 3/8 inch deep was cut to take the bowstring, and at the other end, a similar slot was prepared to take the arrowhead. This was of flint or obsidian (volcanic glass) or alternatively left thick and blunt—one presumes for small game, as was the practice among Neolithic hunters. Feathering, or fletching, involved three 4-inch fletches secured at either end and bound to the shaft. It is of interest to note that Ishi avoided the feathers of certain birds, notably the owl, suggesting that perhaps Neolithic arrow makers were similarly selective.

We return now to Ötzi's bow. Made of yew, heartwood alone, it is a little over 71 inches in length and compares with his height of 5 feet 3 inches. A length that is 8 inches beyond the man's height might seem excessive, but the length of a bow dictates the ease with which it may be drawn. For comparison, late medieval war bows of English origin were habitually longer than their user's height.

Material suited to the construction of bows naturally varied with geographic location, and not all early bow makers had an ideal choice. Within northwestern Europe, the area in which the simple self-bow thrived, wherever yew was found, it seems invariably to have been used, presumably in preference to other woods and, one may fairly assume, by trial and error. Where yew was not indigenous, as in Scandinavia, elm was used as well as pine. In passing, it is interesting to note that in early historic times, the southern Welsh on England's western border are said to have used wych elm (*Ulmus glabra*) for their bows, perhaps in preference to yew, although yew is the superior wood and was commonly available.[13] It is of incidental note that while wych elm is arboreally similar to common elm (*Ulmus campestris*), it has better elasticity. Inevitably there were areas beyond the tree line where suitable bow wood was either nonexistent or extremely scarce. Such was the case for the Inuit people living in the far north. Obliged to use whatever wood came to hand, including driftwood found on the seashore, they adopted an ingenious solution both to safeguard a scarce resource from breakage and to compensate for indifferent elasticity. Limbs were fashioned with wide tapering sections, while a skein of sinew, held in place by lateral bands, was fastened under tension between the string nocks.

Of those regional variations in the simple self-bow, perhaps the most outstanding and significant is the stiffened center section. This is the most unusual feature of bows made of yew and used during early historic times by Alamannic tribes living in southern Germany. Examples of these weapons, dat-

ing, it is believed, from the sixth century AD, are unique for their period and
come from graves excavated during the
mid-nineteenth century at Lupven,
near the village of Oberflacht in
Würtemberg.[14] Three bows were
recovered with stiffened center handle
sections ranging from 9 1/8 inches in
length on a bow of 67 inches in overall
height to 12 5/8 inches on a bow of 72
inches overall. The working limbs are
similar among the bows, since the difference in overall length is absorbed by
the longer handle. Sections are broadly
comparable between bows, with the
handles having a shallow convex back,
straight sides, and deep-cambered convex belly, while the limbs have a shallow convex back, straight sides, and a
ridge (or keel) belly.

Neolithic hunter equipped with bow
and quiver, circa 3300 BC. Illustration
by Wolfgang Bartl.

The stiffened handle bears explanation and comment. Both prehistoric
and early historic self-longbows relied for their power upon just one arc of
force, conveniently called a force curve. Although slightly stiffened at the handle to allow a grip, the whole bow, both limbs and handle section, bent in a
semicircle, a feature that persisted well into modern times. As we would say
today, it worked in the hand. A well-stiffened handle prevented such an occur-
rence, and each limb therefore worked in concert with, but independently of,
the other. The effect was to produce two arcs of force, one associated with each
limb; and with these, arguably, came improved cast. Curiously, this principle
was rediscovered in the nineteenth century for use on recreational longbows.
The feature is known today as "Buchanan dips," after the bowyer whose innovation it was.

The translation from theory to practice was not without its problems however. A rigid handle infers shorter working limbs, and with shorter bow limbs
comes considerable additional stress. Care needs to be taken that this stress,
while undoubtedly adding to power or cast, does not fracture the bow by doing
so. Modern bow makers replicating Oberflacht-style weapons have found by
trial and subsequent breakage that they cannot be drawn either to the eye or

the ear as was practice in medieval times; even a draw to the chin, the shorter modern distance, puts them at risk. The study of early woodcuts, confirmed by disastrous practical experiment, shows that these bows may be drawn successfully only as far as the chest and no further, limiting their effective range, and therefore not capable of taking advantage of any potential increase in cast through shortened working limbs. Thus much do we learn by applied replication.

Again of interest in the context of later design are the string-groove arrangements. The Oberflacht bows are side nocked to take the string; that is, instead of wraparound nock grooves that today would be considered conventional, these bows had string grooves cut on opposite sides of the bow on upper and lower limbs. Side nocking, a feature of bow making that survived into the eighteenth century and beyond, is believed to have been a regular feature of the English medieval and later war bow, a development to be dealt with in greater detail in a later chapter. The perceived wisdom was that it allowed ease of bracing, since the thumb alone was used to slip the string into position on the bent bow, which is of significant advantage when the heavy draw weights of war bows and certain early recreational bows are considered.

Despite their originality, those stiff-sectioned recovered Oberflacht bows seem to have been no greater in draw weight than is a traditional field, or hunting, longbow of today, or so recently constructed replicas indicate. Unless these recovered bows are unrepresentative of contemporary practice, the reason for side nocking in their case remains unclear. We must leave the Oberflacht bows with their unusual handles now and turn to other archaeological finds.

The bows and arrows recovered from a site at Nydam Moor in Sleswig, southern Denmark, are important for the insight that they give into early Germanic weaponry.[15] They were recovered in remarkably good condition from among the remains of a trio of longships that had foundered in what was during the fifth century AD an inlet of the Holsatian sea, and from them has been gleaned much knowledge of Germanic archery equipment.

The entrepreneurial brothers Hengist and Horsa, who, if we are to believe the Anglo-Saxon chronicle, set out from Jutland to land in Britain at around the time these vessels sank, may well have owned and, one assumes, used similar archery equipment to that recovered. In fairness to the skeptics, some doubts attach to the authenticity of these names. In Old English, hengest means stallion, and horsa, horse or mare. Æsc, the name of the son of Hengest, means ash or spear. It may be argued that perhaps the names are allegorical: by horse and spear the British were subdued. We will leave it to others to pursue this path.

Roger Ascham in the preamble to his book *Toxophilus* mentions that Sir Thomas Elyot (Elliot), a distinguished sixteenth-century man of letters, told him that he had

> read and perused over many olde monuments of Englande, and in seeking for that purpose, he markes this of shootynge in an exceedynge olde chronicle, the which had no name, that what time as the Saxons came first into this realme, in kyng Vortiger's dayes, when they had been here a whyle, and at last began to faull out with the Brittons, they troubled and subdewed the Brittons wyth nothing so much as wyth their bowes and shafte, whyche weapon beynge straunge and not seen here before, was wonderfull terrible unto them, and this begyning I can thinke verie well to be true.

Be that as it may, Nydam, the resting place of these Germanic weapons, is now a moor. Geographically it lies near the Alsensund, opposite the town of Sonderburg and was once a deep bay or fjord. Since the late sixteenth century, however, it has been cut off from the sea by a dyke and is now meadowland, and it is here that in 1863 the galleys were discovered.

Of the three boats, one alone survives intact. Another was recovered in small pieces, and a third was broken up and used for cooking fires by Prussian troops billeted nearby during the 1864 war against Denmark. Within these boats, and around their immediate vicinity, literally hundreds of iron weapons, shields, harnesses, spears, the remains of garments, and implements for shipping and fishing, including nets, have been found. Among this treasure trove of ancient artifacts were discovered 40 bows, over 100 arrows, a quiver, and the bronze mounting of another. Surprisingly, for the length of time that they were immersed, and due perhaps to the exclusion of oxygen by heavy silt deposits, all items have survived in a remarkable state of preservation; some look almost new, and they may now be seen in Kiel Museum.

The bows, mostly of pine (fir), although a few are of yew, measure between 67 and 72 inches in length, and their diameter is around 1 1/4 inches. All are self-bows, that is, constructed of one billet of wood, and those few of yew are a little thinner than those of pine. The yew staves are particularly knotty and pinned, suggesting staves of bough wood rather than from the trunk of a tree. Strengths have been variously interpreted, but informed opinion suggests bows of some 50 pounds in draw weight. This would have been adequate for close-quarter fighting such as would be expected during those sea battles reported so faithfully by the saga men and equally so for hunting and for personal protection.

Each of the Nydam bows is permanently bent; we would say they "follow the string" or have "taken a set," which is an indication that they were either

The upper face of a whalebone casket, circa AD 750, depicting a Saxon householder successfully defending his property with bow and arrows. Notice the circular shields and the arrows descending from above. British Museum, London.

permanently strung or were kept strung for long periods of time, a suggestion enhanced by the lack of conventional grooves suitable to hold the eye of a string loop. There are small notches at the limb terminals, sometimes on the belly, sometimes on the back; but these seem inadequate for loops, and it may be that the string was knotted to the limbs in a manner similar perhaps to that used historically by eastern archers. If this was the method used, then these notches would prevent the knots, which are by their nature self-tightening, from slipping down the limb. Not all bows were so notched however; variations include shouldered ends or even a bronze button.

Of passing interest is the presence of one Nydam bow tip of a cone of iron placed beyond the string groove and some 3 1/2 inches in length. Tapering to a sharp point this formed a potential stabbing weapon or perhaps a javelin, potentially useful in close-quarter fighting when the bow proper could not be used.[16]

No bowstrings were found, and since other vegetable matter was found in the soil around the ships, the assumption is that these were not of hemp or linen, the material of which later strings were habitually made. Speculatively the strings for these weapons were of animal material—sinew, gut, or even horsehair—none of which survives. This speculation is borne out to some degree by examination of the arrow string groove nocks that are wider than those of later historic examples known to have been used with hemp.

The arrows themselves are quite formidable, with knobbed, or bulbous, nock ends to accommodate a partial pinch draw.[17] They are made of a coniferous wood (*Abies pectinata*), as are many of the bows, and are between 29 and 37 inches in length. Size isn't everything, however, as some knowledgeable person once said, and the supposition from their length that these arrows were drawn to the head is not necessarily tenable. While the sighting line between eye and arrowhead is demonstrably the more accurate, what few illustrations of Germanic archers there are suggest arrows drawn to the chest. The reason for a 37-inch shaft remains enigmatic.

In another nearby place, more arrows were found that are similar in overall appearance to those of Nydam moor but with applied bulbous bronze nocks fastened to the shaftment by a conical pin. The reason for this can only be speculated, but they would clearly have been readily recognized in circumstances where perhaps it mattered; for example, if the archer was a person of importance whose deeds required recording.

We move on. It is customary today to feather an arrow with three fletchings, and where it can be determined, this appears to have been common practice in prehistoric times. Ötzi, the iceman, fletched his shafts with three. The Nydam arrows are provided with four, however, with each lodged in a groove cut into the shaftment. These grooves are between 4 and 5 inches in length into which the fletches would have been held by resin. It would seem that for completeness, they were bound on using thin thread soaked in a form of pitch or something similar. This would be entirely consistent with their use at sea.

Many of the wooden arrow nocks are decorated with scratch marks and almost all bear some form of marking such as runic characters, which could have been marks for identification purposes or may have had some religious significance. Where runes can be identified, the meaning of one at least suggests a rough humor. The *Geofu* rune, a simple X, means "gift." One can imagine the Saxon humorist smiling to himself as he marked it. A millennium and a half later, his descendants would chalk a similar message on a bomb. The rune *Elhaz*, marked on another arrow shaft, stands for "protection." It is not difficult to see the connection.

The arrowheads recovered were of either iron or bone and designed primarily for penetration, although a few were barbed. Some iron heads were attached by socketing and some by inserting their tangs into a split in the foreshaft and subsequently secured with pitch-covered twine. The heads differed in weight, the heaviest being some 15 grams, while the arrows themselves weighed between 45 and 50 grams. This was a comparatively heavy shaft, and if used with a bow of around 50 pounds in draw weight, it probably would have been effective at little more than 150 yards. This would have been a more-than-adequate distance, nevertheless, for contemporary close-quarter warfare. Also found were whetstones and a hollowed hardwood object that has been thought by some to be a quiver but that may have been a simple multipurpose container intended for domestic use.

Despite the undoubted use of archery by our forebears, there has been discussion and some dissension among historians concerning the position and importance of archers within early Anglo-Saxon armies.[18] Supporting the nobleman's hearth troop, or heorthwerod, of elite personal retainers was the fyrd (or fierd), armed with swords or huge battle-axes, which were wielded with the left hand and capable of felling a horse. There was the great fyrd—a motley collection of peasants armed with missiles and a variety of weapons, including the axe, club, and perhaps the bow, who were required only to defend their shire—and the select fyrd, who would fight elsewhere on command. These latter were rather better equipped and trained and thus more capable. Although the ash spear, round shield, and broadsword predominated, it is with the select fyrd that the archer, trained or otherwise, may have been more likely.

It is possible that an Anglo-Saxon warrior, the remains of whom were excavated at Chessell on the Isle of Wight, was a member of a select fyrd, since he was buried with a 60-inch bow and 24 arrows, examples of bows and arrows with which invading Saxon warriors would have been equipped, both for personal protection and as "gifts" to subdue the Romano-Britons they encountered on their forays across the North Sea. A millennium later, the arrow storm of their bowmen descendants would defeat the might of royal France.

2 | *Medieval Hunting and the Longbow*

The search for food is as old as humans themselves. Our early proto-ancestors supplemented their meager vegetarian diets with protein obtained by scavenging scraps from kills made by more successful predators. This was a dangerous and uncertain way in which to eke out an existence in a world where they were at once both predator and prey—a savage and unyielding world in which through skill and cunning they survived—a world that in the course of time, their remote descendants were to dominate.

We have already noticed how in prehistory people hunted with the bow; rock paintings in Spain and southern France are explicit. It is time now to move forward, to examine the ways in which the bow was used, but first, what of the bow itself? Antiquarians who study the weapon separate it into four types: the hunting bow (with its subdivision, the birding bow); the peasant's, or rural, bow (also known as the drovers' bow); the war bow; and the recreational bow.

While it is not surprising that the medieval peasant used the same weapon for all purposes, the bow possessed and used by foresters and others whose profession or status required them to hunt was a different thing entirely. Because it needed to be held partly drawn in readiness for the driven prey, it was significantly lighter in draw weight than the contemporary war bow. Called either the English or, rather curiously, the Turkish bow (see Chaucer's description below), it was described in some detail within *Le Livre du Roi Modus et de la Royne Racio* (The Book of King Method and Queen Reason), a fifteenth-century treatise published in France that dealt with all aspects of the chase and formed the basis for much of English hunting practice.[1]

The bow was ideally to be of a length between nocks of 22 "poñies," believed to be poignées, or, in English, "handfuls." If one takes a handful to be about 3 1/2 inches, then the recommended length would be around 6 feet 5 inches, with a preference for construction of boxwood or yew.

It used a bowstring of plaited silk that was made to whatever thickness the archer required. Silk offered more elasticity and, when well made, was more deadly (or so it was said) than the hemp with which the war bow was strung, since it would cast a longer and heavier shaft and, moreover, was more durable. It was also said to be quieter; silence was paramount for medieval hunters. The tips of the bow limbs are thought to have been protected by horn sheaths, or nocks, and it is possible that the arrow pass was softened by a piece of buck-skin.

The arrow used with the hunting bow was ten handfuls, or about 35 inches in length; this was a longer-than-usual shaft, which seems to bear out the claim for the bowstring above. The heads used with it were viciously barbed to kill by hemorrhage; they were as long to the end of the barbs as the breadth of four fingers (about 3 inches) and five fingers in length overall (about 3 1/2 inches).

For shafts with lighter heads, low-cut fletchings were appropriate; but longer, high-cut feathers were used for the heavier hunting heads. Barbs were always to be in the same plane as the nock. Bracing height—the distance between the taut string and the center of the handle, for which archers use the archaic term "fistmele"—was described as a palm's breadth plus two fingers. A delightfully imprecise measurement, it translates to perhaps 5 1/2 inches, which seems a little low for a bow of that length, since a fistmele is usually taken to be not less than 6 inches, the fist plus extended thumb being used as a measure today. The draw to be used was the three-finger Mediterranean release. The author of *Roi Modus* divides the forms of bow hunting into two: hunting from a hide (known as a bow-and-stable stand) and stalking. It is for the former that a weak bow is recommended, since it needed to be held par-tially drawn in order not to distract the animal as it approached the stand.

Stalking, it was said, could be carried out in three different ways. The first way was on foot in company with others, but always with a scenting hound. The second was on horseback with two men riding slowly through the forest cover-ing the presence of several archers. These, with bows strung and arrows notched, walked in the lee of the horses until getting downwind of the game and took up position in complete silence in front of trees or in cover. Once positioned, the horsemen then rode past the game, turned, and drove it toward the waiting bowmen. A third method involved a cart, the wheels of which, rather curiously, had to squeak. Seemingly the deer were attracted to the noise and came to investigate. Inside the cart, camouflaged by greenery, the archers huddled, waiting in patient anticipation until the game came within bow shot.

The *Roi Modus* also suggests one or two methods for the solitary hunting archer. Mounted is preferred, since deer are not disturbed by horses and will continue feeding as they approach. The author recommends that the archer put his horse into a position from which he can shoot at the rear of the prey animal, not sideways or to its front. To do this comfortably, he recommends that the left stirrup leather be made a little shorter than the right, since this offers support as one draws up to shoot. If on foot, then the archer must get out very early in the morning, alone, and upwind. The best time, we are told, is between August and mid-September, or at the time of the rut when the animals are otherwise engaged.

After King Method has explained how hunting is properly performed, he seeks comment from his queen, Queen Reason. Her approach is womanly and aesthetic; she classifies the prey as the sort that smells and the sort that does not—*bestes doulces* and *bestes puantes* (sweet beasts and stinking beasts). In the former category she places venison, the stag, the hind, the fallow buck, the roebuck, and with them, the hare, for these all have a pleasant color, don't smell, and what is more, don't bite. Into the latter category fall the boar, the sow, the wolf, the fox and—rather strangely—the otter. These not only smell, but they do bite! Queen Reason much prefers the venison.

There were essentially three forms of hunting. Of these, the bow and stable and that perennial forest activity, poaching, involved the bow and arrow and will concern us here. The third, known as "par force," is not our concern beyond a brief description. Each style survives today. The pheasant or grouse coveys that are beaten into the path of the static, or stable, guns is a modern representation of the former. Poaching speaks for itself of course, while fox and stag hunting, where an animal is chased to its death are each examples of the hunt par force.

Central to all hunting in medieval times was the forester—a man who, in Chaucer's words, knew woodcraft "up and down."[2] His hierarchy was not extensive; within the New Forest in the southern English county of Hampshire, foresters-in-fee were, as the name indicates, paid for their work. Closely associated with them were riding foresters, foot foresters, and under-foresters.[3] In addition to regular foresters, there were in the royal forest of Kingswood near Bristol arrow men whose day-by-day task was, it would seem, to keep order within the forest boundaries. Housed within a tower of Bristol's castle, contemporary documents suggest that they had a less-than-savory local reputation.

The medieval forester was a man of many parts and varied duties, and a contemporary description of these makes interesting reading.[4]

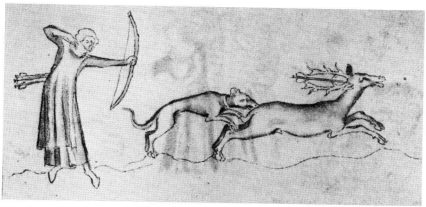

Hunting with bow, arrow, and gazehound (greyhound). Medieval English drawing.

> He must know how to shoot well in a bow. To train his scenting hound to fol-
> low a trail of blood. To stand properly by his tree [stable stand]. To remember
> the placements of the archers with him. To observe the wind, by which he
> should know the direction that the beasts will take, and thus where he should
> place his archers. He must know how to cut arrow shafts. To be handy with a
> cross-bow. To make a new bow-string if necessary. To skin and unmake [cut
> up] a Hart. To direct his scenting hound well, which needs much experience.
> To sound his horn in all the ways which a Hunter needs.

To aid him in all this, he could call upon the services of hunting dogs. Each of
these had their purpose: the lymer, an animal rather like today's bloodhound,
was used for scenting. The greyhound, or to give it an earlier name, the "gazehound," was used to run and bring deer down either after they had been shot
or if they had evaded the bow and stable. The brachet was also used for scenting but often accompanied the forester as a lone animal, riding across his saddle. The mastiff was a large, powerful animal designed to deal with larger prey
and used for guard purposes. One slept well if a mastiff guarded the door.
Finally, the alaunt—an animal no longer bred—was a huge beast of aggressive
and uncertain temperament, virtually untamable and bred with one purpose in
mind: to kill. It was occasionally fitted with armor, and its savagery was pitted
against the wild boar.

When the deer hunt and drive took place in forested areas, then the archer
stood by his tree, camouflaged in green, to await the arrival of the prey. If his
face was "nut brown," as was that of Chaucer's forester, then no further cam-
ouflage would be required. If he was fresh faced, however, then perhaps he
would hide his features with ivy or leaves. Here one may recall the many examples of the English Green Man inn signs. The hunter would be stationed down-

wind and about a stone's throw apart from his fellows if the area was lightly forested, closer if the trees were denser. Rather than hide behind a tree, the archer stood in front of it motionless but with arrow nocked and bow partly drawn.

As had been prehistoric practice, all medieval treatises on hunting included drawings intended as guidance both for the forester and for the archer alike. Thus, a deer coming head on was best shot in the middle of the chest, and numerous hunting drawings show this. If this was not possible, and the animal passed to the left, then it should be shot in the side, with due allowance for the speed at which it moved. This was important, for if one missed, then other archers could be vulnerable. Animals that passed to the right were difficult for right-handed archers, since the whole body had to be turned in order to aim at the beast.

If the arrow had brought down the deer, then all was well. If it was merely wounded, then the archer would sound his horn to bring the lymerer with his lymer, or scenting hound, to follow the beast or perhaps a fewterer with his greyhound to catch and bring the prey to the ground. If the arrow had fallen from the deer, then it was recovered and the blood closely studied for clues. If it was thick and sticky, then the end was near, and the deer would not be far away. If it was clear and bright, then the wound was probably not mortal, and the animal would need to be dispatched by other means.

Where the deer drive took place in open country, artificial stands called "hays" were set up, and the deer were driven towards these, hastened on their way by shouts from the stable. The archer's alleged war cry, "Hey, hey," may have come from this practice. The word "hay" is a common prefix or suffix to the names of many areas today within a onetime forest.

The hunt proper, particularly any that involved royalty, had a carefully orchestrated procedure—almost a ritual. The correct arrangements were set down in the early fifteenth century by Edward, Duke of York, brother to Henry V, in his book, *The Master of Game*, published in 1412.[5] This was essentially a translation into English of *Le Livre de Chasse*, an earlier work by Gaston Phoebus, Comte de Foix, embellished with certain English practices.[6] Sadly, Edward was a casualty—virtually the only one of note—at the battle of Agincourt and was thus spared little time to appreciate the popularity of his treatise. A major addition to *The Master of Game* was the detailed sequence of requirements for English royal bow-and-stable hunting, a practice with which monarchs who used the bow for taking game were well familiar and took very seriously.

Edward's chapter is headed "The maner of huntyng when the kinge wil hunte in foreste or in parke for the hert [hart] with bowes, greyhounds, and stable." The regulations are set down in precise detail, and the whole thing is a guide to proper protocol with a proper accent upon safety. As one might expect, the forester plays a leading role, advising the local sheriff of the number of men, both archers and stable, and the amount of cartage likely to be required to remove the animals killed. Everyone had to reach the forest edge, or the park, at first light and be in position ready for the arrival of the royal party.

When all was ready, and the king and queen were comfortable in their positions in the stand, then the master of game got matters under way with three long notes on his horn. Placings were vital of course, since hunting by bow and stable was a potentially dangerous practice. One monarch, William II, had already been accidentally killed while hunting with the bow, and Edward was doing his best to ensure that he remained unique.

A specific additional duty of the fewterers—those who kept the greyhounds—was to build bowers. "Fayre logges of green bowes [boughs] at [t]her trestes [stands] for to kepe the kyng and the quene and the ladies and gentil women and eke [as well] the greyhounds fro the sonne [sun] and fro evil wedir [bad weather]."

With the hunt itself now under way, the deer herd was expertly partitioned. First the harrier hounds moved the younger red and fallow deer, the barren does, and hinds. In hunting parlance, this was known as "voiding the rascal"—that is, driving them toward those in the stable, whose task it then was to funnel them to the archers waiting at their stands. There they were killed and put to one side. Alternatively, they were herded away to live for another day. The wily old harts mostly stayed put, although if one was raised by the harrying hounds and dispatched by the archers, then the master of game would blow the death on his hunting horn, break up (cut up) the beast, and reward the dogs with blood-soaked bread before returning to the main business of dealing with the herd.

With the rascal out of the way one way or another, the interesting part could now begin—the raising of the harts and their chase. The hart hounds could be uncoupled, and the scenting out could begin. One of the tasks undertaken by the forester was to establish likely hiding places; his intimate knowledge of the forest and its cover equipped him perfectly for this. Indeed, with the king and queen awaiting a good day's sport, his reputation rested on this ability, and it is probable that for several days beforehand he would have carefully noted such places.

Although harts were killed in other ways, it was the king's privilege, if he so wished, to kill one with his bow and arrow as it was driven past. The subsequent curée, or cutting up (unmaking), of the carcasses was a major feature of the hunt, and a ritual was carefully followed. Those animals selected for the king's larder were laid aside to be cut up by the huntsmen and fewterers. The heads of these animals were held up, and the hart hounds were encouraged to bay at them to remind them of their task. The offal, or numbles, from the deer was spread in the hide of the finest hart. The lord or the king, if he was there, had the choicest pieces of these delicacies, and they were his by right to keep or present as favors as he chose. In the ballads of Robin Hood, when our forest hero entertains his guests at a woodland feast, he offers them numbles.[7] The meaning is quite clear and would be so to his audience. He, Robin, is lord of the forest, and they are inferior beings.

Those involved in the hunt were rewarded with a complicated system of hides and venison. In order to preserve some semblance of fair play with everyone getting his proper share, each person with a claim was required to mark the beast accordingly. "Every man, bowe and feutrere that hath out slayn [killed anything] shuld mark it that he myght chalaunge his fee [seek his due]." Rewards to the bowmen for accurate shooting varied between forested areas. In one at least, they were recompensed for their work by receiving the skin or hide of the beasts they slew, but only if they had observed the correct procedure. "And as of fees it is to wete [right] that what man be sette or smytt [shoot] a deere at his tree with deethes [deaths] stroke, and he be rekeveryd bi the sonne going doun [recovered by sundown] he shal have the skynn, and if he be not sette or goo from his tree or do otherwise than it is sayde he shalle non have."

How the beasts were marked is left to the imagination, but one might speculate that archers personalized their arrows; one such marked shaft left in the carcass would be evidence enough of claim. In other areas, or perhaps if the master of game followed a different set of rules, rewards varied. For bow-and-stable hunting, *The Craft of Venery* recommended that "he that draweth furst blode of hym, yf it be withynne the IIII quarters [fore-quarters] schall have the hide, and yf he smyte without the IIII quarters [anywhere else] he that smytithe last schall have the hide, be it hert, or bucke."[8]

Although matters were not balanced exactly in the archer's favor, he was rewarded whenever his arrow struck a beast. An animal that escaped attack by a greyhound but was subsequently shot and wounded and then finished off by the greyhound was accredited, perhaps correctly, to the dog. However, the

Cutting up, or unmaking, of a hart. The numbles, or entrails, are being removed for presentation to the lord. Notice the master forester (with horn) holding a leg. Gaston Phoebus (Gaston III, Count of Fois), *Le Livre de Chasse*, ed. Gunnar Tilander (Karlshamm, 1971).

archer received "a peny for hys shote." The agent whose activities had caused the death of the animal was inevitably a controversial area, and there were unavoidable disputes. These were recognized and went to arbitration. Once again, it was the master of the game who had this responsibility of decision. "If he be at strif with hym that asketh the fee thereof, the maister of the game shal deme [judge] it, and right so shal he do of alle the strives [contentions] for fees betwene bowe and bowe."

It seems apparent that claims, when they were made, would be based on the identification of arrows, and this implies the marking of these at an early date. We have already noted the marking of shafts by the Viking warrior bowmen of Nydam, no doubt with much the same purpose in view.

As we have seen, bow-and-stable hunting was a primary method of taking deer in quantity, and its organization was conducted with care and meticulous

On the track of prey: bowman carrying an unstrung bow and two hounds accompanying a mounted forester. Medieval English drawing.

attention to detail, particularly when royalty or nobility was involved. On occasion, however, the activity was a cover for something rather more radical: the pursuit of warfare.

The border country between Scotland and England had long been debatable land, and the desolate rolling Cheviot hills that separate the two countries have been the scene of many bloody battles in the past. One such is recorded in the "Ballad of Chevy Chase" (Chevy is a diminutive for Cheviot), when English bowmen from the warrior house of Percy, Earl of Northumberland, clashed with the border clansmen of Scottish Earl Douglas.

At the beginning of the ballad, a large hunting party sets out from Bamborowe Castle, a Percy stronghold, and it is immediately apparent that something more than a good day out is planned.

> The Percy out of Bamborowe came.
> With him a mighty meinye [gathering]
> With fifteen hundred archers bold,
> Chosen out of shires three.

Although he was well aware of the implications, Percy's immediate intention was to kill deer for venison.

> The drivers through the woods went
> All for to raise the deer,
> Bowmen bicker'd upon the bent [grass][9]
> With their broad arrows clear.

As midday drew on, "a hundred fat harts there lay." However, nemesis was fast approaching. At last, a

Squire of Northumberland
Looked to his hand full nigh,
He was ware o' the doughty Douglas coming
With him a great meinye.

Earl Douglas had not come to join in the sport; instead, he was there for retribution, since Percy was hunting on the border, and Douglas had a claim to the deer taken. Battle was joined, and during this, both Percy and Douglas were slain: Earl Percy by a Scottish spearman and Douglas by an English arrow from a hunting bowman.

As a social activity for the well-to-do, and for the work it provided for lesser mortals, bow hunting attracted much interest in early times, and the alliterative, anonymous medieval Arthurian poem "Sir Gawain and the Green Knight" sets the scene admirably with a vivid description of a bow-and-stable hunt.[10]

The wild beasts quivered at the cry of the questing hounds
Deer ran through the dale, distracted by fear,
Hastened up the high slopes, but hotly were met
By the stout cries of the stable, staying their flight. . . .
The does driven with din to the depth of the dale,
Then the shimmering arrows slipped from the bowstring and slanted
Winging their way from every tree in the wood,
Their broad-heads pierced the bonny flanks of brown;
The deer brayed and bled, as on the bank they died.
The hurrying hounds still chased them, and harried them still
Hunters came after with high hue of the horn
Cleaving the cliff with the clear noise of their cry.
The beasts which ran on and broke through the ranks of the bowmen
Died at the resayt, seized and dragged down by the dogs.

Forest areas were vital places where peasant and yeoman alike lived out their lives. With venison in quantity around them, the temptation to augment a meager diet was unavoidable. Statutory law had of necessity to be ignored, however, when poaching deer, and regulations there were in plenty. Anyone passing through a forest area was required to carry his bow unstrung and to have his arrows bound by the bowstring to the limbs of his weapon. Whenever any dogs, particularly greyhounds and brachets, were taken by a highway through a forest, the dogs had to be coupled and the greyhounds tied firmly with a knot.

If a dead or wounded deer was found, and with it an arrow, then the arrow was retained by the forest verderer and enrolled; and its details—including a mark if one could be found—were set down for a subsequent inquest. Understandably, it was an offense to carry in the forest either a braced hand bow and arrows or crossbow and bolts, to run brachets or greyhounds, or, in fact, to possess any device that could harm the king's deer. Penalties, originally brutal and involving mutilation or death by hanging, were muted later to imprisonment. This was only a difference of degree, since of those committed to jail, many died there. Later still, imprisonment was replaced by a system of fines.

Dogs were permitted to those who lived in the forest but were restricted in size. Within the Speech House in the Royal Forest of Dean in the English county of Gloucestershire, where a verderers' court was regularly held, an iron hoop was set into the floor. If a dog could pass beneath it, then it was allowed. The hoop is still there.

Despite statutory law administered by the venery court and the penalties involved, the poaching or harming of venison regularly took place. In the New Forest, created in the county of Hampshire by William I as a royal hunting preserve, the illegal taking of venison was part and parcel of everyday life, and an examination of New Forest documents for offenses against the venison makes interesting reading.[11] Although not normally a lawless place, occasionally the villagers took matters into their own hands. On August 6, 1256, William Curdy was found in the forest with bow and arrows; and it being apparent that he was up to no good, he was handed into the custody of Simon Richs and William Cruys until such time as he could be charged.[12] William, however, seems to have been a servant of the abbot of Beaulieu (pronounced "Bewly") and was obviously well connected. The following night, 19 of William's colleagues from the abbey, armed with sticks, bows and arrows, and other weaponry, set upon Simon and William Cruys and beat them both severely. They then forcefully removed the transgressor and took him back to the safety of the abbey, no doubt with the overt blessing of the abbot whose pantry he had perhaps been told to fill.

The law is no respecter of persons or circumstance. Nicholas de Barbeflet, having been apprehended taking a doe and a buck, vainly pleaded that he had already been fined once for the offense of the buck and that regarding the doe, he had been given this by writ of King Henry.[13] Authority was having none of this unlikely tale, and Nicholas was duly committed to jail. In the fullness of time, however, it appeared that this story was true. Payment was confirmed and the writ discovered; the unfortunate Nicholas was set free, one imagines, with mixed feelings about the majesty of the law and royal gifts in particular. In a quieter moment though, he might have contemplated such a position 50 years earlier—he would have been either summarily hanged or mutilated, writ or no writ!

From *The Assize of the Forest*, 1184, we have the following:

This is the Assize of the lord king, Henry (II), son of Maud, concerning the forest, and concerning his deer in England; made at Woodstock with the advice and assent of the archbishops, bishops, barons, earls and magnates of England.

1. First, he forbids that anyone shall transgress against him in regard to his hunting rights or his forests in any respect; and he wills that no trust shall be put in the fact that hitherto he has had mercy for the sake of their chattels upon those. Who shall offend against him hereafter and be convicted thereof, he will that full justice be exacted from the offender as was done in the time of King Henry his grandfather Henry I.

2. Item: he forbids that anyone shall have bows or arrows or hounds or harriers in his forests unless he shall have as his guarantor the king or some other person who can legally act as his guarantor.

Occasionally there is direct evidence of royal displeasure at the activities of "offenders against venison."[14] In 1276, King Edward I, not a man to stand for nonsense from his subjects (or anyone else, for that matter), appointed his "beloved and faithful Matthew de Columbar to look into these transgressions against the royal prerogative."

Because certain malefactor archers have recently taken and carried off beasts from the New Forest, against the peace and without the permission of Queen Eleanor (of Aquitaine) we have appointed you to inquire into the matter. At the day and place appointed you will hold an inquest and do full and swift justice according to the law and custom of our realm, and the sheriff has been commanded to make the witnesses attend.

No doubt wishing to retain the royal pleasure, the beloved and faithful Matthew moved swiftly. The finger was placed firmly upon Robert, the son of John Waleraund; his man, Gervas; and an unknown stranger. All had entered the forest illicitly with bows and arrows and a red hunting dog and taken a doe. Also identified were John le Lust and John le Haver, seen with bows and arrows and a white hunting dog on the following Friday, who took a buck. Shortly afterward, Walter de Bosco and Nicholas de Paulmer, again with a red dog, shot and killed another buck. This was deemed a sufficient haul of malefactors to satisfy the king's majesty, and they duly went to trial. With regard to the implied menace in the king's writ, it is a little curious to record that all were merely fined.

It would be entrancing to continue with anecdotes of the taking of illicit venison in New Forest by bow and arrow, and there are very many of them, but such is not the purpose of this book. However, one last tale from July 1270 is worthy of record.[15]

> On the night of the Tuesday before the feast of St. Margaret the Virgin about sixty malefactors entered the forest with bows and arrows, dogs and grey-hounds, to harm the venison. They remained in the forest on the Wednesday following and took about fifteen harts, fawns, and other beasts. The same day at vespers they went to Beaulieu Abbey wishing to spend the night but were forbidden entry, and on account of this they spent the night at the Grange of Hareford and took food they found. On their departure in the morning they took 180 lbs of cheese, and they remained the day of Thursday in the forest until vespers. Then about forty of them went to the house of John de Brutesthon and took and ate food they found there, and afterward they went off and remained the night at the house of Roger de Langeford at Westashely.

This incursion is the largest recorded in the verderers' court rolls and is interesting in the occupations of those involved. This was no motley collection of peasants out on a spree. Among them were a hayward, four foresters (who were paid to know better), a Dominican friar (who was subsequently found to be Franciscan), and two parsons.

Although the illegal taking of the king's venison was the principal crime, deer were not the only animals at risk. The taking of herons by snare or artificial means was an act punishable by fine and imprisonment.

> If any person slay or take, or cause to be taken, but in his own ground, by mean craft or engine, but with hawking or with long-bow any Herons upon pain to forfeit of every Heron slain or taken vi.s. viiij.d (6 shillings 9 pence in old English coin) nor take any young Heron out of the nest, without licence of the owner of the ground upon pain to forfeit for every Heron so taken out of the nest x.s (10 shillings).[16]

The shooting of birds, and the heron and pheasant in particular, was achieved with a birding bow, a light weapon used for the taking of both feather and fur, since small game would succumb to the special arrowheads used. Of these, there were two, although there is less evidence for the one than the other. These two were the blunt and the forked pile, or forker. The blunt pile, in use well within living memory (I have my own example), headed an arrow heavily fletched (today's are often helically fletched and called "flu-flus") in order to bring a shaft to earth within a short distance. They are, or were, in use for Continental *tir a le perche*, or "popinjay," shooting and are named "maquets." It is believed by some that the forked pile, or the crescent broadhead, to give it a more correct description, was also used to take birds on the wing, although I know of no recorded examples of its use for this purpose and remain to be convinced.

A hart at rest: stalked, surprised, and shot by archer and crossbowman. Medieval French woodcut.

Other game besides venison was hunted with the bow and arrow, and we will spend a moment looking at this. The chief target was the wild boar. This was a dangerous adversary and one that was best approached with an alaunt in close attendance. Boars enjoyed wallowing in mud and while engrossed in this activity were vulnerable. In *Roi Modus*, King Method suggests that this is a task best left to a solitary archer who prepares a hide some two feet above the ground so that his scent doesn't reach the animals. There is also a brief reference to boar hunting with the bow in "Sir Gawain and the Green Knight."

> *A baneful boar, of unbelievable size*
> *A solitary long since sundered from the herd,*
> *Being old and brawny, the biggest of them all*
> *And grim and ghastly when he grunted, great was the grief*
> *When he thrust though the hounds, hurling three to earth*
> *Then men shoved forward shaped to shoot at him,*
> *Loosed arrows at him, hitting him often*
> *But the points for all their power could not pierce his flanks.*
> *Nor would the barbs bite on his bristling brow*

Though the smooth shaven shaft shattered in pieces,
Yet wherever it hit, the head rebounded.

Even in its modern form, the alliteration is evocative of the perils of a boar hunt. One hopes that perhaps this old warrior lived to fight another day, and certainly the poem ends without his capture.

A rather tamer beast of the field, if not the chase, was the hare. As King Method reported—and, one presumes, his queen approved—hares were best taken in April when they were among the young corn. The method was to place hounds in a position where the hare might see them, then circle behind it on horseback. A weak bow was recommended, to be shot while the horse was moving. Alternatively, an archer might go on foot, covered by a horseman. On viewing the hare, the horseman rode on, and the archer made his shot.

Though not an exact science, hunting was an activity that was closely controlled; and with regard to the size of the area of a forest involved, this could only be achieved by sound. The requisite noise was provided by the hunter's or the forester's horn. Horns of course provided then, as they do now, just one note, and it was by a sophisticated sequence of these that skilled hunters and archers at stable knew what was going on some distance away. It is an intriguing possibility, even a probability, that one or more of these horn calls (strokes or mots) was commonly used in battle. There is, for example, some circumstantial evidence for the use of the *menée* stroke, or assembly call, as a preliminary to the battle of Agincourt in 1415.[17]

This pitting of human wit against animal instinct, with success by no means assured, is the pleasure of silent stalking today with either bow or camera in hand. How different it was in times past, when hunting par force or by bow and stable was the order of the day, for noise there was aplenty: the commands of lymerers managing their mastiffs, the voices of fewterers as greyhounds strained at the leash, the low hum of conversation as the master huntsman discussed tactics with his lord or king, and the noisy jesting of archers and woodmen as they waited together in readiness to be directed to their stands. The very air of the forest would have vibrated with noise as the strident tones of hunting horns sounded across the forest glades—the music of the chase as both hunters and foresters passed information back and forth.

The horn is still in use today in England, blown to direct the whipper-in and the hunt followers by the master of hounds at fox or stag meetings—the last vestiges of medieval English par force hunting—as he prepares to uncouple the hounds and move off, and it is blown again at various stages during the hunt. It is no longer quite so fundamental to the activity, however, and there

The kill: hound and bowman carrying a bow and accompanying a mounted forester. Gaston Phoebus (Gaston III, Count of Fois), *Le Livre de Chasse,* ed. Gunnar Tilander (Karlshamm, 1971).

are very few today who would recognize all the ancient hunting calls and their functions, including the *chemin, assemblée, queste, chasse, vehue, prise, retraite, appel de gen,* or *menée*—even if the modern master of hounds knew how to sound them! Each had its meaning; each was understood and obeyed by those to whom it was directed. It is not unlikely that from these calls originated the military bugle commands recognized by soldiers today. But before we look more deeply into the purpose of these calls and their place in the complexities of medieval hunting, let us look at the horn itself, for we have a contemporary description of it and its making from *The Master of Game.*

> There are divers [many] kinds of horns, that is to say bugles, great Abbot's, hunters horns, ruets [trumpets, or curved horns perhaps of metal], small Foresters horns—and meaner horns of two kinds. . . . one kind is waxed with green wax[18] and greater of sound, an they be best for good hunters, therefore I wil devise [explain] how and in what fashion they should be driven [made]. . . . First, a good hunter's horn should be driven [made] (of horn) two spans in length (about 12 to 14 inches) and not much more or much less, and not too crooked or too straight, but that the flue [mouthpiece] be three or four fingers uppermore than the head,—that unlearned hunters call the "great end" of the horn" [This apparently meant that when set down flat, the shape curved upward toward the mouthpiece.] . . . And also that it should be as great and hollow driven as it can for the length, and that it be shorter on the side of the

baldric [the shoulder sash on which it was carried] than at the nether end [This is unclear, but it is thought to mean a natural curve to hold the horn close to the body when suspended. This is certainly the shape of nineteenth-century replica forester horns.] . . . And that the head be as wide as it can be, and always driven smaller and smaller [tapered] to the flue and that it be well waxed, thicker or thinner according as the hunter thinks it will sound best. And that it [the waxing] be the length of the horn from the flue to the binding [again a little unclear, although the binding may have been intended to secure the head from cracking] . . . And also that it be not too small driven from the binding to the flue, for if it be, the horn will be too mean of sound . . . . As for horns for fewterers [the man who held the greyhounds, or gazehounds, in check] and woodmen, I speak not, for every small horn and other mean [unimportant] horns, unwaxed be good enough for them.

The forester involved in bow-and-stable hunting was specifically required to sound a horn in all the ways a hunter needs, and classes were regularly held to instruct in the complexities of the calls. These were essentially simple combinations of its limited musical range grouped as mots or strokes in long and short notes, spelling out a functional message, rather like Morse code.

There were around 14 separate calls, each one specific to a situation. Although some variations existed between English and French practice, mots were explicitly named and their purposes described in a fourteenth-century French poem.[19] These included the *chemin* (the road, or the way to the meet), the *assemblée* (the gathering), the *queste* (the search for the quarry), the *chasse* (the hounds running), the *vehue* (the sight of the quarry), the *mescroy* (the changing of the line of scent), the *requeste* (the search anew when the quarry had returned to cover), the *l'eaue* (a water obstacle), the *relaies* (the need for relays of hounds), the *ayde* (at bay, or request for help), the *prise* (the death of the quarry), the *retraite* (the withdrawal and return homeward), the *appel de chiens* (calling together of the hounds), and the *appel de gens* (calling the hunters together).

In addition to the horn calls, one or two oral "halloos" were made by hunters. These were in imitation of the horn's sound; "huer" is an example of these, perhaps indicating the sight of a quarry. In England and within living memory, Cornish fishermen used a lookout called the huer when searching for shoals of pilchards. "Hue" comes from the old French "to shout," thus we have "hue and cry," a well-known derivative phrase.

Back to the hunting weapon and an often-asked question. Was poison ever used on arrowheads when stalking with the longbow? It is believed that to a limited extent, it may have been. There are occasional unsupported references to the smearing of juice derived from the root of helleborus (*Helleborus foetidus*, perhaps) on English arrowheads; and there is a long-standing, but as yet unproven, myth that English longbowmen dipped their arrows in a certain noxious substance of a biological nature preparatory to battle.

Stone-Age hunter-gatherers who used the bow and arrow stalked their prey; Ishi, the Californian Yana Indian, taught us that. Not for him was the field arrow shot at 80 yards or more. His need to fill his belly was too great to risk such precious magical things. He used his skills in woodcraft to creep close before he loosed his shafts. And to secure his success, occasionally he turned to the darker side of Mother Nature for her help.

Although quite properly we link the poisoned arrow with the techniques of traditional hunters from the rain forests of Brazil and the Kalahari Bushmen from the deserts of southern Africa, the advantages of poison were as evident to the medieval English forest dweller as it was to hunters elsewhere. The common names of certain English wayside plants are redolent of their poisonous qualities. "Wolfbane" and "henbane" are names not to be trifled with, a mere scratch from these would be enough to cause eventual death. Picture the peasant archer, in company with a hound perhaps to flush out prey from cover, a light bow in his hand to deliver a shaft tipped with a poison derived from one of these. That he used it we are as certain as we can be; that he used it so seldom is surprising.

One option was *Atropus belladonna*; even the name has a ring of menace. This is a member of the Solanaceae family and a most potent killer. English countryfolk know it as deadly nightshade and learn of its properties at their mother's knee. Woe betide anyone who mistakes it for a blackberry among the brambles. As an aside, all of the genus *Solanaceae* are poisonous to some degree, and one should leave black nightshade, bittersweet, and henbane (especially henbane) very strictly alone.

With few exceptions—notably tribes in central Africa who smeared the arrowheads with liquid from rotting carrion and others in South America whose method was to induce eventual tetanus—most arrow poisons work rapidly. This is not an unrealistic arrangement of course, since all animals had to be pursued on foot until they fell. Poisons that affected respiration quickly were derived from the corms of aconites (*Aconitum ranunculae*) and widely used in Asia, Africa, and South America. When prepared for use by peasant English bowmen, its local name was and still is monkshood; and we should beware of it, for every last part is poisonous. It is a matter of some curiosity that Mother Nature, benevolent in her distribution of sweet-scented flora, has hidden both life and death within the bouquet, leaving humans in their wisdom to seek it out. We have not too far to look for the moral!

It would leave this chapter incomplete if we were to omit a reference or two to hunting with the bow in the various early English ballads, for they reflected an activity that was as much a part of medieval life as plowing, harvesting, or, for that matter, attendance at church. Robin Hood features as we would expect, although, oddly, his bow-hunting exploits are not dwelt upon to any extent. However, in keeping with his supernatural ability to keep one step ahead of the Sheriff of Nottingham, when he was apprehended by foresters while about his nefarious business, he makes a wager of 20 pounds, which is accepted, to shoot a hart "Two hundred yards me fro(m)."[20]

Then Robin bent a very good bow,
And at him he let flee [fly]
Of the near side he did break two ribs,
And on the far side he broke three.
His arrow being sharp and keen,
Quite through the Buck did flee
By the force of Robin Hood's strong arm
It girt into a tree.

Amazing as Robin's feat was, it was matched by others of his merry band. While they were relaxing one day, "some would leap, and some would run, and some would use Artillery" (the bow, in this context).[21] Robin watches the shooting and asks, "Which of you can kill a Buck, or who can kill a Doe, or who can kill a Hart in grease, five hundred foot him fro(m)?" Put on their mettle by Robin's implied doubts, "Will Scadlock then, he killed a buck, and Mitch (Much the Miller's son) he killed a doe, and Little John he killed a hart in grease, five hundred foot him fro."[22]

To conclude, we should say a word or two about remedies for arrow wounds, since even the best-prepared hunting arrangements occasionally went awry. The remedies ranged from the mundane to the exotic.

"Take a nettle, pound it well, boil in unsalted butter and make an ointment for the wound."

"Take equal quantities of holly bark, mallow, and the middle part of elder, add thereto lard, and wine in the same proportions, boil well until it becomes thick, then take a cloth, spread the ointment thereon and cover the wound with this. By the help of God it will be healed."

One cannot but think that a healthy trust in the divine was an essential to

Robin Hood attending an archery tournament. Woodcut by Beswick. Joseph Riston, *Robin Hood: Poems, Songs and Ballads* (London: 1885).

most medieval medicine! For an arrowhead that has entered and cannot be extracted, it is advised to "seek the roots of a spear thistle, and the white of an egg, mix together and apply to the wound—it will extract the foreign substance." Will it indeed? One feels a certain faith in the process might be needed here as well.

Arrow injuries were sufficiently common to enjoy a specific remedy. This was *Inula helenium*, known by its common name of elecampane, or alecumpayne. Either drunk as a distilled liquid or eaten in the form of candied root as a sweetmeat, it was an almost-universal cure-all and considered particularly potent against the poisoned wound. References to it abound in those early English masques and mummers plays performed by village guilds on feast days to entertain the villagers. In the traditional fight between St. George and the Turkish Knight, the Doctor carries a bottle to heal the wounded hero and says, "here, take this essence of elecampane . . . . Rise up Sir George, and fight again." Perhaps the oddest prescription though appears in a medieval Welsh manuscript. It is for the poisoned wound arising from a snake bite or from an arrow. We are advised to "hold the anus of a red cock to the wound until the bird be dead . . . . If it be a woman, let the same be done with a hen." It is surely time to move on!

3 | *Early Warfare and the Longbow*

It is a measure of people's inhumanity that they are forever discovering fresh and ingenious ways to eliminate each other. It cannot have been long before the Mesolithic hunter, evaluating his new weapon, realized that it had a secondary and very useful purpose. Those that were adept with it could settle both an old score and an intertribal dispute in a most satisfactory way.

Rock paintings from eastern Spain clearly show groups of archers in combat with each other. A typical example from a rock shelter at Las Dogues, Castellón de la Plaña, has a group of ten standing their ground against a sortie from another group, 17 or more strong, who are running at them, shooting their arrows as they go.[1] As seems to have been the practice when early humans went hunting, spare arrows for immediate use are carried lying parallel to the bow's limbs.

Although there is little doubt that at this time, one bow served for more than one purpose, skeletal remains containing flint and bone arrowheads, some lodged in vertebrae, are testimony to the use of the bow—if not for early warfare, then certainly for aggression. What form this belligerent activity took we can only guess. If the hunter caught his game by stalking and ambush, then it might be natural to use this expertise to gain advantage over an enemy. Ambush was a low-risk strategy; in later historic times, sudden attack without warning would become recognized as a favored military tactic where odds were uneven and the set-piece battle with all its chivalric trappings was inappropriate to the situation.

However, there is circumstantial evidence from an early Danish excavation to suggest that standoff engagements, with archers projecting arrows at a high trajectory from some distance, were also a feature of prehistoric warfare. The skull of a male skeleton recovered from this excavation contains an arrowhead that has penetrated the nasal cavity and the roof of the mouth, a position consistent with an arrow coming from above.[2] The arrowhead was of bone in this case and is a reminder that flint and metal were not the only substances used to arm shafts. In passing, we may note that among the arrows found at Nydam Moor and dating from early historic times were some armed with bone heads. In fact, the bows and arrows discovered during the excavation and recovery of the Nydam longships draw our attention toward their prospective use. The Scandinavians were a seafaring folk, and many of the engagements that were fought for political or territorial reasons took place at sea.

In sea warfare, once battle was joined, ships were locked together—invariably, prow to prow. Men then took up their prearranged places. Those with stabbing spears and axes were hand picked to protect the king's banner and stood at the forward part of each vessel to hew or stab frenetically at each other while all the time endeavoring to remain upright. It was more than useful to have good sea legs if one was a Norseman. Behind them might be placed berserkers, an assembly of bloodthirsty fanatics used to throwing fits of homicidal mania whenever the mood took them, which was often. Those with sense steered well clear of the berserkers when they were about their business. Meanwhile, behind the mast and at the stern of the vessel stood men with light throwing spears or javelins and archers with their war bows, loosing arrows whenever a suitable opportunity presented itself. This was not an easy task; the vagaries of wind and weather added to the difficulty of targeting one's enemy while carefully avoiding one's leader in the midst of performing fearless feats at the sharp end. As might be expected, the Norse saga writers relished these furious engagements and reported them as faithfully as scansion, poetic license, and the need to stay on good terms with the victor would allow. No doubt, they lose some of their atmosphere in translation, but a sample or two will give the flavor of what was recorded.

The sea battle between King Magnus the Good of Norway and Earl Svein Ulfson of Denmark that took place on December 18, 1043, was one such heroic struggle. We need not trouble ourselves unduly with the politics of the matter. Suffice it to say that the bellicose Svein was a significant thorn in Magnus' side and, moreover, a pretender to the throne of Denmark—a seat to which the Norwegian monarch was rightfully entitled and one on which, come what may, he was determined to sit. Hearing of Earl Svein's unwelcome presence with his ships and a great force of men at Aarhus in Jutland, King Magnus gathered his troops, and their natural enthusiasm for a satisfying fight having been stimulated by the customary oration, weapons were sharpened, mail was donned, and off all rowed with retribution in mind. As the saga writers subsequently recorded and the scalds and minstrels sang, the battle that followed was heroic—it was a point of principle among that genre that all battles were heroic.[3] Eleventh-century Norse victors liked to reflect on their achievements, and the more overstated the hyperbole the better. One may contemplate the successful scald selecting the choicest pieces with which to regale his lord at the cold wash up.

> *Steel-pointed spear, and sharpened stake*
> *Made the broad shield on arm to shake,*
> *The eagle, hovering in the air,*
> *Screamed o'er the prey preparing there,*
> *And stones and arrows quickly flew,*
> *And many a warrior bold they slew,*
> *The bowman never twanged his bow*
> *And drew his shaft so oft as now;*
> *And Dronheim's bowmen on that day*
> *Were not first tired of all this play,*
> *Arrows and darts so quickly fly,*
> *You could not follow with the eye.*

Though not earth-shattering verse perhaps, the translation scans in a jingoistic rumpty-tumpty sort of way, and one certainly gets the picture. It is satisfying to report that after all that effort, King Magnus finally gained his throne. Although the hand bow (from which the longbow emerged) has from time immemorial been the weapon of the common man, across the centuries, it has also had its royal patrons. Monarchs and persons of high rank did not disdain its use; skill with it was a recognized and respected achievement, and in this, the early Norse kings led the field.

Some 50 years after Magnus the Good departed for the great mead hall in the sky, another king of that name, Magnus Barefoot, featured in an archery event—one enshrined in a curious twist of fate. Let us contemplate the scene. It was the island of Anglesey in north Wales. Gruffyd ap Cynan, a charismatic Welsh prince of the north Welsh cantref (province) of Gwynedd, was struggling to retain his independence at a time when national Welsh politics were increasingly subject to external interests as Norman power expanded ever further to the west. Matters had come to a head when an expedition mounted with the express authority of William II, king of England, made its ponderous way across the border into Wales to remove Gruffyd—an increasing irritant for the English king—from the equation. Led by Hugo "the Stout," Earl of Chester,

An early sea battle. Depiction of the battle of Sandwich and the death by beheading of Eustache Busquet (Eustache the Monk) in 1217. Notice the archer at the stern of the ship shooting what may be a bag of lime.

and Hugo "the Brave," Earl of Shrewsbury, in whom regal responsibility had been dually vested, this force had traversed the coast of north Wales and crossed the sea to land on Anglesey, which was separated from the Welsh mainland by the straits of Menai.

Well aware of this incursion into his birthright, and with full panoply of battle, Gruffyd ap Cynan stood four-square on the shore accompanied by two other Welsh lords, each anxious to protect his hereditary rights against the Norman French. In preparation for the forthcoming conflict, Gruffyd, a cautious man well aware of Norman intentions, had prudently contracted for several shiploads of Irish Danes to take the brunt. Matters had not gone as they should however. Having sized up the opposition, or perhaps having been offered better terms, the mercenary Danes had rewritten their terms of reference and had joined the Earls—the bellicose Hugo the Brave and, puffing slightly from his exertions, Hugo the Fat. Facing them, their forces now significantly diminished, amid an air charged with nemesis, were three unhappy Welsh lords. The scene was set for royal retribution.

But by one of those fortuitous tricks of fate that change events from time to time, help was unexpectedly at hand, for slipping slowly through the swirling mists of Menai en route to the mainland and territorial expansion appeared the fearsome dragon prows of huge seagoing Viking longships. It was King Magnus Barefoot's royal Norwegian battle fleet, crammed to the gunwales with hand-picked, hard-bitten Viking warriors, with King Magnus in personal command. Shipping oars with, one imagines, more than a flicker of interest among his rugged battle-hardened crew, Magnus inquired through an interpreter where he was and what was going on. Having been properly briefed, and having sized up his prospects (which included, among other things, neutralizing a substantial slice of mainland opposition), we are told the king "grew angry." Peeling off three ships from his fleet, he approached the shore and engaged both recreant Danes and Anglo-Norman soldiery alike. A Welsh history takes up the story with evident satisfaction.[4]

> The French fell down from upon their horses like fruit from fig trees, some dead, some wounded by the arrows from the men from Llychlyn (Norway). And the King, unruffled, from the prow of his ship hit, with an arrow Hugh, Earl of Shrewsbury in his eye, and he fell a humped-back to the round, mortally wounded from his armed horse, beating upon his arms. And from that incident the French turned in flight and presented their backs to the men from Llychlyn.

It makes a splendid, if perhaps enhanced, piece of early Welsh rhetoric, since it was actually Hugo, Earl of Chester, who succumbed to King Magnus' shot. Not one to let such an event pass unrecorded, the saga writer had a field day.[5]

> *On the panzers, arrows rattle,*
> *Where our Norse king stands in battle,*
> *From the helmets blood-streams flow,*
> *Where our Norse king draws his bow.*
> *His bowstring twangs, its biting hail*
> *Rattles against the ring-linked mail.*
> *Up in the land in deadly strife,*
> *Our Norse king took Earl Hugo's life.*

While the sea-borne warriors of Scandinavia used the bow as a matter of course in their naval engagements, and it features large in heroic sagas of derring-do, their land-bound Saxon contemporaries disdained it as a primary weapon in warfare. True, it features in their literature, for the epic poem "The battle of Maldon," in which Ealdorman Byrhtnoth of Essex was killed, contains the lines "bogan wearan bisige" (bows were busy).[6] But the context is not clear; those busily using their bows might just have been the invading Danes.

Unequivocal, however, is a reference to the bow's use in warfare in one of the riddles that appear within the Saxon *Exeter Riddle Book*, a collection of folios thought to be of eleventh-century date.[7] Riddle 23 is unambiguous about its subject. Although given here in modern English form, its opening word was originally spelled "agof," which when reversed makes "foga," an early English alternative for "boga"—the bow.

Wob's my name, if you work it out
I'm a fair creature fashioned for battle,
When I bend and shoot a deadly shaft
From my stomach I desire only to send
That poison as far away as possible.
When my lord, who devised this torment for me,
Releases my limbs, I become longer
And, bent upon slaughter, spit it out
That deadly poison I swallowed before.
No man's parted easily from the object
I describe; if he's struck by what flies
From my stomach, he pays for its poison
With his strength—speedy atonement for his life.
I'll serve no master when unstrung, only when
I'm cunningly notched. Now guess my name.

For all the reference to the weapon in warfare, its appearance in set-piece battle was seemingly low key and its exact employment unclear. We turn once again to those tireless combiners of fact and fiction, the saga writers and their account of the battle of Stamford Bridge, precursor to Hastings and a hard-fought engagement that the Saxon king, Harold Godwinson, convincingly won.

Harold Sigurdson, king of Norway, a veritable giant of a man with pretensions to the English throne, had landed on England's east coast and, having gained success at the battle of Gate Fulford, had encamped outside York. Accompanied by Harold's disaffected brother Tostig, he was surprised by the unexpected arrival of the king with his huscarles, picked men of his bodyguard, accompanied by the Northern fyrd, and during a fierce battle, was killed (so it was said) by an arrow in the windpipe, shot by a Saxon bowman.[8]

The king, whose name would ill-doers scare,
The gold-tipped arrow would not spare
Unhelmed, unpanzered, without shield
He fell among us in the field.
The gallant men who saw him fall,
Would take no quarter; one and all
Resolved to die with their loved king,
Around his corpse in a corpse-ring.

We have no exact way of knowing the construction or the draw weights of these eleventh- and twelfth-century bows.[9] No examples exist to be studied, and the few prints from contemporary woodcuts that survive evidently owe as much to artistic license as to fact, for wood cutting of plates was an inexact science. Representations are of crude, lumpish weapons shorter than one would suppose they actually were, their strings tied rather than looped. Although used to some extent effectively in battle, they were not designed exclusively for warfare as was the great English war bow, their fourteenth-century successor. The dual purpose of the Saxon weapon was for hunting and personal protection.

The most compelling practical proposition is that they shared a similarity with the bows and arrows of half a millennium earlier—those recovered from the longships on Nydam Moor. Certainly those arrows of the period that are represented in contemporary illustrations invariably have the bulbous string notch (nock) of earlier times, which is an incidental indication of the form of draw and release in use at the time (the assisted pinch) and testimony that insofar as this important detail was concerned, the status quo remained.

Little evidence exists of the style of shooting adopted by these early bowmen. Contemporary pictures suggest two distinct techniques: for distance shooting, drawing to the chest, and for at least some point-blank shooting, drawing to the face. The Bayeux Tapestry—that most enigmatic reflection of early archery—depicts each of the 27 Norman archers with their arrows drawn to the chest and elevated above the horizontal.[10] This is consistent with the discharge of the arrow storm that we are told fell among the Saxon shield wall.

Similarly, the single Saxon bowman depicted also draws to his chest, although he appears to be aiming point blank. Whether Saxon archery played any significant part at Hastings (in distinction from the earlier affair at Stamford Bridge) is debated by historians. What records there are suggest not, and we have only the tapestry as witness. However, in passing, it has been claimed—on dubious authority it is true—that a dead soldier in the lower margin with an arrow in his face and leg is a Norman knight, which is corroborative evidence perhaps that at least one Saxon bowman was modestly successful at Hastings. A point that may be overlooked when studying the engagement as pictured, and one of some importance, is the prominent presence on the tapestry of one fully harnessed (mailed) archer among William's motley band of bowmen. If this represents a leader, as it might seem to do, then it is an argument for the planned and disciplined use of archery controlled by someone in authority in the context of William's tactical battle plan.

The fyrd in which the Saxon bowman fought was composed differently. He was one of many whose primary purpose was to embarrass the opposition with various assorted missiles, including, among other things, arrows. The intention was to leave the elite house-carles facing an enemy disoriented and in disarray. The tapestry has a mace or something similar hurtling through the air in evidence of the fyrd's presence and purpose.

That the Saxons had and used the bow there is no possible doubt; all knowledge-able authorities are agreed that practice at archery was a feature of early English life. That it was used to effect in warfare is less evident however. The English military ethic involved hand-to-hand combat in the heroic style. The devastating standoff capability of the great English war bow, the weapon that above all others humbled French chivalry at Agincourt, had yet to emerge. It remained for Duke William of Normandy to show the way and for his royal successors to carry the baton onward.

A Norman mailed archer as depict-ed on the Bayeux Tapestry. Notice the waist quiver and the replace-ment arrows carried on the bow.

The battle of Hastings was a close-run thing, for locked in combat were two divergent styles of warfare. There was massed Norman archery to soften resistance, followed by determined cavalry attack—an innovative combination tested successfully on the Continent—pit-ted against professional warriors wielding the murderous two-handed Saxon battle axe, massed together to form the famed shield wall, and their stubborn attrition of an attacking force dominated by cavalry.

Although only archers using the hand bow are pictured on the tapestry, there is some historic evidence for Duke William's employment of the cross-bow at Hastings.[11] However, it seems likely, if not probable, that since it was most effective and accurate at comparatively short range against specific tar-gets, its use would of necessity have been limited to the preliminaries. For while the hand bow could continue in use, hurling its heavier arrows at high trajectory during the time that the cavalry was in action, the limitations of the crossbow with its lighter bolts seemingly precluded its continuance throughout the battle. Such may be the reasons for its nonappearance on the tapestry. Finally, of note in the context of later warfare is the depiction of an archer on horseback pursuing the defeated English. Mounted archers were not to become a staple of the medieval English armies until a later date.

For all its devastating impact on Anglo-Saxon England's ability to defend itself, the demolition of the shield wall on that October day was less traumatic than it may have seemed. While the death of Harold and the downfall of the House of Godwin left a power vacuum eagerly filled by William and his entrepreneurial entourage, the principle of dedicated bodyguards remained. The house-carles, introduced by the Danish king Canute and maintained by his successors were displaced by a very similar organization, the *familia regis* of King William. This body owed direct allegiance to the king and was the fighting core of the Norman army. A twentieth-century historian neatly summarizes the glue holding this elite corps together as "friendship and money."[12] The new king was generous to his friends—and they remained friendly to him while gifts in money or kind flowed freely.

Supporting the elite *familia*, William employed mercenaries (soldiers not motivated by loyalty to a cause whose services were purchased as commodities are bought) while the old select fyrd, hitherto effective in their duties as primary support for the house-carles, now underpinned the *familia*. They were assisted by the great fyrd, a raggle-taggle of county militia, more than occasionally lukewarm in their enthusiasm and rather less well armed than their peers, who served up to and, when needed, sometimes beyond their county borders. It is not surprising that mercenaries who were well paid performed well—the very word illustrates the point—and besides providing a safe passage home, Duke William paid his professional soldiers handsomely for the victory at Hastings. Other monarchs have not always been so careful of their housekeeping. Mercenaries whose pay is delayed quickly lose their passion for the cause; while those who are not paid at all are downright liabilities and very likely to turn to other ways of obtaining the promised plum.

Professional soldiers apart, the new king was not slow to appreciate the fighting qualities of the men he now ruled. As early as 1068, at William's direction, the Anglo-Saxon foot soldiers of the Devonshire fyrd were called out in his support. The occasion was the siege of Exeter, erstwhile Godwin territory, and the date a bare two years after the defeat of a king to whom they were previously loyally bound. Whether those men of the southern fyrd who had opposed William at Hastings would have been quite as enthusiastic might be more open to question.

That the Saxon fighting men in much of England now accepted William as he accepted them is evident from a circumstance at the battle of Gerberoy in 1079 when, unhorsed and wounded, his life was saved by an English soldier.[13] But we must move on, for we have too long departed from the purpose of this story.

The nascence of the great war bow, the crooked stick that forms the title of this book, is lost in time. There are those who aver that it is wrongly named—that it should be called the Welsh war bow—and others who just as passionately claim it for England. Surely, each played their part, did they not? Who are we to deny them? But before credit is ascribed to either, let us examine each claim in context; and as we do, let us look closely at certain constraints. You, the reader, unbiased in the matter, must pass your judgment!

Professor J. G. D. Clark, an eminent authority on prehistoric and early historic archery, succinctly summarizes the case for England. He writes, "In approaching the immediate origin of the English longbow one enters terrain with little firm ground," to which I prudently would add, "We move with care, for we tread on the stuff of legend."

There is little, if any, evidence from archaeology for archery in Wales during the pre-Roman Iron Age, and from this one may with caution draw the conclusion that the Welsh either did not have the bow or if they did, then they had it in such small numbers that its chance survival was remote. There is the benefit of doubt, however, and this we must readily acknowledge.

With the coming of the Romans, auxiliaries arrived whose weapon was the recurved eastern composite bow of complex manufacture. Many bone fragments of these weapons have been recovered from archaeological excavation at the Roman legionary fortress of Caerleon in south Wales, and their presence is evidence that the composite bow of horn, sinew, and wood, rather than the simple wooden self-bow of European tribes, was the one that was in customary use.

Enter the Normans—more particularly, Richard de Clare, Lord of Chepstow Castle. His sobriquet, "Strongbow," is significant; and his place in the history of Welsh archery is important, for Chepstow is in Gwent, and it is the men of Gwent whose fame as archers surpassed all others. It is these men of whom Giraldus Cambrensis (Gerald of Wales) wrote they "were more accustomed to war . . . and more expert in archery, than those in any other part of Wales." Furthermore, it is these men that the warrior king Edward I chose to use to support his men-at-arms.[14]

In support of his claim, Giraldus records the penetration of Welsh arrowheads "nearly a palm's breadth" into an oaken door. Assuming a palm's breadth to be some 3 1/2 inches and assuming a bow shot at close range, this is evidence indeed of the power of the Welsh weapon. Despite occasional flights of fancy consistent with a period when fact, fiction, and pure imagination were the stuff of life, this account bears the hallmark of truth. Welsh archers were men with whom it was unwise to trifle.

An uncomplimentary depiction of Welsh bowmen. Thirteenth-century woodcut. Notice the crude appearance of foreshortened bows. Public Record Office Liber A (E36/274) f.32 & f.36.

But how did they learn their trade? Did Richard de Clare, he of the "strongbow" who chose to identify himself so closely with the weapon, encourage its use among those over whom he held sway, men who accompanied him on his Irish wars? Did he act as a powerful leader and a strong bowman inspiring others? Is it to the Normans, and one Norman in particular perhaps, that we owe the genesis of the great war bow? What of the English and their own weapon? That they had the bow there is no doubt; many are the early woodcuts that prove its use for hunting, if not for warfare—although as we have seen, there is circumstantial evidence from the Exeter riddle for its use in battle. While there may be doubt over the use of the bow in immediate pre-Roman and Romanized Celtic Britain, there is no such doubt about its use by Saxons, either in their homeland or after their arrival in Britain.

As we have already seen, Roger Ascham in his preamble to *Toxophilus*, *the Schole of Shotinge*, records that Sir Thomas Elyot believed the Saxons to have dominated the Britons by the power of their bows alone. So if the Saxons, predecessors of the postconquest English, had the bow and used it to effect, then where is the controversy? It is a rhetorical question. The Welsh had and used the heavy bow for warfare and hunting, the Saxons had and used a lighter weapon for hunting and, perhaps to some limited and unorganized degree, for war and protection. To the volatile Celt, warfare was a way of life; each Welsh male owed allegiance to a *twysog*, or petty chieftain, and would expect to accompany him upon military expeditions as a matter of course. Warfare was a bond that tied able-bodied men to their leader. Warfare was an expected way of life and something at which the warrior Celt had proved himself to be rather good. With an economy that ensured summers spent on the mountain and winters in the valley, there was an in-built mobility to early Welsh life—a fluidity of movement that was denied the Saxon peasant tied to his land. The poet Thomas Love Peacock exemplified this Welsh ethos exactly in his poem "The War-song of Dinas Bran."

> *The mountain sheep are sweeter,*
> *But the valley sheep are fatter,*
> *We therefore deemed it meeter*
> *To carry off the latter.*
> *We made an Expedition,*
> *We met a host and quelled it,*
> *We forced a strong position,*
> *And killed the men that held it.*

Inflamed by raiding Welsh from across the border, many so-called expeditions were sent by Norman marcher lords irritated by Welsh incursions to teach these untamed mountain men a lesson; such forays ended in inevitable failure, for the forests and mountains of Wales were made for ambush. The Welsh bow was employed to devastating effect as a sudden rush of spearmen, backed by accurate archery, laid the intruders low.

But what of their bows? We turn to Giraldus again.[15] The Welsh bow, he tells us, was of wild (wych) elm (*Ulmus glabra*), unpolished and uncouth but powerful. Not calculated to shoot an arrow to any great distance, but deadly effective at short range, it made an ideal weapon for ambush warfare in the confined space of forest glade or mountain pass. Yet one wonders why, with forest yew available, wych elm with its poorer elasticity was seemingly preferred. However, the Welsh bow served its purpose adequately, even admirably, since it caught the royal eye. It did so to such effect, in fact, that the carriage of bows and arrows (and pointed weapons generally) was forbidden east of the river Severn. There is more than a suggestion here that the Welsh bowman was more than a match for contemporary English opposition.

Although England's early Norman kings were well supplied with archers, these were largely crossbowmen—mercenaries who served well and were paid well for their service. Cost is a powerful stimulus for change of practice though, and with the native product close at hand, albeit drawn from a nation not yet fully subjected to Norman rule, Welsh bowmen from Gwent slowly replaced the mercenaries. However, there was a problem. There are two elements to an archer: the bow and the person, and here we may speculate a little about national character. Undoubtedly a fine archer and a brave fighter, the Celt was a volatile being and sometimes a stranger to the essential discipline of warfare. Moreover, his loyalty to the cause of England was more than occasionally in doubt, as those who administered the king's writ in authority over him were prone to find to their cost.

But battles are won by dogged determination and slavish loyalty, and in England, there was an immense untapped source of potential warrior bowmen, phlegmatic by nature and dogged of character, whose loyalty to their lord was absolute. It was to these men that their king and country turned, and as history records, they served them well. There was indeed already a nucleus of such native archers in early English armies. From the northern English county of Cheshire were drawn the Macclesfield Hundred, an elite body of bowmen whose pay of threepence a day reflected their skill and the esteem in which they were held.

The stirrings of military interest in this pool began during the reign of Henry I (1100–1135) when a law was passed exonerating an archer from charge of murder or manslaughter if while at practice on a recognized archery ground and after calling "stand fast" he accidentally killed a passerby.[16] Although the freedom from prosecution has long since gone, 900 years later, this cry (now abbreviated to "fast") is still a principal tenet of archery discipline while on the shooting line.

While the bow in use at that time in England is most likely to have been a lighter weapon than the fully developed war bow, it is speculative that during the twelfth century there was an understanding of a need for accurate distance shooting. Certainly by 1242, with the publication of Henry III's *Assize of Arms* and recognition of the bow as a primary national weapon, all males between 15 and 60 years of age were required not only to practice archery but to keep arms, including bows. The age of the English and Welsh military bowmen, the dreaded "goddams"—so called from their constant use of the term—whose presence on French battlefields would strike terror into the hearts of nobility and peasant alike, was about to begin.

A consequence of the more general use of the bow was the growing threat associated with forest dwellers whose practice with the weapon was taking an increasingly practical turn to the detriment of the king's deer herd. They were required to arm their arrows with blunt heads and forbidden on pain of dire penalty to harm venison. A cabalistic verse succinctly outlined the circumstances in which a malefactor might be apprehended. "Dog draw: Stable stand:

Back beround: Bloody hand." (With scenting hound or with bow ready, carrying a carcass, or having cut it up). From New Forest documents for 1247, we have proof that the forest law had teeth. "It is presented and proved that on the Monday before St. Nicholas (December 2) John the son of Edonis de Lyndhurst and Simon le Theyn were taken by the foresters with bows and arrows for harming the deer. Afterwards they were hanged for theft."[17] No doubt, this was *pour encourager les autres.*

Before they could be fully effective, however, Englishmen needed to be weaned from the lighter hunting-style bows that they habitually used (and with which they were most familiar) and introduced to the more powerful war bow, a weapon capable of lofting a 3-ounce battle shaft over 200 yards to bring down horse, knight, and advancing infantry alike. We may reasonably speculate that there was a period when this occurred—one undoubtedly accompanied by predictable rustic opposition as bow strengths doubled.

While there is no direct record in support of this inferred reluctance, we may confidently believe that it existed. Within the early ballads of Robin Hood, a rich source of archery lore, there are faint echoes of what may have been entrenched attitudes among those who listened; attitudes that authority would wish to overcome. A feature of the early ballad "Robin Hood and the Potter" will serve as an example.[18] Our forest hero has assumed a disguise to enter Nottingham Town for some nefarious purpose, and having done so, is made aware of an archery tournament. He is persuaded to enter this, and arriving late on the scene, he is offered a bow by the sheriff, the best there is available.

Thou shalle haffe a bowe, seyde the scheffe [sheriff]
The best that thow well cheys [choose] *of thre,*
Thow sems a stalward and a stronge [man],
Asay [proved] *schall thow be.*
The scheffe commandyd a yemen [yeoman] *that stood hem bye,*
Affter bowes to wend [go]
The best bowe that the yemen browthe [brought]
Robyn set on a stryng.
Now schall y wet [I know] *an* [if] *thou be god* [good]
And polle het op to they ner [thine ear]
So god me helpe, seyde the prowde potter,
Thys ys bot rygzt weke gere [This is but right weak gear].

Weak gear or no, that was all that was available, and Robin then goes to his cart to select an arrow from his "quequer" (itself an early and interesting word with an Asian origin for what today we know as the quiver). With this arrow and the borrowed bow, he not surprisingly wins the tournament. The interest of this brief snatch from a lengthy ballad lies in two subliminal messages: the reference to "weak gear" and in the admonition to "draw to the ear." Robin, the role model for medieval man, disdained weak bows. They were for weaklings; real men used the heavy weapon. Moreover, real men drew their arrows to the ear, not to the chest or part way to the face as may have been the custom at that time. They got their backs into their weapons, and in that way, they got distance and accuracy.

There is just a hint from another early ballad (the earliest, in fact: "A Lytell Geste [Tale] of Robyn Hode") of a time when perhaps bow draw weights changed from low to high poundages.[19] Robin has aided a poor knight with money to repay a debt, and in gratitude, the knight has given him a present. He has provided a parcel of 100 new bows and 100 sheaves of arrows, which surely is a generous gesture, but an interesting one if they had replaced earlier, weaker weapons.

> *He* (the knight) *purveyed him an hondred bowes,*
> *The strynges well ydyght* [dressed]
> *An hondred shefe of arowes gode,*
> *The hedys burneshed full bryght*
> *And every arowe an elle long,*
> *With pecok well idight* [fletched]
> *Worked all wit whyte silver,*
> *It was a semely sight.*
> *But what will these bowes do? sayd Robin,*
> *And these arowes fethered fre,*
> *By God than sayd the knyght,*
> *A pore present to the*(e).

The Lytell Geste cannot be positively dated, but informed opinion has suggested a thirteenth-century oral origin. Such a time, in fact, would be consistent with Henry III's *Assize of Arms* and the emergence of the bow as a national weapon. Let us not leave this unexpected present just yet. If we are to assume that these bows were superior to those that Robin had, then perhaps they were made from the bole rather than the branch of a tree. We know that bough bows are inferior to those from the trunk, or bole, for Roger Ascham, the sixteenth-century father of modern archery, tells us so in *Toxophilus*.

> But turne we againe to know a good shotinge bowe for our purpose. Everye
> bowe is made eyther of a boughe of a plante [sapling] or of the boole [bole] of

Woodcut (thirteenth century) depicting Edmund, king of the East Angles, saint and martyr, being shot to death with arrows by drunken Danes from an army led by Hingwar (Ivar the Boneless) and Hubba after the battle of Hoxne in AD 946. Notice that the arrow is being drawn by two fingers. From Royal MS.

the tree. The boughe commonlye is very knottye, and full of pinnes, weake, of small pithe [sapwood, to provide tensile strength] and some will follow the stringe, and seldom werith to any fayre coloure [wear to achieve a patina], yet for children and yonge beginners it may serve well enough. The boole of the tree is cleanest without knot or pin, having a faste and harde wodde, by reason of hys full growth, strong and mighty of cast, and best for a bowe.

Confirming all this, if confirmation were indeed necessary, are the ballads again, but this time involving Robin's trusty lieutenant, Little John. In the ballad "Guy of Gisborne," John is apprehended by foresters while about his business and stands four-square to defend himself.[20]

Then John bent up his longe bende-bow
And fettled him [got ready] *to shoote*
The bow was made of tender bough,
And fell down at his foot . . . .
Woe worth, woe worth thee wicked wood,
That ever thou grew on a tree,
For now this day thou art my bale [woe],
My help when thou should be.

Resulting from this (perhaps predictable) equipment failure, Little John is captured and led away. A moral is clearly there for the avid listener. Bough bows, the weapon used, no doubt, by many of those familiar with the tale, are out! Sensible archers use real bows, cut from the bole and not the bough; a subliminal message is hammered home yet again. A century earlier than Ascham, Geoffrey Chaucer chooses the bow made from a "plant" (sapling) to exemplify the wholesome and pure in his romantic verse drama "The Romance of the Rose."

This bachelore stood beholding
The daunce [dance]*; and in his honde holding*
Turke bowes two had he.[21]
That one of them was of a tree
That bereth fruit of savour wicke(d)
Ful croked was that foul stycke.
And knotty here and theer also,
And black as bery or any sloe
That other was of a plante
Without wenne [knot]*, I dare warrante*
Ful even and by proporçioun [proportion]
Treitys [graceful] *and longe, of good facyon* [fashion]
And it was painted well and twitten [narrowed or tapered]
And overall diapered [decorated or inscribed]
With ladyes and with bacheleres.

The foul and crooked stick of a tree that Chaucer so vividly describes (although not typically "knotty"as Roger Ascham noted above) would doubtless have been more familiar to his audience than the graceful weapon, epitome of excellence, that follows; but he had a moral to convey, and what more natural than to elaborate upon the well-known qualities and characteristics of bough and plant bow in order to emphasize it?

There are numerous references to painted bows in early records, and these are not yet satisfactorily understood. It has been suggested that painting in this context may be no more than a protective coat of shellac or something similar in contrast to the more usual finish of oil or wax. The reference warrants explanation, but none so far is convincing. Whatever it meant to Chaucer and his audience, however, the resultant surface was such that it could be decorated, and this may provide a clue.

Sadly, in fact, we know very little about these early bows. It seems probable that at least some, perhaps all, were of yew. Whether this was native wood or from Youghal in Ireland, whence we know bow staves to have come, we cannot say. We may guess that their sections were similar to those of later times, but whether they were fitted with horn sheaths, or nocks, to protect their vulnerable tips as were later versions is unknown. The length of these early weapons is also uncertain. We may regard their appearance in early representations with some suspicion, although the illustrator of the Luttrell Psalter does seem less inclined toward artistic license than do others.

Let us turn once more to ballad for our clue, for there is enigmatic and circumstantial evidence here. Wishing to kit someone out with cloth, Robin instructs Little John to measure "thre yerdes (rods or roods in this context) of every color" when providing the wherewithal for the clothing. We are told that "Lytell John toke no other mesure but his bow tre" (tree, or stave). If the allusion is truly literal, then three linear "rods or roods" of 7 feet 6 inches (the northern measure) would provide 22 feet 6 inches of cloth. Tradition tells us that Little John was a tall man, but a 90-inch bow might seem more than a trifle adequate. As an aside, and not to be taken altogether seriously, the bow traditionally associated with him and held for centuries at Hathersage Church in Derbyshire is 81 inches long. We will leave the matter there.

If the length of the early medieval bow is a mystery, then what of the arrow used with it? Again, we have guidance from the ballad. Robin's gifted arrows are "an ell long" we are told. That is fine, but there is an immediate problem; unfortunately, the ell had no fixed standard. Taken originally from the length of a part of the body, as were other early measures, it measured about 18 inches, or the length of a man's forearm from elbow to extended middle finger. Clearly this is not of arrow length. Across the years, however, variations occurred; and for reasons that seem not to relate at all to anatomical dimension, we are offered a Scottish ell of 37 inches, a French ell of 47 inches, and a Flemish ell of 27 inches. To complete the picture, we have an English ell that is seemingly standardized at 45 inches in the sixteenth century. So, where are we in this maze of figures? We may discard the concept of a 47-inch arrow, and since the ballad clearly predates the sixteenth century, the 45-inch measurement must also go. We are left with the Scottish ell of 37 inches or the Flemish ell of 27. Each is tempting. The longer version suggests the clothyard shaft of nineteenth-century fiction, and certainly this could have stood, or been drawn, within a full-sized war bow. However, although short for warfare, the 27-inch arrow does make its appearance later on, since early recreational shafts were of this length. Adding to the confusion, early sixteenth-century war arrows, those that were used with 77-inch war bows, were 31 1/2 inches in length. Clearly, we are no closer in defining the length of early medieval arrows than we are with the early medieval bow.

Fletchings present no problem however. These were mainly goose, although the ruddier brown of peacock seems to have been preferred by some over the rather drab gray goose feather. In his *Canterbury Tales*, Chaucer reflects the Yeoman's taste for the mildly exotic, and he may have been mirroring a trend. In modern English, it reads thus:

> *This Yeoman wore a coat and hood of green*
> *And peacock-feathered arrows, bright and keen,*
> *And neatly sheathed hung at his belt the while*
> *For he could dress his gear in yeoman style,*
> *His arrows never drooped their feathers low.*

Although two profiles (the swine backed and the saddle backed) are known and can be found in a hunting context, the fletching profile of the war arrow may have stabilized quite early. Although, unsurprisingly, none survive in the original, almost without exception it is the long, low, triangular shape that appears on early woodcuts.

With the arrowhead we are on slightly firmer ground. Where arrow shafts are conspicuous by their absence—nature having effectively recycled them— arrowheads are present in some numbers and, within the parameters of their various purposes, in considerable variety. A thoughtful London museum has cataloged them, using two principal categories: those designed to penetrate mail and plate armor and those designed to cut through flesh and bone. Among these, we now recognize many different shapes and profiles. Inevitably, there are variations within a general shape, and some are better known than others. The head that is probably best known is called Type 16; to the cognoscenti, this conjures up a lightly and closely barbed socketed broadhead ideally suited to penetrate flesh and to cause hemorrhage. Scarcely less well known is the one called Type 7, a needle-sharp socketed head designed to deal with mail. While today we define these two distinctions as broadhead (Type 16) and bodkin point (Type 7), in earlier times, they had other, vernacular names descriptive of their characteristics or perhaps their shape.

Thus, from a fifteenth-century inventory of arrows, we have "dokebyll-hedys" (possibly deriving from "duck's bill," the dialect word for a boring instrument used in a stock like a center bit, and employed chiefly by chair makers) and "bykere" (the related word is "bikkern," meaning beaked or pointed), "brodhoked" (broad hooked or barbed), "hoked" (hooked), and "sperhedys" (spear heads).[22] To these may be added the "forker," the "swallowtail" or "horsehead," and the "conical," "short square," and "fluted" bodkins. Each had

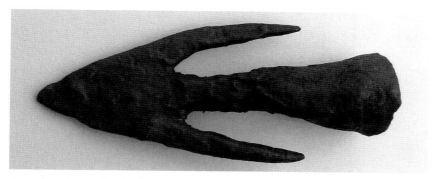

A medieval arrowhead, plan view. London Museum Type 16. Jessop's alternative typology M4. Notice the wide-spaced barbs. Photo by Mark Stretton.

its purpose. The curiously named "forker," or crescent broadhead as we should correctly call it, was used to slice the necks of ostriches in Roman amphitheaters. Its alleged ability to cut a ship's rigging has assured it a place in fictional history, and we have Sir Arthur Conan Doyle's nineteenth-century adventure story "The White Company" to thank for this piece of fanciful whimsy.

This then was the armament with which the early warrior archer went to war. In the next chapter, we will examine how it was used and the organization of its making.

The Rise of the War Bow

Had the battle of Hastings gone Harold Godwinson's way—as so nearly happened—it is a matter of some speculation whether the longbow would have emerged in the form in which it did. Indeed, it is a matter for conjecture whether it would ever have formed a significant part of Anglo-Saxon armies. Had the shield wall stood firm, then it is entirely possible that the light Saxon bow, more suited to its purpose as a hunting weapon than to standoff warfare, would have remained an ancillary weapon, with no greater role than as part of the ill-disciplined, general missile-hurling fyrd.

King William had long been convinced of the effectiveness of the bow and arrow, whether it was the longbow or the crossbow; and the presence of his archers at Hastings, mercenaries to a man, was an expenditure coupled to carefully calculated purpose. If crossbows were indeed present at Hastings, as many believe they were—and they are referred to by the author of the "Carmen de Hastingae Proelio" (The Song of the Battle of Hastings) when he mentions that shields would not stop crossbow bolts—then this was their debut in England. Be that as it may, William's employment of archery had played as significant a part in softening up Harold's Anglo-Saxon opposition as perhaps it had in his earlier Continental adventures.

For all its obvious potential as a weapon of mass destruction, the early hand bow was restricted in the distance it would cast an arrow, though perhaps not quite as limited as one eminent modern authority on Norman warfare might believe, for he has credited it with a maximum effective range of under 90 yards, or fractionally more than a third of the distance achieved by the English war bow in its prime. The contemporary crossbow is credited with the greater range of 150 yards.[1] However, the seed was sown, and from the fertile soil of

England was eventually to grow and flourish the military bow along with the English and Welsh archer and those military tactics that made English armies well-nigh invincible for two centuries and more.

Anglo-Norman armies were small and compact, partly because a proportion of their forces was composed of mercenaries but partly, perhaps, because (to paraphrase an oft-quoted observation) it isn't size that matters, it's what can be done with it. Consisting of mounted knights, foot-slogging infantry, and horsed archers in varying numbers, but with a preponderance of cavalry, they were in the main a well-led and effective fighting force responsive to the need, on occasion, for tactical maneuver.

Archers are specifically mentioned in a number of twelfth-century battles, and although it is not always entirely clear whether they were crossbowmen or hand bowmen (I use the term deliberately to distinguish from later true long-bowmen), their presence was tactically significant.

Two battles will serve to make the point: Alençon, fought in 1118, and Bourgthéroulde, fought in 1124; each illustrates the developing use of archers in support of cavalry.[2] Alençon had famously figured some 60 years before, when Duke William had been seriously irritated by the action of the inhabitants, who had hung animal skins over the walls to taunt him as the bastard son of a tanner. In retribution for the implied insult, he had 32 leading citizens paraded in front of the rest and summarily sliced off their feet and hands. William, Duke of Normandy, future conqueror of England, had his dark side!

But, we turn to the battles. Perhaps for reasons of injured pride (since William's son, Henry I, was not victorious), Alençon does not feature in Anglo-Norman accounts of engagements fought. In 1118, the town and castle were held for Henry I by his nephew Stephen—an immoderate man with few saving graces—whose cavalier treatment of townsfolk and their wives had led them to invite a sympathetic nearby Angevin, Fulk of Anjou, to take over control. This he had accepted with alacrity and was even now arranging to besiege the castle. Faced with the prospective loss of an important stronghold, Henry had gathered his forces and had set off to deal with the overenthusiastic Fulk, who was encamped in a nearby park. Militarily, the position was complex. While the castle was held by men loyal to Henry, the townsfolk were, to put it no stronger, ambivalent about their allegiance. Meanwhile, between the king and both castle and town was a not-insignificant force of knights and mounted archers, three groups of whom had, with a great deal of clamor and general hubbub, been repulsed when sent to test Henry's defenses.

Matters were approaching stalemate when a second Angevin noble, Lisiard of Sablé, appeared on the scene. Having heard the noise of conflict while some way away, and ready as ever to help a fellow countryman (after, one may assume, carefully weighing up the opposition), Lisiard dismounted his men in a nearby wooded valley and ordered them to prepare for battle. Having equipped themselves with leg armor, mail coats, and helmets and generally readied themselves for battle, knights, archers, and infantry on foot formed their lines and, at a trumpet call, engaged Henry's forces. Once in position, the Angevin archers played havoc with Henry's knights and their horses. It is not clear whether Lisiard's men were mounted or had dismounted for the attack, but a subsequent cavalry charge supported by archers and crossbowmen finished matters, and leaving Alençon, its castle, and its relieved townsfolk to the victorious Fulk, Henry retired in discomfort with the remnants of his army to lick his wounds. It was an early lesson in the decisive power of massed archery and one that would not be lost on the defeated king.

A second early battle in which the bow featured prominently took place in 1124 either at or near the town of Bourgthéroulde. Waleran of Meulan, an intemperate young nobleman in conflict with King Henry, was returning to his stronghold after attempting to relieve one of his besieged castles when he was unfortunate enough to find his way blocked by a force of royal household troops collected from nearby castle garrisons. Against advice from his more prudent captains and without the caution born of experience, rather than accept the inevitable and make a detour, the hotheaded Waleran decided to take on this professional opposition and prepared his cavalry to fight.

The royal troops dismounted, and their commander outlined his battle tactics: a plan of particular interest, since archery was to play a significant role. One section of the force of men-at-arms was to dismount and fight on foot, while the rest were to remain mounted for action as cavalry. Household bowmen were to be placed forward of the front line to disrupt the expected cavalry charge, and a force of mounted archers was also sent forward to the left of the line to engage the right flank of the enemy. It is uncertain whether these men fought mounted or on foot. Matters went exactly according to plan; horses were brought down by arrow volleys, the charge was broken, and the survivors fled. Waleran himself was taken prisoner to cool his heels at Henry's pleasure.

It is evident that during the eleventh and twelfth centuries, if archers and archery were not fundamental to Norman battle tactics, then they were valued sufficiently to play an important role in their Continental successes (and conversely their occasional failures). But we must now leave the Continent to its devices and return to England, for opportunities to use the bow tactically to effect were fast approaching.

The battle that took place at Northallerton in Yorkshire in 1138, known colloquially as the Battle of the Standard, was fought between the Anglo-Normans and their old enemy, the Scots.[3] We will set the scene. Henry I of England had died three years previously, and with the sad demise of his son and heir in the White Ship disaster in 1120, the English throne had been in some turmoil. Stepping with confidence, if not authority, into the breach, Stephen, Count of Blois and Henry's nephew, had taken up the reins of power and was as firmly in control as most monarchs at that time. Bubbling with barely suppressed fury, however, was Henry's daughter Matilda. The king had extracted promises of support for her as legitimate claimant to the throne from his barons, and Stephen's summary takeover rankled. In full knowledge of this, her uncle, King David of Scotland, ever ready to find excuse to invade England, made the first of three punitive assaults on the northern counties. Although Stephen's arrival with a very large army successfully countered this threat, the concessions that David subsequently obtained convinced him to make a second attempt at unseating the king. Accordingly, 1137 saw Scottish clansmen once more south of the border, again to be bought off by truce.

Matters were now taking on a distinct air of déja vu, and 1138 saw King David again on what was fast becoming familiar territory, this time with the overt support of an English baron, the influential Eustace fitz-John. His confidence boosted by this recruit to the cause, King David had encouraged his Galwegian troops to plunder the northern countryside, and they had been particularly thorough. The contemporary chronicler Henry of Huntingdon recorded the following:

> His followers dealt most barbarously with the English. They ripped open pregnant women, tossed children on the points of their spears, butchered priests at their altars and, cutting off the heads from the images on crucifixes, placed them on the bodies of the slain, whilst in exchange they fixed on the crucifixes the heads of their victims.

However, temerity brought retribution. With Stephen away in the south dealing with a rebellion, the northern barons, responding to an appeal by Archbishop Thurston of York, now took matters into their own hands. Thus it was that on August 22, 1138, on a hillock outside Northallerton, the sacred standards of St. Peter of York, St. John of Beverley, and St. Wilfred of Ripon were raised; and defending them, ready to deal with King David and his murderous Galwegians, was the fully armed avenging might of northern England. The northern army was ranged in three battalions: a forward rank of dismounted men-at-arms and bowmen, a phalanx of knights gathered around the standards to defend them, and the shire levies to the rear and the flanks. Facing them, on a hillock some 600 yards away, David had deployed his troops. Men-at-arms and archers were to the fore, with Galwegians and Highlanders initially to the rear. However, this arrangement was not to the liking of the men from Galloway, who volubly asserted their hereditary right to lead the charge; and to King David's military discredit, he acceded to this claim.

Matters therefore opened with a wild charge by the unarmored Galwegians. Although they were mown down in their hundreds by arrow volleys from the English bowmen, their impetus was such that initially they passed the archers and burst through the English lines. Those who gained a foothold were quickly dealt with, however, and once more the shield wall stood firm. Repeated attacks followed, all of which were repulsed by northern men-at-arms. Finally, in an endeavor to break this stalemate, David's son Prince Henry led a small mounted charge. Unfortunately for the prince, this proved rather too successful; he and his horsemen rode straight through the English lines to reappear at their rear. Before advancing Scottish infantry could take advantage of this breach, the shield wall had once more reformed, and unable to return or to be of much more use, the discomforted prince and his mounted men were obliged to discard their insignia and merge with the opposition until they could once more regain their own lines. With the Galwegians now a steadily diminishing force, the cavalry disoriented, and a lack of enthusiasm mounting among David's remaining Highlanders, the Scottish army disintegrated and, leaving their king and his bodyguard to their own devices, departed the field. With their horses some way away, the English men-at-arms were unable to deploy promptly enough to catch the retreating Scots, and the usual slaughter of fleeing troops did not occur.

Since this book concerns the bow and its use, it is appropriate to speculate a little here. While archers certainly took part in the Battle of the Standard and, from their apparent positioning, played a significant role in disrupting the Galwegian charge, their weapons are most unlikely to have had anything approaching the power and the range of the later war bow. Sir Charles Oman is of the opinion that the lighter, hunting-style bows would have been in use.[4] If this is so, then they are unlikely to have exceeded 70 pounds in draw weight and may well have been less. Assuming an arrow of sufficient heaviness to do effective damage, a bow of this capacity casting an arrow of, say, 60 grams in weight will make little more than 140 to 150 yards at maximum trajectory and will be point-blank effective at considerably less distance.

Broadsword-wielding Galwegians, fueled by testosterone and blood lust, would cover 150 yards in rather less than a minute, during which time the

Northumbrian bowmen had not only to halt or at least disrupt the charge but to move swiftly through the line of infantry behind—if indeed they would allow them past—in order to leave the way clear for men-at-arms to deal with the remnant. For many archers, it was surely a choice between the devil and the deep blue sea; lightly armed and vulnerable, faced with well-motivated Scots to their front and a locked shield wall behind, in this context it is difficult not to see them as expendable. Nevertheless, they performed well and with bravery; and there is little doubt that as in Continental confrontations, the inclusion of archers as part of an overall tactical plan paid significant dividends. It was not until a century later, however, that Henry III's *Assize of Arms* (1252) gave the bow an official position among the country's primary armament.

Although the finest archers in those thirteenth-century days were still from south Wales—for the English peasant had yet to master the heavy war bow—it seems probable that the bowmen facing the Scots at Northallerton were locally born and bred. There may in fact have been a stronger tradition of archery in the north of England than in the south. During the protracted wars of Edward I, while the Welsh archer provided the core of English military archery, pockets of English bowmen were also regularly present—notably, from Cheshire. A body purely of archers unmixed with spearmen and known colloquially as the Macclesfield Hundred was employed without break throughout this period. The only other solely bow-armed corps to serve for a similar lengthy term was drawn from Gwent and Crickhowell in Wales. Members of each of these elite bodies were paid the considerable sum—for the time—of threepence a day.[5]

Archery was a feature of certain midland counties during the thirteenth century. Exchequer accounts for Nottingham Castle during the years 1266 and 1267 show a mix of 30 crossbowmen—20 mounted and 10 on foot—with 20 hand-bow archers. This small force was engaged at the king's behest to serve against an enemy deep within the forest of Sherwood, where in one particular engagement, the account notes, several horses were lost. Flying in the face of accepted academic fact, it is tempting here to draw Robin Hood into this particular circumstance! It would not be an entirely fanciful exercise, since although it has to be said that for every enthusiastic identifier there are two others who just as fervently think otherwise, one of the more believable accounts of the English forest hero makes him a defeated Montfortian (a supporter of Simon de Montfort, leader of the baron's revolt against the excesses of King Henry III). There is one slight clue, though, in support of the battle of Sherwood, and it comes from an alternative story of Robin's death following his wounding in a significant clash with authority. It is included here as a diversion from stolid historical fact, and no other excuse is offered for its presence. The ballad (which, unlike many others, has no pretensions to age) is interesting only in its relating a believable conclusion to the "reign" of Robin Hood the outlaw, longtime thorn in the side of authority.[6]

"Sir William" (surname unspecified) is called by the king (also unspecified) to gather together "one hundred bowmen brave, all chosen men of might" and on Midsummer Day, they marched away "with long yew bows and shining spears, they march'd in mickle pride." Once in the forest, Sir William bids them prepare their bows and await his call while he moves off in search of Robin. Having found Robin, he asks for his surrender, to be told, predictably, that he has no intention of being taken prisoner. Robin is prepared to fight for his freedom, and both he and Sir William summon their men by blast of horn. A fight then takes place between the opposing sets of bowmen. "The archers on both sides bent their bows, and clouds of arrows flew." Sir William is killed early in the engagement, but his troops battle on from morning until noon. "Both parties were stout, and loath to give out." Matters finally end, however, with honors even, and the forest invaders depart for London. Robin is taken ill; one suspects he has been wounded, although the ballad does not say as much. He sends for a monk in order to be bled, but loses his life in consequence. With their leader gone, his archers leave the forest. "Some went on board and cross'd the seas, to Flanders, France and Spain, and others to Rome for fear of their doom, but soon return'd again." This then is an alternative to the conventional story of Robin's death. It is a late ballad, true, but perhaps it is the reworking of a more ancient folk tale—one with just a soupçon of fact to bolster its authenticity.

In passing, it may be noted that transgressors against the venison in Sherwood and Barnsdale forests were granted free pardon if they joined the king's forces to fight in Wales. This is evidence, if any were needed, for recognition of their skill with a bow.

Simon de Montfort, manipulator of the weak King Henry III and the power behind the throne, fought his last battle in 1265. Leading a smaller force (from which much of his Welsh infantry subsequently defected during the conflict), he was pinned down outside Evesham in Worcestershire by Prince Edward, who later was to become the warrior king Edward I. Putting his faith in a desperate but unsuccessful cavalry charge, after fighting bravely, de Montfort was killed along with the vast majority of his men. If Robin of Sherwood had really been a Montfortian, then his escape from the carnage of Evesham truly bears the mark of good fortune.

Although Prince Edward was to wait a further seven years before succeeding to the throne, the battle of Evesham showed his military acumen in full measure and, when he was king, set the scene for later victories against rebellious Welsh and belligerent Scots alike.

We move forward a generation to 1297 and 1298 for two battles that set the scene for a forthcoming dominance of bowmen and their weapon. The one was a totally avoidable disaster for the English under Lord Surrey and the other, a resounding victory for King Edward I.

The battle of Stirling Bridge was notable for the presence of three men: William Wallace, a brutal fighter for Scotland's cause and a gifted tactical leader of huge strength and charismatic appeal; the Earl of Surrey, an indolent and vacillating ditherer who commanded the English force; and Sir Hugh Cressingham, King Edward's thoroughly unpopular penny-pinching treasurer.[7] With Wallace on the rampage throughout Scotland and Edward fully occupied in other parts of his kingdom, responsibility for re-establishing the status quo fell upon the reluctant shoulders of Surrey. Having finally accepted his role in the matter, he gathered together an army and, accompanied by ever-watchful Treasurer Cressingham, moved slowly and with no noticeable enthusiasm northward to bring the insurgent Scots to battle.

Arriving at Stirling, he found Wallace and his spearmen securely entrenched and awaiting him on the north side of the river Forth a mile to the northeast of the wooden Stirling bridge. While debating with his commanders the necessity of crossing, it was suggested that this should be achieved by way of a wide ford downriver of the site in order to mount a flank attack. This proposal was turned down by Cressingham, probably on the grounds of expense, since it would have added time (he had already dismissed one contingent of the army in a cost-cutting exercise). Here, in front of them, was a perfectly adequate bridge, he said, why should they not use that?

Indeed, there was a bridge there, but it was a narrow packhorse affair over which two men could barely ride abreast. Moreover, on its northern side was marshy ground with just a causeway on which to marshal. However, Cressingham was adamant; and, watched by an incredulous Wallace and his valiant spearmen, two by two the English men-at-arms, including Treasurer Cressingham, rode ponderously across to form up with difficulty on the other side. Waiting until a significant but, he estimated, a manageable proportion had crossed and were milling around in some disorder, Wallace struck. Leading his enthusiastic spearmen, he advanced toward that half of the English army that had reached the northern side and engaged them in battle. The result was chaos. The English were routed. Men-at-arms retreating across the bridge were met head on by those endeavoring to reinforce. Ultimately the bridge collapsed. Some Welsh archers and knifemen swam to safety, but the half of the English army that was attacked by the Scots ceased to exist. It is recorded that Wallace captured the parsimonious Cressingham and had him flayed to make a sword belt from his skin.

Although archers were undoubtedly present at Stirling Bridge, they seem not to have been used to effect. It became customary later that when fording or bridging a river, archers would first be sent across to establish a secure bridgehead—a necessary and an effective tactical ploy, as later events were to prove. Had the original proposal to ford the river been accepted, with archers used for this purpose, then matters may well have turned in Surrey's favor.

Falkirk was a very different matter however.[8] With other matters settled or satisfactorily on hold, Edward himself was now able to devote time and energy to his Scottish borders, and the army he gathered together was evidence of his determination. From north and south Wales, he requisitioned 10,500 men, of whom 2,000 from the south were probably archers. Of the English, 1,000 were required from Chester and the same number from Lancashire. Again, it is probable that these men used the bow. A corps of some 500 foot crossbowmen made up the infantry contingent. An estimated 2,400 cavalry brought the strength of the army that was to face Wallace and his spear-armed schiltrons to around 15,000 men. In opposition, the Scottish army, which included a contingent of cavalry and a small corps of archers with hand bows, was somewhat less.

Providing victuals was, as always, a difficulty, since in those early days, supplies were irregular. A rather nasty incident arose when Edward, with unaccustomed lack of judgment, allowed his Welsh troops sole access to a shipment of wine, to the forthrightly expressed concern of his English archers, who drew knives and braced bows in support of their rival claims to this bounty. Following the resultant melée, put down with some difficulty, the Welsh threatened to defect to Wallace, occasioning the alleged xenophobic response by Edward, "What matter if enemies join enemies. Welsh and Scots alike are both our foes. Let them go where they like, for with God's blessing in one day we shall get revenge on both Nations." Matters were calmed, however; and Wallace and his pikemen having been located, on July 22, 1298, the two armies met in battle.

The Scots had devised and adopted a defensive formation of squares or circles of pikes, with the front ranks kneeling, their weapons at breast height, and the rear ranks standing. All were behind a hedge of stakes. This formation was

A nineteenth-century engraving depicting the collapse of Stirling Bridge.

almost invulnerable and able to withstand cavalry attack with considerable success. Edward, however, had a formidable card to play: his Welsh and English bowmen; and after his cavalry had routed and killed the corps of Scottish archers placed between the schiltrons, he brought them into play. Loosing volley after volley of their murderous battle shafts with steady deliberation, they slowly but surely demolished Wallace's tightly packed squares of pikes. Unable to retaliate, troops fell where they stood, and great gaps appeared where once had been a solid mass of men. When it became certain that his cause was lost and defeat was now inevitable, Wallace and his commanders escaped into nearby Callendar forest.

It would be tempting to say that Falkirk was the catalyst for acceptance of the bow as a principal infantry weapon, but this was not so; its time was yet to come. There would be catastrophic failure at Bannockburn and success at Boroughbridge before the French wars were to prove its true worth.

Edward, warrior king of England, died in 1307. Dynamic of personality but also cold, ruthless, and calculating, at Orewin Bridge he had destroyed the power of Prince Llewellyn of Snowdon and brought a smoldering Welsh nation to heel. He had decimated the Scottish schiltrons with the power of his arrow storm at Falkirk and returned the upstart Wallace to the woods. And now he was dead. His son, Edward II, a pale imitation of his father, had inherited the throne. A lonely man, frustrated in governance by more dominant opponents, he was unduly influenced by his association with Piers Gaveston, a close (rather too close, some thought) personal friend.

Falkirk and William Wallace were history. Robert I "the Bruce" was on the Scottish throne, and Scottish affairs had taken a distinct turn for the better. By 1313, virtually all Scotland was under King Robert's control; and in 1314, determined to capture Stirling Castle, he laid siege to this, the last significant fortress still in English hands. Edward Bruce, brother of the Scottish king, had been chosen for this task. A chivalrous man, whose sense of fair play was not shared by his brother, he had been approached by Sir Philip Mowbray, guardian of the castle, and had agreed to a suggestion that if the castle had not been relieved by the English by Midsummer Day, then the keys would be handed over and the occupiers would move out. Forced to respond to this cozy arrangement, Edward II gathered a formidable army from the northern and midland English counties, leavened it with Welsh archers and spearmen, and set off for Scotland. His force was estimated at around 20,000 men, of whom some 2,500 were heavy cavalry, and the remainder were infantry, both mounted and on foot. Of the infantry, a considerable number (perhaps 5,000 or more), were Welsh and English archers. Opposing this substantial force, Bruce may have mustered some 6,500 spearmen and men-at-arms and a contingent of 500 lightly armored cavalry. In addition, he had a small force of archers and the theoretical assistance of 3,000 "sma" folk—a euphemism for a gaggle of poorly armed and ill-trained but fervent locals whose undisciplined motivation was largely self-interest.

Edward had encamped within the timescale and the stipulated distance from the castle necessary to satisfy besieger and besieged, and as was pointed out by those versed in such matters, the terms of the arrangement had been met and there was no need for the castle to surrender. More than that, in fact, there was no prescribed need for battle. However, having got this far with the cream of the country's fighting men—and faced by a significantly smaller force—Edward was having none of this pacifist nonsense. Although he had little of the martial acumen and military skill of his father, he was a brave man and was well able to face danger. Here he was and here he would stay to defeat King Robert (via Edward Bruce) and eliminate the Scottish menace as his father had successfully done before.

The battle of Bannockburn was spread over two days. The first brought two incidents. First, there was a severe mauling of the English heavy cavalry before they could return to their lines by well-disciplined and expertly led Scottish spearmen as the horsemen sought unsuccessfully to gain access to the castle. Second, there was an ill-conceived and subsequently widely publicized attempt to gain personal glory and indelibly stamp history by an English knight, Sir

Henry de Bohun. Seeing King Robert girding up for the battle but not yet mounted on his war horse, this aristocratic fellow seized the initiative and, lance couched, made for the king at full pelt. Unfortunately for him, as was reported, "Scher Henry myssit the nobill King." The noble king, however, did not miss Sir Henry. Turning his agile palfrey quickly, he brought his huge battle axe down with a solid thump on the ambitious knight's head and "cleft de Bohun to the brisket." The bellicose Sir Henry had indeed made history—as most schoolchildren will know—but not, one may fairly assume, as he had wished. Questioned later about the wisdom of this encounter, Bruce replied laconically that he had "lost an aye guid axe"!

Day two dawned with Edward's army dispirited. Efforts to maintain resolution were only partially successful, and the king seized at straws to bolster morale. Seeing Bruce's men kneeling in prayer, he convinced himself that they were on their knees begging for mercy and, against the judgment of his commanders, ordered a general advance. Once more, matters went decidedly wrong. The English cavalry was unable to get into the closely packed schiltrons, and Edward, unlike his father, had not yet brought his archers into play. This he now belatedly did, and for a time, they did their work and did it well. However, they were undefended by infantry and were quickly dispersed by an attack from the Scottish horse troops. Buoyed by success, the schiltrons leveled their spears and now moved forward inexorably toward the dejected English troops, who broke and fled. Flight became rout, and the battle on the banks of the Bannock burn was over.

With the barbarous murder of Edward II at Berkeley Castle in 1327 and the accession of Edward III to the throne of England, matters changed. Archery became more prominent and the English bowman more valued. The foreign mercenary crossbowmen, for many years a significant part of English battle tactics, were dismissed and replaced by native English and Welsh longbowmen. Gone now were the light hunting bows of the preceding century; the mighty English war bow and the indomitable warrior bowmen who used it to such effect had finally come of age. No longer expendable peasants tolerated by men-at-arms only for their disruption of approaching troops, archers were now mounted, relatively well equipped, and of a higher social class. Bowmen were of yeoman stock whose pay of 6 pence a day made them a cost-effective force which rode in retinue as respected companions to armor-clad chivalry. Hard-bitten fighters, powerful of arm and strong in mind, intolerant of foreigners and xenophobic to a man, they were those whose skill and courage could by itself turn the tide of battle in England's favor.

Let us set the scene. Outlasting Edward II, his English rival, by two years, Robert the Bruce, king of Scotland in all but name, whose warlike skills had welded the disparate elements of his country together, died in 1329 and was succeeded by his son, the child monarch David II. The Treaty of Northampton, signed in 1328 by his predecessor, persuaded Edward to maintain a stance of neutrality; while the pretender to the Scottish throne, Edward Balliol, domiciled in England under Edward's covert protection and with the tacit use of English resources, made military excursions across the border in support of his claim. New brooms habitually sweep clean, and with Edward consolidated upon the throne, English assistance now became more overt. In 1333, Edward Balliol, with King Edward, besieged Berwick on Tweed, an east-coast border town that had vacillated between Scotland and England for centuries as military fortune favored each. In an endeavor to break the siege, the Scottish general Archibald Douglas had brought a huge army together and was encamped by Halidon Hill, some few miles to the northwest of the town. A prosaic English account of the battle is explicit of the use of archery.[9]

> The English minstrels sounded their drums, trumpets, and pipes; and the Scots gave their hideous war cry. Each Division of the English army had two wings of good archers, who when the armies came into contact shot arrows as thickly as the rays in sunlight, hitting the Scots in such a way that they struck them down by the thousands; and they began to flee from the English in order to save their lives.

A curious incident, although an unsubstantiated precursor to the battle proper, is also recorded and is worth repeating here. It would seem that for a time, stalemate ruled. Neither side wished to open the batting. Men grew restless, and in this account, the Scots commanders challenged the English to single combat between champions. One may presume a certain natural stirring of interest at this and a shuffling of feet among both armies as the challenge was accepted on the English side. Stepping forward down the hill came the Scottish champion—a black-bearded giant of a man armed with a variety of weapons and accompanied by a very large dog. Striding purposefully toward him (after having received blessings and, no doubt, words of personal encouragement from the king) came Robert Benhale, an equally substantial man-at-arms from Norfolk. History records nothing about the conflict, just the result. After some preliminaries, Sir Robert duly dispatched the dog with his sword, following this by first killing his opponent and then decapitating him. It is this event, the legend claims, that precipitated the wild undisciplined charge of the Scots. The story has a certain ring of authenticity about it; that there was such a charge is not in dispute. By such strange devices are battles lost and won!

The outcome of the battle of Halidon Hill, a decisive defeat for the Scottish army, was the recapture of Berwick. Once again, this strategically important city was in English hands.

With the true longbow now firmly ensconced and the lighter rustic weapon returned to its place in forest glade, it is time to consider this leap of faith in some detail. Although the twelfth-century conflict at Northallerton had seen its successful earlier use, the introduction of the hand bow (the proto-longbow) by Henry III's 1252 *Assize of Arms* as an acceptable weapon of war brought this form of massed archery into prominence within the ambit of proper military thought. Although not all military strategists recognized its worth—and we may include Edward II among that number—others were convinced of its virtue.

Consider the practicalities of this introduction. A major factor, and one that will appeal instantly to all today's practicing archers, is the problem associated with a change of bow draw weight. The peasant's bow was designed for ease of draw, for hunting and personal protection, and, moreover, for the use by women, who also employed it to hunt for the pot. It is likely, even probable, that this bow continued in use, but in company with it stood a very different object that was the height of a man plus a "fistmele" of some 6 inches. Its 5-inch girth was over half the size of a man's wrist, and its draw weight was double that of the bough bow by its side. This was the formidable weapon the owner was required by statute not only to have but to learn to use.

It would be a whole new generation that would slowly accept this bow as theirs, and this was a significant fact, for whereas at Falkirk, the vast majority of archers were Welsh, at Halidon Hill, English archers predominated. An earlier generation had mustered for Falkirk; it was a second generation that made the new bow truly their own. The tide had turned. Practice at butts on holy days was mandatory, but the English took to the crooked stick as no other nation did. Not for them was the cranequin and gaffle that gentled the arbalest's power; strength of arms and back was needed to draw and use the longbow. The longbow was a strong man's weapon, and accounts of its awesome power occasionally creep into official documents.

During the siege of the Scottish city of Dunbar, the chronicler records the following:

> And now I shall tell you of a great shot made as they skirmished there one day. . . . The arrow pierced the blazon of William Despencer, and through three folds of mail armor, and through the three pliues of his acqueton (a padded jacket), and into his body, so that he lay there dead of the blow.[10]

At the siege of Tournai in 1340, we are told this:

The English returned to the Syr. Martin's Gate in order to shoot and make a great assault; and Locemens was shot in the eye by an arrow, causing him to die. And milord Godemar du Fay was shot in the plates of his armor and the arrow remained stuck in it.[11]

It is fashionable among some historians today to decry the power of this weapon. Bowmen they are not.

Where elm and other woods had been employed to make the earlier bow, now yew from Ireland, Spain, Italy, or Prussia was used. Construction had been improved, and fraternal guilds of bowyers and of fletchers, or arrow makers, headed by wardens responsible to aldermanic councils, were established in major towns and cities to ensure the maintenance of quality. The bole of the tree rather than the bough was now in regular use, and it was decreed that "every man of the said craft make and work all manner of stuff of the said craft well and sufficiently of good, able, and dry timber, and of no false, green, or deceivable timber wherethrough the buyer therof in any wise may be deceived or endamaged."[12]

Penalties for disregarding this important prescription were financial and severe. Besides his obligation to replace the offending object forthwith, the bowyer had to pay the city or town council 1 shilling and 8 pence, and the same amount to his guild, for his misdemeanor. In one sense, he got off lightly. Later, in the fifteenth century, when a guild of longbow bowstring makers was formed after the Agincourt campaign, errant members had their hemp bowstrings burnt under their noses!

Although inevitably, since it was the seat of government and royal influence, London became the prime center for companies or guilds of bowyers and fletchers, others had long been set up in York, Chester, and Coventry. As an interesting aside, the ostracizing expression "sent to Coventry" may have its origin in the guild system. An artisan found wanting and expelled from his London guild would find the next nearest in Coventry. If he wished to continue his trade, then he would need to up sticks and move there in the hope that he would be accepted. He was, in effect, "sent to Coventry."

To ensure that quality was properly maintained, a system of apprenticeship applied. Boys were indentured at an early age, usually for seven years but occasionally for longer, and bound by certain inflexible rules of conduct. An indenture between young Nicholas de Kyghlay and bowyer John de Bradley, signed in 1371, is explicit of the relationship between the boy and the man who was to be his master and mentor for the next seven years.[13] Nicholas was required to "keep his master's secrets, and his counsel," and he was not to "do him damage to the value of sixpence per year or more, nor know of it done without prevent-

Forces under Jean de Hainaut laying siege to Aubenton in 1340. Hainaut was allied with the English at the time and attacked this fortification in the same year Edward III moved against Tournai. Note the archers and crossbowmen. Jean Froissart, *Chroniques*.

ing it to the best of his power or warning his master thereof forthwith." His leisure time was strictly controlled. "He shall not play at dice, he shall not be in the habit of frequenting taverns, gaming-houses, or brothels." At the same time, in anticipation of forthcoming puberty and the onset of carnal thought, he was specifically forbidden to "commit adultery with the wife or daughter of the foresaid master under pain of doubling his servitude, or contract marriage with any woman nor marry her within the period of seven years unless with the consent of his foresaid master." In return for all this, "John de Bradlay shall instruct and inform Nicholas in his craft which he uses of bowyercraft and in buying and selling." He was also to provide food, drink, linen and woolen clothing, bedding, footwear, and all other necessaries. These prescriptions were quite standard, although occasionally other odd things were added. One apprentice was abjured not to leave his master's windows open at night— prompted perhaps by an earlier experience—while another was forbidden to take his lunch break more than half a mile from the workshop. One might speculate that this carefully excluded the nearest alehouse.

Although the first reference to a London company of bowyers occurs in 1363, the craft had been recognized in the City for some years before. Often quoted is the name of Ivo le Bowyere, whose misdemeanors in 1293 brought him into conflict with no less a person than the abbot of Westminster. A free-man of the City of London, Ivo successfully cocked a snook at the injured cleric, defending himself on the grounds that he was not subject to a court outside the City walls.[14] The fletchers company appears to have arisen from a more or less mutually accepted splitting of the combined trade of bow and arrow making.[15] It is not clear at this distance in time from which trade the impetus for this came, but it may have been the fletchers, for on March 7, 1371, those who were presumably predominantly arrow makers petitioned the mayor and aldermen of the City of London for the trades henceforth to be separated "for the profit and advantage of all the Commonalty." This was agreed, and the Worshipful Company of Fletchers henceforth came into being. Matters were not easily accomplished, however, since certain men had apprentices to both trades. After some acrimonious exchanges with authority, minds were eventually made up, although one recalcitrant individual who was summarily directed by the mayor to become a bowyer forthwith turns up in the records as a master of the fletchers.

Unlike the bowyers company, whose master or warden serves for two years, the fletchers company changed (and still change) their master each year. Responsibilities largely involved the maintenance of quality and included examination of arrowheads for hardness. Night working was banned, since it led to the production of unserviceable arrows "to the prejudice of the Company." Shafts produced were essentially of two types: those for war, termed "bearing arrows," although the description has other connotations, and "merke," or "mark," arrows, used for practice. These were later known colloquially as "halfpenny ware," and from them ultimately derived the butt, or "rood," shafts of the eighteenth century and the target and clout arrows of the nineteenth and twentieth centuries.

Best-quality bearing arrows that were "well and cleanly made, cross-notched after the best manner, peeled and varnished" were paid for at the rate of 16 pence for 100. Second-quality bearing shafts fetched 14 pence per hundred. Mark shafts, perhaps because they were "paired," were paid for at 20 pence per hundred. But now let us leave the arrow and return to the war bow and its employment.

Edward III was single minded in his wish to regain his lost French dominions. Overtures to the king of France, although backed up by flexed military muscle, had failed dismally, and it had become increasingly obvious that drastic measures were necessary if Philip of Valois was to be persuaded of the validity of Edward of England's claim. Matters were therefore put in train for a full-scale invasion. In the fall of 1345, to carry troops, horses, and supplies, ships of 30 tons burden and upward were requisitioned from around the coast, as far away as Newcastle upon Tyne, and required to gather at Portsmouth by October 6. Writs were issued to call in archers from across the country.[16] This produced 100 of the "best and ablest" from Chester—perhaps the Macclesfield Hundred again—2,000 from south Wales, led by Rees ap Griffith, Owen ap Oweyn, Thlewelin Eignon Vaghan (Llewellyn Eynon Vaughan), and Rees Dungan, and included, among others, the now-legendary Black Bowmen of Llantrisant, of whom more will be said later. From London, 320 came; from Devon, 60 (to be provided specifically with bows and arrows and other arms); and from the other shire counties, a total of 3,800. Altogether this made a force of some 6,000 English and Welsh bowmen, the balance in favor of the English men. The massed arrow storm was about to come of age.

5) *The War Bow Comes of Age*

It was the year 1346. Although it was their custom to fight on foot, by now many archers were mounted, and they rode on horseback to muster at Portsmouth in preparation for the forthcoming French campaign. One may imagine the scene as thousands of bowmen and men-at-arms with their horses milled around in seeming chaos before embarking on the motley array of large and small ships sequestered by Edward for the purpose. Clerks busied themselves with manifests as food and victuals were neatly stowed, while carts containing weapons and other warlike stores were lifted and placed carefully at hand, ready for smooth transition from sea to land when the invasion fleet arrived. Watching it all from a place on the sidelines, we can visualize a small group of 40 miners led by four master miners from the Gloucestershire forest of Dean. They would be used to dig beneath city walls, for Edward was prepared to deal with whatever confronted him on his planned *chevauchée*. When eventually all was deemed ready, the fleet set sail and, after overcoming the vicissitudes of wind and weather, finally made landfall at the small Normandy port of St. Vaast la Hougue.

Disembarking was accomplished without incident, and Edward turned his attention to the job at hand. Custom required that the countryside around be pillaged and laid waste as he and his army made their slow way towards the city of Caen. Once there, a demand to surrender was scornfully rejected by the proud Norman citizenry, and an invitation to battle was readily accepted.[1] The place was defended by some 1,600 men-at-arms and 30,000 armed fighting men—enough, it was confidently thought, to see off this impudent upstart Englishman and his puny invading force, for the English were not yet rated as a military nation by Continental Europeans. On July 26, they would leave the ramparts and annihilate the English in a well-conducted battle, and all would once more be well.

But Edward had a secret weapon: the mighty English war bow. By now under full control of those who used it, when lugged back to the ear by powerful men, it released its murderous battle shafts to deadly effect. The self-confident citizen-soldiers of Caen had yet to meet it and the English and Welsh "goddams" who had tamed its strength.

The exact form the medieval longbow took is a matter for conjecture. None exist for examination, although drawings, woodcuts, and paintings offer suggestion. There is some not-entirely convincing evidence from these that a proportion, but evidently not all, of medieval bows were made with reflexed limb tips. This feature would have increased their cast (in simple terms their power), and in favor of the suggestion is the apparent distance achieved by these weapons. Modern experience with well-made replicas indicates that a simple straight stave of realistic draw weight will make a distance of around 250 yards, but little more. Unless one allows that to exceed bow shot of 240 yards, medieval archers each drew bows well in excess of 100 pounds (which indeed they may have done), there is argument for a weapon with a more sophisticated draw force curve—one provided by reflexed limbs. A second mystery concerns the arrow used. Reference abounds within a medieval inventory to "cross-nocked" shafts.[2] Now, cross nocking (two string notches cut at right angles) is well known in modern times as a method used in speed shooting, since it allows the shaft to be placed upon the string more promptly than with the conventional single nock. However, was this a method employed in earlier times to deliver more shafts in time of need? Or was it merely a description of the notch cut at right angles to the string groove to accommodate the horn sliver inserted to protect the nock? With no examples to study, we can only speculate.

A third question concerns the arrowheads. We know these today by two distinctions: "broadheads" for hemorrhaging and "bodkins" for penetration. Although the term "broadhook"—which may be an intention for broadhead—appears in a medieval inventory, the term "bodkin" does not. However, there are numerous references to "sperehedes," "dokebyll," and "byker" heads, one or more of which may have been designed for penetration. Suggestions for their purpose and appearance will be found in the appendix. But we must leave this intriguing diversion to return to Caen and the forthcoming conflict.

The day chosen for battle dawned, and as the two forces marshaled, one may suspect a twinge or two of apprehension among the valiant defenders as they viewed the opposing army, for massed-formation archery was no longer a tactical military concept in medieval France. The English rode to the field on horseback, banners and pennants fluttering in the light breeze. Behind them marched the bowmen in tightly ranked units under their vintinars and cente-nars, evenly and with precision.[3] They halted when ordered and maneuvered without fuss.

The Normans, unused to this disciplined deployment, watched with increasing concern. Here was not the expected raggle taggle of unrated bucol-ics cowed by the might of France; confronting them was a quietly determined army of trained soldiers that was well led, ready, and, moreover, armed not with the familiar arbalest but with a new and strange weapon of great length. The Normans were about to meet the great war bow with its murderous battle shaft. As they watched, trumpets sounded, 6,000 longbows were drawn, and a cloud of arrows rose from the English ranks, hung for seconds in the sky, and descended upon them, to be followed by another and yet another. The Normans panicked and retreated into safety. The citizen army defended itself as best it could, but the archers followed the demoralized ranks "without leave or array" and, after a hard fight with casualties high amongst the defenders, took the bridge leading to the town. Edward had the city ransacked for goods and treasure before preparing to move on.

His plan was to travel overland to Calais, perhaps via Paris, subduing as he went, in expectation of meeting and defeating the French army of Philip de Valois en route. On the strength of activity so far he had every reason for con-fidence. After consulting with his commanders and with Calais firmly in his sights (but in expectation of an anticipated encounter with Philip), Edward gave the order to march. Two rivers barred his path: the Seine and the Somme. Each was a problem to be solved, since he could expect destroyed bridges and stiff local, if not national, opposition to his attempted crossing. He was not mis-taken. Leaving Caen on July 31, he reached the Seine at Elbeuf on August 7 only to find, as he had guessed, no opportunity to cross without a significant struggle. With no wish to hazard his small force when another opportunity might present itself, Edward moved on until at Poissy, virtually on the outskirts of Paris, he found what he had sought: a bridge that although broken, was repairable.

While Philip of France dithered, Edward of England was across the Seine with his army intact and en route for the Somme. Covering between ten and fifteen miles a day, in seven days Edward had reached Acheux, some five miles from the river, and conscious of Philip (by now just a day's march behind), he sought a crossing. Now, Edward had been brought up in the area and knew that there was a passable ford somewhere at hand, although he did not recall where. Vainly he sought among his chivalric prisoners for information, only to be met

Stylized representation of a mounted English archer. This woodcut has been used variously to illustrate the *Gest of Robin Hood* (Chepman & Millar Tracts, National Library of Scotland) and to portray Chaucer's Yeoman in the 1491 printed edition of *The Canterbury Tales*. By the mid-fourteenth century it became common for bowmen to travel on horseback.

by polite disclaimers. With time now running out, he offered a general reward for information. This did the trick; Gobin Agache proffered the required detail. The ford, he said, was known as Blanchetaque, or "white spot." It was passable at knee height at low tide. This was the knowledge Edward needed. He gave orders that men should be ready in warlike array to march when trumpets sounded at dawn on August 24. Among the accounts, there is some confusion as to how they proceeded. By one version, the ford was crossable by only 11 men abreast, which suggests a march in column. However, the king's personal account speaks clearly of crossing "one thousand men abreast," indicating a "line of march" and a far more substantial causeway. With the real possibility of attack from the rear and a welcoming party of men-at-arms and Genoese crossbowmen established on the farther bank, this would tactically be a wiser choice.

According to Edward's own account, the crossing was effectively accomplished in one hour—itself indicative of passage en masse—and with only the loss of a small portion of his baggage train to the advancing French.[4] Once within range, his dismounted longbowmen rapidly disposed of the opposing Genoese mercenaries with heavy loss while his men-at-arms struggled and clanked across, knee deep in the tidal river. One speculates on the effect all this water had on the armor, since there would have been little time to dry out thoroughly before battle. Those wishing to face their shining French counterparts in pristine condition would have had little time to clean off rapidly advancing rust!

With the major obstacle of the Somme behind him, Edward rested his men. The road to Calais was blocked by French forces, however, and it was clear that Philip was prepared to fight. The long-expected battle was now inevitable, and after consulting with his commanders, the king leisurely organized his battles (battalions) not far from the village of Crécy. The vanguard, nominally commanded by young Prince Edward, he placed to the right of the line—with the experienced earls of Warwick and Northampton as his advisers. The rearguard, to the left, was under the command of the warlike Bishop of Durham and the earls of Arundel and Suffolk. The center, acting as a fighting reserve and standing back a little, was commanded by the king himself.

All fought dismounted; their horses were placed with the carts and beasts of burden in a sort of laager to the right of Prince Edward's battle. The placing of the archers, who were to play such a vital part, is not entirely clear, but it would be surprising if they were not placed on the flanks of each battle to disrupt the advancing cavalry. Indeed, a French account describes with feeling the effect of arrow volleys.[5]

> On the other side the archers fired so marvelously that when the horses felt these barbed arrows (which did wonders) some would not go forwards, others turned their rumps towards the enemy, regardless of their masters, because of the arrows they felt. Some, unable to avoid it, let themselves fall. The English lords, (men at arms) who were on foot advanced and pierced through these men, who could not help themselves, by their own efforts or by their horses.

A French version of Edward's disposition of his troops is explicit. In this, 1,200 men-at-arms, 4,000 archers, and 3,000 Welshmen (spearmen perhaps, although Welsh archers were certainly present and in some considerable force) are assigned to Prince Edward. To the rearguard the French give 1,200 men-at-arms and 3,000 archers, while King Edward himself retains 1,600 men-at-arms and 4,000 archers as a reserve. All together, this makes a fighting force of 4,000 men-at-arms, 11,000 bowmen, and 3,000 spear and knife men, totaling some 18,000 men. This figure does not accord with other accounts, however, and appears to be a serious but understandable exaggeration, since in battle the vanquished habitually prefers the victor to be significant in either numbers or firepower.

The battle of Crécy opened with a volley from mercenary Genoese crossbow archers. Though brave soldiers, they were quite unready for battle. They had marched for miles with their heavy bows and bolts and were tired; moreover, the protective pavises (great shields) behind which they reloaded their weapons were still on the supply carts, and they were thus highly vulnerable to the longbowmen with their greater range. As the arrow storm rose from the English lines, hung for a moment in the sky, and then landed among them, they turned and ran back, to the rage of the impatiently waiting French nobles and men-at-arms who now put spur to horse and charged their despised enemy, cutting through the Genoese and killing a large number as they did. They in turn defended themselves as best they could, and many French nobles made it no further than their own front line.

The longbow was at its most effective when matched against cavalry, for although in the fourteenth century, the hard pointed arrowheads could still penetrate armor,[6] it was the horses that took the brunt of the attack from bowmen stationed on the flank.

Although archers were habitually placed in ranks, as many as eight deep, demonstrably this arrangement could only be effective while shooting high for distance. For reasons of safety, the front rank alone would have been able to shoot when the trajectory lowered, and this begs the question of how the front line was manned and by whom. It is tempting to think of those to the fore being both stronger and more accurate with their shooting, able to aim successfully for vulnerable places in the plate armor of the day. We are told that in later times certain archers were distinguished as being of the "first sort," but tantalizingly we are not told the qualification.[7]

The bowmen themselves were open to attack however; wooden stakes, later so vital to the Agincourt campaign, were not yet part of an archer's gear. At Crécy, while potholes and shallow trenches dug in front of their positions gave them some protection from direct charge, a determined and sustained cavalry attack could run them down, as Bannockburn had shown. Such attacks as came that day at Crécy, however, were disorganized, with no apparent fighting strategy and totally without discipline. Chaos, not King Philip, reigned supreme.

Two persistent legends are connected with events at this battle—one, it must be said, is more believable than the other. While King Edward established the Order of the Garter shortly after he returned to England—supposedly as a response to retrieving the Countess of Salisbury's fallen garter during a dance—a French account links the order's foundation directly with the battle. It was believed that the word "garter" was the Welsh word used on the day for the rallying of the troops.[8] Although the word "garter" is thought to be in part of Celtic origin—"gar" is the word for "leg" in some Welsh dialects—there appears to be no such Welsh word of that pronunciation; however, *cartref* (meaning "home") or its mutated form, *gartref* (meaning "at home"), are close.

Although it is remotely possible that the Welsh troops with Prince Edward might have responded to a call "for home," its association with the Order of the Garter must be tenuous in the extreme.

The second legend is sustainable. This concerns the Black Army (or the Black Bowmen) of Llantrisant.[9] Llantrisant is a Welsh town that in preparation for Edward's 1346 excursion to Crécy had dispatched a number of bowmen to serve. They appear to have fought in Prince Edward's division, and during the engagement when—as is documented—he was knocked down, they are said to have formed a protective ring around him while he was helped to his feet. For this assistance, the grateful prince on his return allotted them a piece of land to be held in perpetuity; and to this day, those who can prove their direct descent from members of the Black Bowmen have rights to this field. An alternative account has them defending the crossing at Blanchetaque. They are by lineage, if not by choice, the oldest fraternity of archers in Britain, and their recognition is a point of pride among today's traditional Welsh longbowmen and women.

While Edward III was recognizing, more so than any before him, the value of English and Welsh archers, he had of necessity to maintain their numbers in his armies. The following edict, published in 1363 as the French wars got underway, illustrates an apparent decline in the very arm that had ensured victory at the battle of Crécy:

> The King to the Sheriff of Kent; Greeting.
> Whereas the peoples of our realm, nobles as well as commoners, usually practiced in their games the art of archery, whereby honour and profit accrued to the whole realm and we gained not a little help in our wars, with God's favour and now the art is almost totally neglected and the people amuse themselves with throwing stones, wood or iron, or playing handball, football or stickball or hockey or cock-fighting; and some indulge in other dishonest games which are less useful or worthwhile, so that the kingdom in short becomes truly destitute of archers.
> We, wishing to provide an appropriate remedy for this, order you that in all places in your Shire, as well within the Liberties as without, where you shall deem to be expedient, you shall cause to be proclaimed that everyone in the Shire on festival days when he has holiday, shall learn and exercise himself in the art of archery, and use for his games bows and arrow or cross-bolts[10] or bolts, forbidding all and singular, on our orders to meddle or toy in any way with these games of throwing stones, wood or iron, plaing handball, football, stick-ball or hockey, or cock-fighting or any other games of this kind, which are worthless, under pain of imprisonment.
> By the King himself.

The battle of Crécy, August 26, 1346, in which English and Welsh longbowmen out-ranged and outshot Genoese crossbowmen and turned back advancing French infantry. Jean Froissart, *Chroniques*.

With the gradual acceptance of the archer as a vital addition to the tactical military scene was coming a subtle change in attitude. The men who fought alongside English chivalry at Crécy (later at Poitiers and later still at Agincourt) were not the expendable peasant archers of the previous century, placed in front of men-at-arms, useful only to disrupt advancing infantry, and to be discarded when their task was finished. These men had a full role to play, and it did not stop when battle was joined and archery was over and done. Throwing down their bows, they joined in with falchion, sword, arming knife, and in the later battles, with their heavy lead-faced mauls. Independent of spirit when caution might have been a wiser course, they more than occasionally took matters into their own hands. The reported exploits of one man, archer John Dancaster, exemplifies this initiative. Here follows his story, though its veracity is unchecked![11]

In 1352, six years after Crécy, John had been captured and, having no money to pay a ransom, was put to work in the castle of Guines. Accepting his fate with sanguinity, he made the best of the situation; and having employed his free time by seducing a laundry maid, he learned from her that there was an underwater causeway across the moat over which he might escape. This he duly did, having first measured the castle walls with a length of thread. Once outside, he set off for Calais where he gathered together 30 men from the garrison. Wearing blackened armor and carrying scaling ladders, he and his company returned to Guines Castle. After crossing the moat, they scaled the walls with the ladders; and once inside, they surprised and killed the guard and threw their bodies into the moat. The French knights and their ladies, being in bed asleep, were woken and, still in their nightwear, were pushed without ceremony into a castle strong room. The remaining English prisoners were then released from their cells and treated to a good meal.

The following morning, the ladies of the castle were set free and with their horses, servants, and belongings, were dispatched on their way. Meanwhile, word that Guines was now in English hands was sent to Calais. This news was met with mixed reception, however, since England was then in a state of truce with France. With a full-scale diplomatic incident slowly developing, thus it was that backed by the authority of law and with the tacit agreement of the English—who must have savored the situation—two knights sent by an indignant Count de Guines duly arrived at the castle gate to demand it back. The answer from the battlements was brief, impolite, and can be summarized succinctly as "not just yet"! The discomfited knights reported this rebuff to higher authority, and matters moved up several notches. Apprised of the situation, King Edward, no doubt with more than the hint of a smile on his face, ordered through his herald that it be returned to its rightful owner, only to receive a reply from the battlements that it would be handed over to the king and no one else.

There followed a good deal of hard bargaining, with the count offering many thousands of pounds and "perpetual peace with the king of France" for the occupants if it was returned. The new owners were adamant, however, that they would give it only to the king of England; if he didn't want it, then they would sell it to the highest bidder. Faced with what was becoming a fait accompli, the discomfited count retired from the scene with as much grace as he could muster, and King Edward eventually acquired the place from John Dancaster and his single-minded bunch of entrepreneurs. History does not record this archer's subsequent career, but if the story be true, then one may reasonably speculate that his tankard was never empty for long.

Although victory at Crécy was followed in 1347 by truce and comparative peace, by 1350, hostilities had begun again, and Edward was once more faced with warfare to claim his French possessions. This year saw an extraordinary and potentially hazardous action by Edward that perfectly illustrates his character and lack of concern for personal safety.[12]

The governor of Calais had been approached by a leading French commander with a plan for him to betray the town to the French for a large bribe. Seeming to agree, the governor duly reported this to King Edward who, with his son the Black Prince and a few trusted nobles and knights, hurriedly crossed the Channel, arriving a few days before the intended takeover. Once there, he prepared a welcome for the unsuspecting French. Under the vaults, inside the gateway, and around the walls of the gatehouse he had false walls erected, and within these spaces he installed men-at-arms and archers. The drawbridge he had partially sawn through to break when a great stone was dropped upon it from above. The French duly arrived with a great store of gold to be paid for the expected betrayal, found nothing untoward, and retired. Subsequently they returned to take possession. The stone was dropped on the drawbridge, which snapped asunder, and the knights broke free from their hiding places and engaged the occupying French in fierce conflict, eventually gaining the upper hand.

Outside, the French, seeing that they had been tricked, took flight; and Edward, whose identity had not yet been revealed, took 16 men-at-arms and 16 longbowmen in pursuit. Realizing that they were running from such a small force, the fleeing Frenchmen turned on their heels; and in the marshy hinterland beyond the castle, a line of 80 men-at-arms formed ranks against Edward and his men. In response, Edward positioned his men carefully—the archers he placed on dry islands among the marsh, and when they were in position, he revealed his true identity saying, "Do your best, archers, I am Edward of Windsor." Only then did the English bowmen know that it was their king that led them; they bared heads, arms, and chests and concentrated on not wasting a single arrow. The French stood on a narrow causeway across the marsh, wide enough for just 20 men, and were thus vulnerable to attack from either flank. Able to move lightly between pockets of dry land, the 16 archers held them off, killing some and taking prisoners until the Prince of Wales arrived with a relieving force. It was subsequently said that 1,000 knights, 600 men-at-arms, and 3,000 foot soldiers had been sent to take the castle. Although Edward had put himself and his heir at great risk by what some in the safety of England thought a foolhardy venture, his reputation was enhanced. Edward III was most definitely a "hands-on" monarch!

If King Edward was a man of action, then his son, the Black Prince, was cast in the same mold. In July of 1356, Prince Edward led a *chevauchée* from Bordeaux deep into French territory, a foray that was to culminate on

September 19 in a fierce and hard-fought engagement close to the important French city of Poitiers.[13] A young man in his prime, yet cautious with his resources, when needs demanded, Prince Edward relished a fight. While there will always be doubt as to the reality of his avowed wish to "cross swords with King John" of France (and French accounts are clear that he was in retreat toward Bordeaux), when the time came, Edward's will was not found wanting.

We will briefly examine the position. The English army had taken much booty on its journey; the slow-moving carts holding this were groaning under the weight, and not wishing to lose these while he waited for activity from the French, on the night of September 18, the prince wisely started them on their way back to Bordeaux. With the French now barring his path and battle inevitable, Prince Edward addressed his archers, for it was upon them that much of the weight would fall.

> Your manhood he said, hath bin alwaies known to me, in great dangers, which sheweth that you are note degenerate from true sonnes of English men, but to be descended from the blood of them which heretofore were under my father's dukedom and his predecessors, kings of England; unto whom no labor was painefull, no place invincible, no ground impasable, no hill (were it never so high) inaccessible, no tower unscaleable, no army impenetrable, no armed soldiour or whole host of men was formidable.

Continuing in this vein, he reminded them that their bowmen ancestors had "tamed the Frenchmen, the Ciprians, the Syracusians, the Calabrians, the Palestinians, the stiff-necked Scots and unruly Irishmen, and the Welsh also." Thoroughly roused by this eulogy, the English archers were positioned and made ready for battle. Those of the rearguard were deployed along a hedge, protected from direct attack by a ditch and trenches. Once in position, they engaged the French crossbowmen and outshot them for speed and quantity. Meanwhile, their fellows in the vanguard, positioned on pockets of dry land in a marsh at the bottom of a slope, faced French cavalry. These were intended to ride down the English to protect their men-at-arms, and it was the archers' given task to prevent this. However, they were directly facing the horses, and therein lay a problem, for as their forequarters were protected frontally by steel plates and leather shields, arrows aimed at them either shattered or glanced off, falling among friend and foe alike.

Seeing this, the archers were repositioned to their habitual position on the flank, enabling shots to be concentrated on the horses' unprotected rumps. This had the required effect; the wounded chargers reared, throwing off their riders, or turned and galloped away. With the cavalry now disrupted, the

English bowmen in prayer before engaging in battle. Drawing by Wolfgang Bartl.

archers then concentrated upon the men-at-arms, attacking them from their customary position.

Poitiers was a close-run affair, and arrow stocks ran low; at one time, during a lull in the fighting, tired archers were forced to replenish their quivers by dragging arrows from bodies of the half-dead enemy. Finally, during a break in the fighting, the prince commanded his men-at-arms to mount their horses and, in a desperate attempt to decide the outcome, ordered a charge—a maneuver largely alien to the English whose preference it was to fight on the defensive and one that prompted a hail of crossbow bolts from the French. Prince Edward ordered his bowmen to respond, and they did so with verve, darkening the sky with the arrow storm. Then, their quivers now quite empty, they threw their bows down and set upon the enemy in desperation with falchions, swords, and arming knives.

Meanwhile, the prince had dispatched a small force of 60 men-at-arms with 100 archers to gain a position behind the French, and this they did without being seen. At a prearranged signal, the banner of Saint George was unfurled, and archers let fly their volleys to wreak havoc in the rear of the unsuspecting enemy. It was the end. The dauphin had by now fled the field, King John of France was taken, and the French army was in full retreat to the gates of Poitiers. As was customary in those days, it was the victor's responsibility to feast his victims, and Prince Edward duly provided a repast—taken, it should be said, from the captured French cuisine. The royal feast was interrupted by news that a close friend, Sir James Audley, had been discovered on the battlefield in a less-than-marketable condition and had been brought in for treatment. Taking leave of the king, the prince personally attended his old friend, an action that was warmly approved by his captive and showed the tender side of his warlike nature.

To describe the half century between Crécy and Agincourt as peaceful would be to stretch imagination, since sieges and minor skirmishes flourished. England's command of the sea was challenged, and between 1369 and 1396, no less than five *chevauchées* were mounted—not all as successful as intended, it must be said. However, full-blown battle was largely avoided until 1415, when Henry V set sail to recover the vital port and city of Harfleur.

Although the "goddam" and his war bow still gave major substance to English armies' manpower, in the matter of defensive body armor, technology was advancing; and whereas at Crécy this had had been of wrought iron, facing the bowmen now were breastplates of steel. There is much, shall we say, discussion about the thickness of this material when used for battle armor, but practicality suggests a thickness of 1.6 millimeters over vulnerable areas. There is academic dissension here, but allowing the weight factor to influence me, I side with realism. That properly hardened and pointed arrowheads will penetrate this at a point-blank range of, say, 30 yards, particularly if waxed beforehand, is demonstrable and has indeed been satisfactorily demonstrated.

An aspect given less prominence than it perhaps deserves is the condition of the armor worn. Inevitably, metal deteriorates and requires cleaning. It may be presumptuous to think of a knight wishing to appear at his best when on public view, but cleaning may well have involved abrasion to remove rust, and if the armor were of some age, particularly if sand were involved, it is reasonable to assume that this work would have thinned it. The effect may have well been to present a knight whose reflection dazzled all who saw him but whose protection from a bodkin-pointed battle shaft was rather less than it might have been. What a triumph of pride over pragmatism! Military tactics may have altered from previously accepted practice during the Agincourt campaign, for while the armored man-at-arms was protected to a greater or a lesser degree by plate armor, he relied on mail to protect certain areas; moreover, both he and his horse—particularly his horse—were still vulnerable to their side and rear. Progress induces change, and where they would have been largely ineffective against a frontal assault, archers were now customarily positioned on the flank where they were ideally placed to disrupt a cavalry advance.

Although there may have been sporadic use of protective stakes against mounted men in earlier campaigns, and it had long been the custom for spearmen attacked by cavalry to rest their spears on the ground to form a hedge of

When arrow or crossbow bolt stocks ran low, such as occurred at Poitiers, it was common after a battle for the victors to collect them from the field for reuse. Here French valets gather spent crossbow bolts.

spikes (such as at Bannockburn), this form of defense does not figure prominently in the longbowman's armory until the Agincourt affair. During the march from Harfleur to Calais, however, King Henry V was given advance knowledge of a French plan to ride down the archers at the opening of the long-expected set-piece battle, and armed with this advance knowledge, he commanded then that every archer cut a stake of 6 feet in length, sharpened at each end, and carry it with him. When in battle position, each should hammer one end into the earth with his maul and have the other maintained at breast height ready to impale any horse unlucky enough to reach it.

While plate armor was developing to counter frontal penetration, there is some circumstantial evidence that the draw weight of war bows may also have increased in compensation. In this regard, however, Commissioner William Harrison's assessment of the capabilities of his fellow Elizabethan archers—on hearing that Frenchmen and Rutters (Germans) derided English bowmen by offering their backsides as targets knowing they would be safe—is anything but flattering. His subsequent comment suggests a general decline in draw weights and perhaps in the ability of men then to come to full draw. He remarks, "Our strong shooting is decayed and laid in bed. But if some of our English men now lived that served king Edward III the breeches of such a varlet would have been nailed to his bum with one arrow, and a second feathered in his bowels before he turned to see who shot the first." The point is arguable, and we will not pursue it here. The draw weight of Tudor war bows has been assessed and will be discussed in another chapter.

We move on. The principal advantage (indeed, the main purpose) of flank archery was disruption of either cavalry or infantry, and we are privy to some of the vernacular names given to the types of arrowhead used at the time. Two in particular catch the imagination. These are the "byker" (bicker) and the "dokebyll" (duckbill). The former would seem to describe a purpose and the latter, by simile, a shape.

The word "byke," from which "byker" is derived, is an early word for a bee (the English surname "bickerstaff" means a place where bees are kept). To "byker," or bicker, an enemy formation was to assail it with arrows.[14] In context, we would today call this the arrow storm. A fifteenth-century observation will illustrate its use. "Ynglis archaris . . . among ye Scottis bykkeryt with all thair mycht." And a line from the popular English north-country ballad "The Hunting of the Cheviot" stating, "Bowmen bickered upon the bent (grassy plain)" will confirm it.

It is arguable that the arrowhead used for "bykkeryng" was called a "byker."[15] If this is indeed so, then what form did it take? If it was intended to sting or gad a horse or embarrass an unarmored Scotsman, then what better than a lightly barbed broadhead? At Agincourt it was perhaps the byker-head-ed arrows of the flank archers that rendered the cavalry charges ineffective. Defining the "dokebyll" head is more difficult. The "duckbill" was a narrow pointed tool used by certain craftsmen, and this suggests that a "duckbill head" was similarly pointed. Was this what we today call a bodkin? Perhaps, but we will not debate it further.

Speculatively associated with archery and the battle, since they are of the period, are cross-nocked arrows. As mentioned earlier, today's commonly accepted purpose of cross nocking is for ease or speed of shooting; and if fif-teenth-century battle shafts indeed had two string nocks cut at right angles to each other, then it is difficult not to see speedy nocking as the purpose. The arrow storm relied upon quantity for its effect, and the faster the archer shot, the more effective was his contribution.

There is an enigma associated with archery at this time however. Many con-temporary representations of archers show them with arrows resting on their thumb on the further, or "wrong," side of the bow, and it is commonplace today for archers to dismiss this as inaccurate observation by the artist. But it may not be. At least one modern longbowman shooting for speed uses this system, and there is an advantage. An arrow customarily has to be selected and placed across the bow to be nocked before it is shot; if it is placed upright on the ground, the string taken to it, and it is lifted to be held on the thumb, the whole action is quicker. More practical research is needed, but the principle must not be discarded.

As Crécy demonstrated, major battles, particularly those involving the medieval longbow, attract legends. Agincourt has more than its share, perhaps, and therefore selecting two presents no difficulty.

Those familiar with the Great War and the retreat of the English army from Mons in 1915 will perhaps have heard of the "angels of Mons" and how weary troops, outnumbered and outgunned, summoning their last reserves of physical and mental strength, believed they saw shining angels around them and the figure of Saint George mounted on a white horse rallying them to fight on. Whether or not they did is in one sense immaterial; they did rally, and the German advance was halted.[16]

In one English account, much the same sort of supernatural phenomenon was reported as having taken place at Agincourt. One late version of the "Brut" (an early fifteenth-century vernacular record of occurrences concerning England) is relevant.[17]

> On that day the Frenchmen saw St. George in the air over the host of the English fighting against the Frenchmen, and as a result they worship and esteem St. George in England more than in any other land. Thus almighty God and St. George brought our enemy to the ground and gave us victory that day.

The second account is not so much a legend as a factual incident, for it is the record by two contemporary French observers, Messrs. Le Fèvre and Waurin, of the actions of Sir Thomas Erpingham, a senior English commander thought to have been given responsibility for the archers immediately prior to the engagement.[18]

> The king of England ordered a veteran knight, called Sir Thomas Erpingham, to draw up his archers and to put them in the front in two wings. Sir Thomas exhorted everyone on behalf of the king of England to fight with vigor against the French. He rode with an escort in front of the battle of archers after he had carried out the deployment, and threw in the air a baton which he had been holding in his hand.

Here, Waurin adds the following:

> He cried "Nestroque" which was the signal for attack. Then he dismounted
> and put himself in the battle (battalion) of the king of England who was also
> on foot between his men and with his banner in front of him. Then the English
> began suddenly to advance uttering a great cry which much amazed the
> French.

This word "nestroque" has given historians and other academics much
opportunity for ingenious interpretation. Until recently, the more believable of
these has been an anglicized "now strike," given in Erpingham's native Norfolk
dialect. However, another even more likely interpretation has now been
advanced. A word or two of explanation is necessary. Armies were controlled
until recently by commands interpreted by bugle (or in earlier times, horn)
calls. These were once known as "strokes," a term familiar to hunters and forest dwellers of the time. An important one of these was the *menée* stroke,
which signaled assembly or, in this context, readiness for battle. It seems feasi-
ble that having deployed his men, Erpingham called for the trumpeters to
sound the *menée* stroke, which when heard from the French lines, sounded
like "ne stroke" (the stress of the word *menée* is carried on the second syllable).
Is this a realistic interpretation? It certainly seems so, but accurate or not, the
matter must rest there.

The Agincourt campaign was responsible for the radical reappraisal of an
important, if lowly, constituent of the country's military arrangements. The
mighty war bow and its murderous armor-piercing battle shaft so dominant in
battle were of little use without the bowstring. These vital components had
attracted criticism during the campaign for their tendency to break at times
inconvenient to their users, and with the army now back home, matters were
ripe for review.

Anxious to both protect their good name and to assure future business, the
string makers of London applied to the City's aldermanic court for permission
to put their house in order.[19] Thus it was that in August 1416, the Ancient
Company of Bowstringmakers (or "Stringers," as they were known) came into
being by prescription. Before the century had run its course, however, the
company had become known as "longbowstringmakers."

This is a suitable point at which to explain the change, for in 1416, the term
"longbow" (which for convenience, I have used in preceding chapters) had yet
to take hold. The first known written reference to the description "longbow"—
a name that rapidly passed into common usage to replace the then-current
"hand bow"—occurred during the troubled mid-fifteenth century as men and
women looked to the defense of their properties.

In 1448, Margaret Paston (of Paston Letters fame) found herself in difficulty, being pressed by an aggressive neighbor. With her husband, John, away in London on business, she wrote to him in some haste.

> Right Worshipful Husband
> I commend myself to you and ask you to get some Crossbows, and windlasses with which to wind them, and crossbow bolts, for your houses here (Gresham in Norfolk) are so low that no-one can shoot out of them with a longbow however much we needed to.

We will return to the stringers with their new title. Although the customary penalties of fines or imprisonment for poor workmanship were built into the company's rules and ordinances, old practices die hard, and 1499 saw a necessary stiffening of these. Members were to use "well-chosen English hemp" from the female plant, not "tubbed," or "Coleyn" (Cologne?) hemp. Foreign stringers—those outside the City's franchise who had not served apprenticeship—were banned from trading, while poor workmanship was rewarded by the offending article being burnt beneath the workman's nose while he was in the pillory! Adulteration of material may have been a problem. In sixteenth-century Bristol, the trade of stringer was combined with that of barber. The opportunity for human hair to be used to supplement hemp was obvious![20]

Archers with their longbows were now a vital part of the military scene, occupying flank positions from whence their volleys herded advancing horsemen or infantry into increasingly tight formation. However, they were too lightly armed for hand-to-hand combat with heavy cavalry and, in certain circumstances, were vulnerable to attack. Although stakes were now de rigueur and bristled like hedgehog spikes wherever archers gathered for battle, there were occasions when nature took a hand. The battle that took place on the dusty plain outside the gates of Verneuil on an August day in 1424 was one such occasion.[21]

A French army, strengthened by a strong Scottish force, commanded by Alexander Earl of Douglas, and leavened with 600 Lombard mercenaries, faced an English force commanded by the Duke of Bedford. Once the bowmen were in position, the hard-baked earth would not allow their protective stakes to be driven in; and before those on the right flank could properly prepare, the French cavalry rode them down and, flushed with this success, charged pell-mell toward the baggage train. Once there, however, they were resolutely met by the 2,000 archers who formed the reserve division. These men were well prepared, and arrow volley after arrow volley decimated the advancing horsemen. Meanwhile, the mounted body of 600 Lombard merce-

Archers flanking pikemen in combat: a stylized representation of medieval warfare at the time of Agincourt. From an early unidentified French manuscript.

naries, seeing the unguarded wagon train with its valuable potential, rode into it and, having slaughtered the unarmed varlets and pages, began making free with the contents. The reserve archers, having by now dealt summarily with the French cavalry, quickly turned their attention to the pillaging Lombards and engaged them in hand-to-hand combat to drive them in total flight off the field, leaving their booty behind.

Having disposed of two large bodies of well-armed and mounted men, the archers of the reserve division, their blood now fully roused, formed into companies and, seeing the battle raging on their left front between Douglas' Scottish division and Salisbury's infantry, took the initiative, charging into the Scottish right flank with maul, falchion, and sword. Their presence turned the tide, and despite resisting valiantly, during the resultant battle, an army of over 6,500 Scotsmen was virtually annihilated. The valiant defense made by the Scots at Verneuil was recognized by the French king; the Royal Guard of Scottish Archers in France (La Compagnie des Gardes Écossoises) was formed after the battle, and this served French kings loyally for the next two centuries.[22]

Verneuil demonstrated two facets of archers and archery. These were their vulnerability when unprotected by stakes and their innate ability to act purposefully and with effect upon their own initiative. We will now consider a third use. The battle of Towton, which took place in 1461, bears the dubious distinction of being the bloodiest engagement ever fought on English soil.[23] It brought to a head a festering internecine power struggle between the great houses of York and Lancaster, styled by William Shakespeare and popularized by Victorian writers as the Wars of the Roses—although a more inapt name could scarcely be imagined!

Lancastrian Henry VI, a mentally unstable aesthete and England's consecrated king, had been challenged as the country's ruler by usurper Edward Duke of York who, with popular approval, had been proclaimed King Edward IV. The Lancastrian forces were commanded by the Duke of Somerset, a young man of 24, while the Yorkists were led by the even younger 19-year-old Edward, aided by the elderly and unfit Duke of Norfolk who had earlier been dispatched posthaste to raise and follow with his contingent.

A preliminary night-time skirmish with Lancastrians at Ferrybridge went badly for the Yorkists, who had omitted to post sentries (a potentially severe setback), although the victors were subsequently caught, and their leader, Lord Clifford, was killed by an arrow through his neck. The battle proper opened on the bitterly cold and snow-swept morning of Palm Sunday. With the wind behind them and snow flurries restricting the visibility of their opponents, Yorkist bowmen under the command of Lord Fauconberg moved forward and opened the battle with volleys directed against the Lancastrian archers on Somerset's left wing. They then retired. Feeling the effect of the Yorkist arrows, the Lancastrian archers responded; however, a combination of a strong head wind, poor visibility, and the position of the Yorkists meant their shafts fell short, it is said, "by forty tailour yards." Readers who are archers familiar with traditional two-way clout archery will know the effect of a strong head wind well enough when shooting back.

After suffering a number of volleys, and with his own men now short of arrows, Somerset lost patience and ordered a general advance. Although successful for a time, with Yorkists giving ground, the day was finally saved for Edward by the timely arrival of the Duke of Norfolk with a strong contingent of hefty East Anglian fighting men. Gradually the Lancastrian line turned at right angles and then broke. Retirement became retreat, and retreat became rout. Edward's instruction to kill only nobles and spare the common man went unheeded as Yorkist bloodlust gained hold. Accounts of numbers said to have been slain during and after this most dreadful of battles vary, but conservative estimates suggest 28,000.

The gruesome discovery in 1996 of a mass grave associated with the battlefield has revealed the skeletal remains of 50 men.[24] Where skulls have been present, the probable cause of death has been established, in many cases through careful and meticulous osteoarchaeological pathology, and this has revealed the likelihood of deliberate postbattle slaughter through wounds to the skull.

Dreadful as the carnage at Towton was, it did not signal the end of this civil war. The battles of Barnet and Tewkesbury in 1471, which saw the final demise of the Lancastrian cause, were yet to come; while in 1485, the success of Henry Tudor, Earl of Richmond, at Bosworth brought a new player to the throne of England—one who was to establish a dynasty that would reign for over 100 years and provide two of England's greatest monarchs: Henry VIII and Elizabeth I.

6 | *The Decline of the War Bow*

Although comprehensive defeat at the bloody battle of Towton had destroyed the Lancastrian powerbase, and the House of York—by Edward IV's victory— now dictated affairs in England, the bloody struggle for succession had yet to run its full course. Waiting in the Continental wings, conscious of his claim to the throne, was Henry Tudor, Earl of Richmond. It was a complex claim, how- ever, and one that was inevitably disputed, for it rested ultimately upon the relationship between John of Gaunt, third son of Edward III, and Katherine Swynford, his mistress and later his wife. A daughter, Margaret, born to their grandson John, had married Edmund Tudor, father of Henry. Although not supportive of any parallel claim, or at least not one to the throne of England, it is nevertheless interesting to record that the grandmother of Henry Tudor, Earl of Richmond, by a second marriage was Catherine de Valois, widow of Henry V, the victor of Agincourt. The man who was later to become Henry VII, was therefore technically the step-nephew of Henry VI.

Let us return to reality. When Henry set foot ashore at Milford Haven in August of 1485, he could hardly have known that before the year was out he would have begun a dynasty that was to last for over 100 years, for the House of Tudor would give England two of her greatest monarchs: King Henry VIII, the archer king, and his daughter, the first Queen Elizabeth. During that time, the great war bow, proud symbol of England's martial supremacy, was to begin its steady and inevitable decline until by the death of Elizabeth, last of the Tudor monarchs, it no longer featured on the national list of arms.

But we should begin at the beginning. Henry Tudor, Earl of Richmond, landed in Wales with a supporting army of some 2,000 nondescript French mercenaries, men described by a French writer with some distaste as "two thousand of the loosest and most profligate persons in all that country." This was scarcely, one might think, the right tool with which to wrest a kingdom from its consecrated king. But through his uncle, Jasper Tudor, Henry had prepared his ground well. Thus it was that proud of his Welsh blood, on August 7 he raised the red dragon banner—battle standard of the Welsh warrior prince Cadwallader—and confidently waited for supporting fervor to grow.

Gradually the Welsh rallied to him, and with numbers mounting steadily, he marched north through the principality to Ambion Hill in English Leicestershire and destiny.[1] The longbow was to feature on both sides significantly during the ensuing battle.[2] Supplementing his European mercenaries, Henry now had with him companies of Welsh bowmen from Gwent, Monmouth, and southeast Wales. Opposing him, King Richard drew on 1,200 archers led by Earl Surrey, while waiting in the wings were the bowmen and billmen brought by Lord Stanley, nominally under the king's command but not—as things transpired—his control.

Although potentially the royal army was numerically superior to that of the usurper Henry, matters were not developing well for Richard. Stanley's force of some 8,000 men was held back, while Richard's rearguard of 3,500 men led by the Earl of Northumberland was also not engaged. Numbers were therefore broadly even.

The battle opened with an artillery barrage and an exchange of arrow volleys as bowmen from the forests and valleys of Wales engaged yeomen archers from the shire counties of England. William Shakespeare has immortalized Richard's cry to his troops: "Fight Gentlemen of England, fight good yeomen, Draw archers, draw your arrows to the head." Following his ill-conceived and headlong dash against the usurper—during which Henry's standardbearer, Sir William Brandon, was slain by lance thrust—and the critical intervention of Lord Stanley's men on Henry's side, the king was unhorsed. While fact and legend are at odds as to where Richard's death occurred, his crown, found in a thorn bush, was placed on Henry's head.

Yorkist archers had become Tudor bowmen, and the Tudor age had begun. Although this period opened with the longbow still a vital part of the English military scene, Continental ideas were fast becoming accepted, and the more advanced of the country's military strategists were already contemplating what to a generation earlier would have been virtually unthinkable: a battle fought without the massed arrow storm. Powder and shot would supplant the terrifying sound of battle shafts in flight, and handgunners of indifferent skill would replace the formidable "goddams," the legendary English and Welsh longbowmen, backbone of victorious English armies for over 200 years.

But that time was yet to come, for in early Tudor times, the longbow was still the weapon of the people. Required by statute law to own and to use a bow regularly, the Tudor yeoman archer was no mere cannon fodder. His skill and determination in battle had assured him of a place in history, and his weapon the niche in people's hearts it holds today. His forbears had almost overnight turned the fighting men of a nation, mocked as militarily third rate by Continentals, into a force so feared that at one time they were compared to Attila's Huns. Many a Frenchman fervently joined his priest in praying, *"A sagittis hunorum, nos defende Domine!"* ("From the Hunnish archers Lord defend us.") And by "the Hunnish" was meant those English and Welsh who used the bow. The period of Tudor monarchy—that time between the late medieval fifteenth century of Henry VII, victorious at Bosworth, and the opening of the seventeenth century—was one of imposed military change. Marked by a lengthy period of comparative peace at home, it saw the decline of the English war bow with its heavy draw weight and in its place, the emergence of a lighter, recreational weapon shot for pleasure, for the simple crooked stick still exerted its subtle power over people's minds.

In its continuing effort to stem the downturn of interest in regular archery practice, in 1478, Parliament had defined those unlawful games that it specifically forbade as "conducive to dispute and discouraging to the usage of archery." While those games expressly forbidden under penalty of two years imprisonment and a fine of £10 seem innocuous enough today, to those in power during the Yorkist-Lancastrian conflict, they represented a serious threat to archery. Forbidden activities included "dice, quoits, football, closh, kayles, half-bowls, hand-in and hand-out, and chequer board."[3]

For all their advanced military thinking, early Tudor monarchs were well disposed toward the bow, and they encouraged their children in its use. Henry VII's eldest son Arthur enjoyed archery and was trained in the use of the weapon from an early age.[4] Had he lived, he would undoubtedly have fostered the use of the bow just as Henry, his younger brother, did when he came to power in 1509.

Decline in the use of archery was gradual, accelerating as the century advanced; the numbers of bowmen mustered were smaller than hitherto, and their success was not always assured. The confrontation between Scotland and England at Flodden, as James IV sought by invasion to relieve English military pressure on Louis XII, his French ally, illustrates this clearly.[5] The Cheshire archers, once their county and country's finest, were routed on the English right wing; others, however, who were commanded by Lord Surrey and who had climbed an almost unscaleable hill, played a vital part in halting James's reserve division in its tracks, thereby consolidating an English victory.

As we shall later see, the bow continued to appear, albeit as a secondary weapon long after its national obsolescence. The last occasion when it was used tactically en masse in a set-piece engagement is generally supposed to be the battle of Pinkie Cleugh on the east coast of Scotland in 1547.[6] No longer employed to deliver an early and devastating arrow storm, here it featured as a supporting arm late in the battle, after cannon and arquebus had done their work.

It is through a strange quirk of circumstance that the longbows and arrows of which we have most information come from the Tudor warship *Mary Rose*, which foundered in 1545 at a period when the bow was in decline and approaching obsolescence. But we must not cavil at this opportunity to examine in detail the harvest of material garnered from the sea, for recovered from their resting place in Solent mud are virtually pristine examples of the sixteenth-century war bow.[7] Thus, by replicating its dimensions, and also by examining the several thousand arrows recovered, we can define its likely capability with some degree of certainty. Although others may yet come to light, these war bows together with one other linked to Flodden and a broken example stored in a village armory in Suffolk form the sum total of our practical knowledge.[8] It is a reflection of the totality of change that until 1982 when the *Mary Rose* emerged from the depths, virtually nothing remained of a weapon upon which England's martial eminence was founded.

With examples at our fingertips, it is fitting here to briefly picture the equipment with which the Tudor bowman went to war and to assess its strength and power, for in doing so, we may glean some slight insight into the scope of its predecessors. The wood for bows came from a number of sources; there is evidence that staves from Zurich, from which finished weapons were fashioned, were supplied to bowyers in lengths of 84 inches, "three fingers" in thickness (approximately 2 inches), squared and polished, and without knots. In 1574, these staves were sold at between £15 and £16 a hundred.

Among other important information, the long-awaited archaeological report providing details of the archery equipment recovered from the *Mary Rose* will list the lengths of individual bows, and we may expect many to approach 78 inches.[9] The dimensions of a selected bow, MR A812, already in the public domain, show this to be 78 inches in length with a 4 3/4-inch girth at its center.[10] The bow is 1 1/2 inches in width and similar in depth; it tapers gently and evenly toward 1/2-inch round tips coned from 1 3/4 inches at each limb end. The presence of lighter wood suggests the extent of a protective horn tip, while a small cut to the side indicates side nocking. The sections of this bow are broadly ogival; that is to say, the back of the bow is heavily convexed and the sides are cambered. However, as one would expect of a yew bow, the bowyer has followed the grain; and in consequence, sections drawn at 4-inch distances along the stave vary in shape.

Many *Mary Rose* bows have a series of peck marks varying in number and shape on the limb, and it has been suggested that these are arrow passes to indicate the position of the arrow when held on the hand.[11] I do not necessarily hold this view. By balanc-

King James IV of Scotland, grandfather of Mary, Queen of Scots, represented as a mounted archer. From a painting in the Bibliotheque Nationale, Paris.

ing a number of bows on the thumb to determine the hand position, as would have been done in Tudor times, it is apparent that the peck marks are not always adjacent. An alternative, but equally useful, purpose would be to indicate the upper limb, coupled perhaps with a need to identify a bow either to a maker or to a particular batch, and I suggest that this may be the purpose.

It is possible that the bows now recovered were provided by the tower armory when the warship was stored. The maker of the king's bows at that time was John Pyckman, appointed in 1545 to succeed his father Henry Pyckman; it may therefore be that at least some of the weapons were made either by him or under his jurisdiction.[12] We shall never know.

Draw weights are difficult to determine with any degree of accuracy without bracing and drawing a bow; calculation based on girth and length suggests weights of between 90 and 130 pounds as the range of many, although replicas have been made of greater draw weight, and these have provided much useful data. While recognizing the ability of some to handle bows of 150 pounds and more, and respecting the skill of certain of today's archers who use them, it is my view that such weapons were in the minority.

Yew is the best of bow woods, and the *Mary Rose*'s manifest shows "Bowes of eugh (yew) vc (250)."[13] This is the material of which a substantial number of those recovered are made, and therein may lie a tale. During an earlier commission before her refit, things seem to have been rather different; for a letter by Thomas, Lord Howard, written in June 1513 in response to a council reproof about the wastage of bows reads thus:

> And as touching the receiving of bows and arrows, I shall see them as little wasted as shall be possible. And where your lordships write that it is great marvelled where so great a number of bows and arrows be brought to so small a number, I have enquire the causes thereof: and as far as I can see, the greatest number were witch (sic) bows of whom few would abide the bending.[14]

We may not have far to look to find a reason for this wastage. By the 1511 statute of Henry VIII, bowyers had been required to provide two bows of lesser woods, including, among others, bows of wych elm or witch hazel for every one of yew. Understandably, it proved extremely difficult to sell these, since customers rather naturally wanted yew; and faced with unhappy bowyers holding unsaleable products, the government perhaps accepted these for military service. Archers whose lives depended upon these weapons may well have had a negative reaction to the issue of inferior equipment, and it is within the bounds of possibility that therein lies the reason for the wastage! It would not be difficult for a disenchanted archer to overdraw a bow and break it, hoping that the eventual replacement would be of yew.

The quality of weapons may have had some bearing upon early musters, for we know that archers were segregated into those of the "first sort" and those of the "second sort." While the difference is not defined, it may be that the ability to draw a heavier bow, thus achieving a greater length, was a deciding factor. In passing, although not specifically mentioned, a glance at the total numbers mustered shows there to have been archers of a third sort! One speculates upon their abilities and purpose.

The reason for the bow, any bow, is to propel an arrow to a target, whether that target be close or far away, with sufficient impact to damage or immobilize. Modern experiment with replica weapons can provide useful indications of the ability of the longbow to satisfy this basic need. Experiment has shown that a self-yew replica war bow of 130 pounds in draw weight, constructed to the dimensions of a Tudor weapon, with a typical section, and equipped with an inert bowstring will shoot a reproduction 31 1/2-inch war arrow weighing 68 grams through a chronograph at an initial velocity of some 165 feet per second (112 mph). In still air, it will travel in excess of 220 yards. A lighter, 52-gram arrow will exceed bow shot of 240 yards.

Lest it should be thought that all Tudor longbows were of *Mary Rose* dimensions, we should examine a weapon (or to be exact, what remains of it) that is held in the ancient village armory (housed in the parish church) of the

The shaftments of a selection of sixteenth-century battle shafts (top) with evidence for the binding on of fletches. There are approximately 6 bindings per inch (or 36 in 6 inches). The extremities of a selection of sixteenth-century war bows (bottom) showing grooves caused by side nocking. Author's photos with acknowledgements to the *Mary Rose* Trust.

Suffolk village of Mendlesham.[15] Its age is not exactly known, but it is believed to date from the late sixteenth century. The broken stave of this yew longbow is about 53 inches long and comprises the whole of one limb, the handle section, and a part of the other limb. The handle area is defined by a little extra wood to make this almost circular. The limb has a rectangular cross section, and the surviving tip is coned to take a horn nock. As with all well-made yew bows, the grain has been followed, with knots and pins carefully enhanced.

From examination of the remaining limb and the central grip, it would seem that the original length was a mere 67 inches, some 9 inches shorter than many of the *Mary Rose* bows. Now, the relation of bow length to draw length is critical, and a rule of thumb suggests a bow no more than two and one half times the arrow length. The maximum arrow length suited to a bow of this length would thus be 27 inches, a length appropriate for a recreational arrow. However, taking the *Mary Rose* arrows as markers, battle shafts are 31 inches in length; it seems to follow that if the bow had been used to shoot a 31-inch battle shaft, then its breakage cannot have been a surprise.

Since the limb taper increases over the last 12 inches, this suggests a possibility that the bow has been piked, or shortened, from an original length. There is a clue to its possible age, for in a 1590 treatise on archery, the author, Sir John Smythe, writes the following: "The imperfections of the longbow do consist only of the breaking of the bow or the bowstring, for which in times past there was special care taken that all Livery, or war bows being of the wood of yew were longer than they now use them."[16] Thus, comparison between the shorter Mendlesham bow and its lengthier counterparts from the *Mary Rose* would seem to confirm a later origin.

We will briefly examine the war arrow. To the several thousand recovered from the Solent mud we may add one more, found at Westminster Abbey in the nineteenth century.[17] Unlike those arrows from the *Mary Rose*, which cannot be later than 1545, that from the abbey is not datable. Although it is armed with a lightly barbed broadhead (London Museum Type 16) and is evidently not a recreational shaft, its effective length is 29 inches, 2 1/2 inches less than a war arrow. It has a barreled profile and with the head in place weighs 42.6 grams. Beyond a suggestion that it is perhaps typical of lighter medieval arrows used for distance shooting when opening a battle (for bickering), we will leave it. It may be seen in the Undercroft Museum of Westminster Abbey.

We should not depart from the Tudor longbow scene without a brief mention of the bracers, or armguards, worn by bowmen, since these are the most personal of things.[18] A total of 24 were recovered from the *Mary Rose* and are thus presumed to have been worn by military archers. All but two are of leather, and these are of ivory and of horn (the horn example is damaged). A number are decorated with religious or secular motifs, and these include a nimbus, St. Peter's keys and sword, a possible "Sunday Christ," and *aves*. Secular symbols include fleur-de-lys, crowned and uncrowned roses, a sunburst, bearded faces, a gridiron, and an eagle erased and regally crowned.

In addition, two bracers are ornamented on one side by quartered charges on which are centered the royal arms within a crowned and inscribed belt, the whole being surrounded by an Ave Maria, or prayer to Mary. The presence of

these bracers gives rise to speculation (so far unsubstantiated)
that members of the royal bodyguard were aboard on that fateful
day.

While there is evidence from
the location of bows and bracers
that archers were in position
when the *Mary Rose* foundered,
their presence at other contemporary engagements seems not to
have attracted the euphoria
accorded to their ancestors. An
illustration of the siege of

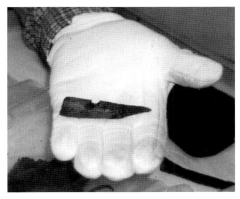

A side-grooved horn nock from a Tudor war
bow. Author's photo with acknowledgements
to the *Mary Rose* Trust.

Boulogne in 1544 has just five archers present shooting among a multiplicity of
artillery and harquebuses.[19] Careful scrutiny shows one to have a broken bowstring; another, a broken bow; and a third, a broken arrow. One feels a certain
prejudice to have crept in!

For all the fast-accumulating military rejection of the bow as a favored
weapon, statute law still required that it continued to be given proper consideration, and archers formed the substance of many of the shire county musters.
The Somerset County muster for 1584 shows the position well.[20] Charged to
provide 800 shot, 700 bowmen, and 700 corslets (armor-clad pikemen) totaling
2,000 men, the county actually mustered 762 shot, 998 bowmen, and 661
corslets for a total of 2,421 men, of whom the excess was largely formed of
archers.

A drill apparently associated with an earlier muster in 1569 is interesting,
since it is one of few that specifically mention archers.[21] The officer in charge
(the centenier, or perhaps the vintinier) is said to have called, "Rank yourselves,
archers." On hearing this, the men formed up, eight or more to a rank. The
officer then moved to the flank and called, "Front to me, archers," whereupon
all the men turned toward him. Crossbows and longbows having been found in
order, the archers then mounted and rode off. Passing some mark set up for
them, they each drew two or three arrows one after the other and, drawing to
the head, shot them three or four score yards off.

While accepting the inclusion of this drill as an addendum to the 1569
muster document, I have some misgivings about its age and relevance. These
misgivings are compounded by the instruction to use not two fingers to draw

the string but three, called here "a fond new fashion." A three-finger draw had been in vogue since at least 1544 (according to Roger Ascham[22]), and it seems odd to have it described as "new" some 30 years later.

During the sixteenth century, drilling based on companies of 100 men was certainly regularized. Each company was marshaled as a solid square, arquebusiers were in front and at the rear in two ranks each of ten men. A file of ten archers was then followed by two ranks of ten pikes. The ensign with his attendant halberdiers, drummers, and phiphes (fifers) was in the center. This was the theoretical ideal; in practice, numbers varied from company to company, reflecting both resources available and, to some extent, the feelings and traditions of individual captains or areas.

Below the vintinier, or "twenty-man," were the decentiers, each of whom mustered ten men. These were more closely associated with their charges and were expected to know where each lived, where each might be found in an emergency, and, even more importantly, what physical condition each was in. The decentiers had the additional title of "whifflers," an ancient term for those responsible for crowd control, for which they were provided with a wooden baton or sometimes a ceremonial sword. Although not specifically included in their terms of reference, they were almost certainly also expected to weed out and have retrained the "mishandy" archers among their flock, including perhaps the occasional sinistral, for while sinistral pikemen are mentioned specifically for retraining, whether left-handed archers were retrained is open to question. There is a curiously persistent folk memory in Middleton, Manchester, that the village archers who served at Flodden were all left-handed; whether this was so it is impossible to say today, but the tale persists, and it is perpetuated by the presence of a bronze statue of a left-handed archer affixed to the wall of The Middleton Archer public house.

Although as the century drew on, there was mounting opposition to the national emphasis upon archery among those of the country's military leaders who had been influenced by Continental reliance upon the handgun; the more conservative, including the monarch herself, sought to strengthen the use of the bow. Archers had been singled out for special attention by Queen Elizabeth who "from her special studye and care to strengthen the courage of her subjects and better their days" urged that the use of the bow should be encouraged in the villages and some "pleasant means" be found to "draw youth thereunto so that all and everyone, being viewed, arrayed, and prepared may be ready always to serve."

Commissions of array mustered all potential soldiers, including archers, and at these, able men were selected to serve.[23] In theory at least, these were

The "Flodden Window" at Middleton Church, Manchester, circa 1514, which portrays in stained glass the departure of the archers from Middleton to fight at the battle of Flodden. Notice their unstrung bows above their heads and fletched arrows by their hands.

chosen "without partiality, malice, injury or distemperance," however, age was taken into account, and those between 18 and 46 were preferred—as was bodily ability and probity of character. Weapons were allotted to men "fit by their stature and aptness, the strong to be bowmen." By statute law, it was a requirement that men "not lame or having no lawfull impediment and being within the age of xl years, except Spiritual men, Justices etc. and barons of the exchequer, to use shooting in longbows and have a bowe continually in his house to use himself."

As Roger Ascham had dryly observed earlier, however, "generally men everywhere, for one or other consideration, muche shootinge use not," and there seems little doubt that in this respect, statute law was honored more in the breach than the observance.[24] The law had teeth, though, and used them. In January 1575 at Winchester, Christopher Smyth, Justin Cheapman, and 13 others were presented at court "for that they and everye of them have not frequented archerye nor used to shote in longebows by the espace of one moneth contrary to the Statute" while at Cheltenham, even the town bailiff himself, responsible for providing the town's butts and overseeing archery, was presented at the hundred court for "using illicit games." The picture, therefore, is one of slow decline in the use of archery as a viable force in warfare—a decline hastened by military modernists influenced by Continental practice but vehemently resisted by conservatives dedicated to retaining the status quo.

By 1572, matters within the City of London had evidently reached a position where the apprentices, from whom the City's armed forces were substantially drawn, had become something of a liability, since despite statute law and, one hopes, proper encouragement from their masters, seemingly many were either not practicing archery properly or were not practicing it at all. From the minutes of the City of London Court of Aldermen, we hear this:

> Sir Thomas Offley, and Sir John White are appointed to go to my Lord Keeper for the delivery of the Certificates for archery and to inform his Lordship that it is very inconvenient and perilous to suffer apprentices within this City to go a-shooting according to Statute and therefore in their Certificate they have certified that they have taken Order for such as use shooting as conveniently can, or may, and to understand how his Lordship hath liking of that word "convenient" and make report to this Court.

We do not know whether the Lord Keeper of the Certificates for archery liked the term "conveniently" or not, but he had little alternative but to accept the inevitable. The selection of Alderman Offley and Alderman White for the task by the City's Aldermanic Court suggests an archery interest in common, and it is not impossible that they were charged with reversing the situation.

One suspects that both bowyers and fletchers, and not just those who worked in London, were inevitably feeling the pinch, as men observed the letter but not the purpose of the law, for as Roger Ascham had commented 40 years before, it was one thing for a man to have the statutory bow in his house, but his reasons for not using it were legion, and it was quite another matter to persuade him to do so.[25]

It is about this time that the defunct society of Prince Arthur's Knights was reformed, and it may be no coincidence that within it Alderman Offley became a leading light. Although there is no certainty of this, since knights are identified only by initials, those of J. W. appear on lists, so perhaps John White joined him.

While the purpose of the society has never been clearly defined, circumstantial evidence suggests its reformation to have had a practical as well as a recreational purpose. It would have been very much in keeping with the need for men trained in the use of the bow for the rank and file to have been drawn from the City militia. Certainly a contemporary fraternity, the Black Train, headed by the Black Prince of Portugal had a military purpose, since it was reviewed on occasion by Offley in his aldermanic capacity, en route for practice in Mile-end fields.

Debate—if one may so dignify the wordy and acrimonious exchanges between entrenched protagonists of gun and bow—was rife, and military gentlemen took sides according to their strongly held beliefs. Such beliefs were influenced, one suspects, by Continental practice and the perceived need to be seen as at the cutting edge of military thought. The military council was in something of a turmoil about the matter. On the one hand, archery had its proven track record and a string of battle honors. On the other, there was the uncomfortable fact that notwithstanding statute law, as an activity, archery had lost its appeal. Cards, bowls, "dicing," and other less moral pastimes were a more popular choice among the male citizenry.

Although there seems little real doubt that history apart, the gun was preferred over the bow by those able to anticipate the future, the council sat firmly on the fence, patronizing the bow as a weapon most suited to rustics, being "a weapon familiar and naturall to them" while insisting when ordering the suppression of illegal games that "the reputation of the bow should not in any way be obscured or taken away."

Faced with this official ambivalence, counties chose their own ways.[26] Warwickshire, Derbyshire, Buckinghamshire, and Wiltshire took measures to enforce the statutory regulations, while Hertfordshire refused to muster archers except "suche as are bothe Lustye in bodye, and able to bide the weather, and canne Shoote a good Stronge Shoote, for heretofore we have allowed manye simple and weake archers." Meanwhile, Dorset attributed the weakness of their archers to the fact that "the harquebuz are of better accompt [account]." In fairness to men who either enjoyed shooting with the bow or who feared reprisal under statute, life had been made increasingly difficult for them by the intemperate actions of landowners who enclosed shooting grounds for tillage or pasture and who had no compunction whatever about setting dogs on honest archers aspiring to hone their skills.

A number of treatises extolling the virtues of either bow or gun were now published by those with a metaphorical axe to grind. Liberally embellished both with historical fact and fiction, they argued the case for one or the other with verve and supercharged Elizabethan hyperbole. Among the more restrained of these was "A Briefe Treatise to prove the Necessitie and Excellence of the use of Archerie."[27] This 22-page booklet was sponsored by the bowyers and fletchers companies of London, whose commercial interests were transparent. Combining various accounts of the power of longbow archery, this concluded with a sanctimonious prodding of authority following the recent strengthening of statute law.

A considerably longer eulogy, in rumpty-tumpty verse but covering much the same ground, was compiled by Thomas Churchyard, a practical man with extensive knowledge of archery and the longbow. This formed the introduction to Richard Robinson's fanciful History of Prince Arthur's Knights and is notable for his enigmatic reference to a device that Churchyard predicted would re-establish the use of the weapon.[28] Of this interesting reference, more follows below.

Head and shoulders above the differing factions, however, were Sir John Smythe, an ardent supporter of archery for whom the longbow reigned supreme, and Sir Humphrey Barwick, a choleric dyed-in-the-wool handgunner who dismissed the bow as irrelevant to the modern scene. Smythe's *Certain Discourses Military*, published by him in 1590, followed the omission of the longbow from the official list of arms.[29] Although acknowledging the place of the musket in the late sixteenth century—one feels a certain inevitability here—Smythe's treatise was a practical panegyric for the longbow, not simply as a weapon, but as symbolic of England's past military glory. In the course of his rhetoric, he takes issue with the arguments advanced by handgunners against the bow. "Among many other of their fancies, they do allege that the archer's bows being by them used gainst the enemy in the heat of summer will grow so weak that they will lose their force and effect." Smythe dismisses this out of hand as a "new fancy and a very dream" pointing out (incorrectly, as it happens) that yew—of which the bows were made—does not "decay" in strength whatever the weather. Yew does in fact become more pliable when under extreme heat, and its elasticity decreases accordingly, and this would be a factor for commanders to consider on a very hot day. In answer to Barwick's contention that bows break, Smythe counters by observing that "in times past bows were so well backed and nocked that they seldom or never broke." Concerning the climate and its effect, he adds the following: "Besides that the archers used to temper with fire a suitable amount of wax, rosen and fine tallow together in such a way that, by rubbing a little on their bows with a woollen cloth it protected them against all weathers, of heat, frost, and rain."

Smythe is on safer ground when he observes that arrows will wound and even kill both men and horses from a greater distance than will gunshot. He also points to the relative simplicity of carting the lighter bows, arrows, and bowstrings compared to the carriage of harquebuses, powder (with its attendant dangers), and heavy lead shot. Finally, he draws attention to the advantage of the longbow as a weapon ancillary to the pike, seeing herses of archers as effectively flanking squadrons of pikemen. Flushed with enthusiasm for the cause of the longbow, a little surprisingly, he dismisses the archer's stake as being superfluous, but he has made his point. Far from being an obsolete weapon, Smythe is convinced that the longbow has not yet run its course.

Sir Humphrey Barwick, on the other hand, has very little time for the bow and very much time for the handgun.[30] He dismisses Smythe (whom he insists on calling Smith) as a "King Harry Captain," and advances the virtues of the handgun in all respects. Wedded absolutely to his subject, at a dinner that he (Barwick) attended, a fellow officer was asked about the rate of fire per hour of the musket and answered ten shots (or one every six minutes). Although Sir Humphrey kept quiet during the meal, which, given his choleric temperament, must have taken some effort, as loyal as ever to his chosen weapon, he button-holed the captain afterward and wagered him that he could shoot 40 bullets in that time—or one every 90 seconds. Fortunately for Barwick's purse perhaps, the wager was not accepted.

After advancing the cause of "fiery weapons" and dismissing Smythe's claim to wound or kill at 9, 10, or 11 score yards, Barwick issued a challenge.

> For triall thereof I will stand at six score yards distant from the best of the archers aforesaid, and let him shoot 10 arrows one after the other at me, and if I do stir from the place, let me be punished and I will be armed as before is said of the Pistoll proofe, and if I be therewith wounded, I am contented to take my mends in my own hands: and againe, let me be set in the same place where this lustie archer stood to shoot his ten arrows, and let there be a whole complete armor set right up where I did stand, and let me have but two shootes with a Musket or Harquebuse, and let it then appeare what the one and the other is in force.

Predictably perhaps, Smythe also did not take Barwick's challenge seriously, laughing it off by predicting that he (Barwick) would be knocked off his feet and would be hit in the bum while trying to regain his stance.

Whether a 68-gram bodkin delivered from a heavy draw weight war bow would have penetrated pistol-proof armor, or indeed any armor, at that distance is open to doubt of course; but 120 yards is virtually point-blank range for a heavy bow, and there is no reason to suppose that this "best of archers" archer would have aimed at Barwick's breastplate rather than his throat or his legs. In retrospect, it is a measure of Smythe's humanity (and humor perhaps) that he did not accept the challenge.

We will leave the debate, but not before quoting from a treatise entitled "The Practice, Proceedings and Lawes of Armes Described," published in 1593 and written by Matthew Sutcliffe. Aimed with forthright directness at the sixteenth-century armchair military strategist, he wrote, "You that knowe the

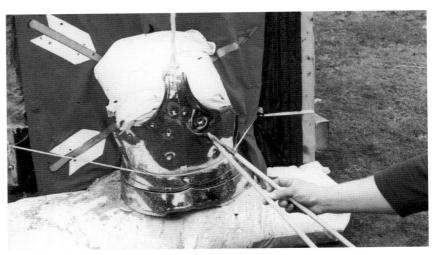

The penetrative power of a medieval-style bodkin head, which was forged by master arrowsmith Hector Cole. Author's collection.

traine of armes, yeelde here the testimonie of your experience to this discourse, and if you hear any cavil against it, yet let not such as never marched further, than out of the kitchen, or parlour censure that which they understand not." Sutcliffe provides a balanced view of the advantages and disadvantages of archery. Summarized, it is of little use in assaults against towns, but comes into its own when, in the field and protected by stakes, it is used against horsemen. It will outshoot the handgun for speed and distance, but when faced by armed men, it needs the protection of armed men.

Despite the dismissal of the longbow by many as a weapon suited only to "rustics," it was still considered to have a place in important projects. Sir Walter Raleigh was recommended to include longbows when arming the settlers who were to found the colony of Roanoke Island. Whether he took this advice is unknown.

Although the longbow was now discounted as a primary weapon for warfare, its military use was not yet finished. With the death in 1603 of Elizabeth and the accession of James I of Scotland to the throne of England came the renewed patent "concerning Archerie," bringing with it a requirement for farmers and other occupiers of land to reduce the height of fences and to bridge ditches to allow archers free passage over ground that had habitually been used for shooting.[31] Those who supported the old weapon were not yet disposed to desert it, and the stage was set for a revolutionary idea that had germinated in the mind of William Neade, an "ancient archer." It had long been considered a sensible military tactic to combine archers with pikers or pikemen, so, reasoned Neade, why not couple the two weapons to create a double-armed man? He published a treatise in 1625, addressing it to King Charles I, in which, after reminding his monarch (perhaps a little unnecessarily) of the nation's declining moral fiber, he extolled the advantage of shooting with a bow.[32] "Much more may be spoken of this laudable Exercise of Shooting, for the exercise thereof expels drunkennesse, swearing, dicing, carding, quoyting, cat-playing, besides many other vaine and ungodly vices." He then sets out arguments for the advantage of bow and pike and the drill by

The "double-armed man by the new invention," 1625. A coupling of bow and pike invented by William Neade and approved for military service by King Charles I.

which they should be used. Whether Neade's idea was his alone is a matter for conjecture.

Neade's mechanical coupling, although unwieldy, seems to have had some modest success. It received the monarch's blessing, and he was given letters patent authorizing him to make the "engine" necessary to link the two weapons. To my knowledge, no detailed drawing now exists, but the device seems to have consisted of two metal sleeves able to be varied in diameter, coupled by a universal joint. The military advantage would be to allow archer-pikemen to influence the preliminary activities of a set-piece engagement by embarrassing approaching infantry or cavalry, subsequently presenting pikes when at close quarters. Neade was required to demonstrate the principle to Charles in St. James Park before approval was given and proclamation made "To Use the Bow and Pike together in Militarie Discipline."

There is some circumstantial evidence for the use of the coupled weapons, if not in actual battle, then in a warlike context. The reference in a dispatch during the Civil War in England to a "Company of Bows and Pikes" stationed at Hertford on guard duty suggests that Charles's direction was observed.[33] The coupling was cumbersome, however, and for it to be of functional value and not an obstruction required a quite detailed sequence of preliminary drill. Neade was equal to this, though, and his treatise was explicit in both written word and accompanying drawings, although what is not made clear is whether the bow is braced before or after coupling; practicality suggests the former.

In 1622, 400 longbows and 800 sheaves of arrows were sent to America to help rearm Virginian colonists after a massacre by Indians. Their preference was for guns, though, and the bows and arrows were diverted to Bermuda, "near enough to be readily procured in time of need." It is possible that this stock was eventually drawn upon, but its ultimate fate is unknown.

One of the last occasions on which the longbow was used—or to be precise, was intended to be used—concerned an abortive attempt by King Charles I in 1627–1628 to succor the Protestant inhabitants of La Rochelle. Alexander MacNaghton (or MacNaughton), a Scottish mercenary soldier, was given the responsibility of engaging a company of 200 Scottish archers for service on this campaign, recruiting if necessary from "fugitives from our lawes," and from their subsequent intemperance, he appears to have observed this direction to the letter!

MacNaghton's levy of Highlanders came from the Campbell lands of Glen Shira, and since clan Campbell had superiority in the glen at that time, the force was perhaps largely drawn from them. In the matter of weaponry, although highland Scots were well accustomed to the longbow and used it frequently and to effect, Charles provided MacNaghton with a parcel of 500 English weapons for his company's use. It is relevant to report that after the La Rochelle expedition had foundered, for one reason or another, only 121 bows were returned to store. Of MacNaghton's recidivist Highland bowmen, it is recorded that they had had a particularly difficult sea journey to the south and caused such mayhem when they finally got ashore that it was necessary to declare martial law before they could be rounded up and returned to their native soil.

Although by now the longbow was long obsolete as a primary arm, the council was obviously reluctant to lose it altogether. One or two of the poorer and more remote shire counties had continued to muster archers long after the decreed change to handgun and pike, and perhaps in recognition of a groundswell of concern for the old weapon—leavened no doubt by the commercial interests of the bowyers and fletchers—a more-or-less successful attempt to form archer regiments in London took place in 1629. These were required to be formed from volunteers, although in anticipation of unwillingness to serve, authority was given for men to be drafted in to make up numbers. A carrot was offered in the form of monetary awards for skill at shooting at annual musters in, more than probably, Finsbury Fields. However, while there is some evidence of meetings for a year or two after their formation, enthusiasm soon cooled, the impetus was lost, and it is not until the Civil War that we hear of the longbow again.

During the struggle, the bow made its appearance in a supernumerary role, when companies armed with it were formed in London for what today we might call home guard duties. The committee appointed by the Court of Common Council of London presented an account in respect of the formation and arming of city auxiliaries into six regiments. These were to be equipped with the following arms:

3,000 muskets and rests at 15 shillings each
3,000 bandoliers at 1 shilling and 6 pence
1,000 English pikes at 5 shillings and 4 pence
4,500 belts at 10 pence
1,500 swords at 5 shillings and 6 pence (These were in addition to 5,000 swords already held at Cutlers Hall.)
300 longbows at 4 shillings and 8 pence
300 sheafs of arrows at 5 pence
300 pathradoes and engines at 2 1/2 pence (What these were and what their purpose was is unclear.)
300 leather cases for arrows at 1 shilling

At least three regiments of these auxiliaries were actually formed, and they were marched to Uxbridge on April 19, 1644. On September 30, they were again called out, together with the trained bands of Westminster.[34] They were in existence as late as 1648, when they were ordered to be brought to strength with City apprentices and other persons not already in the trained bands. This is a direct parallel with the British Local Defense Force (later, the Home Guard) of the 1940s.

The bow seems to have been carried as a personal weapon by individuals, since it appears occasionally as a means to launch messages into and out of besieged towns; and there is some evidence for its use as a deliverer of fire arrows, a particularly effective way of disturbing an opposing force at rest.

The constituents of a fire arrow in earlier times were 8 parts bruised gunpowder, 1 part saltpeter in the crystal form, 1 part saltpeter in loose form, 1 part sulfur in loose form, 3 parts rosin in the crystal form, 1 part turpentine, 1 part linseed oil, 1/2 part verdigrease (acetate of copper), 1/3 part bole

Armeniac (earthy material from Armenia), 1/3 part bay salt (from the Bay of Biscay), and 1/6 part colophonia (made from a distillation of turpentine and water). If the maker thought it appropriate, arsenic (1/8 part) could also be added. A molten solution of pitch, linseed oil, sulfur, tar, and tallow was then prepared and poured over the concoction. When it was cold, it was secured to the arrow stele, covered with light canvas, and tied into position. Holes were then bored in front, fine powder was rammed in, and a fuse was fitted. now it was ready for action! Advice to the archer was to have "a certain strong bow with which to shoot fiery shafts and something stronger and longer than ordinary arrow shafts for making the firework fast to them, the which being discharged out of the bow by a skillful archer having a strong arm will do excellent service for diverse occasions."

Earlier, John Bartlet, a notable enthusiast for fire arrows and author of *A New Invention of Shooting Fire-Shafts in Longbowes*, published in 1628, had taken matters somewhat further (rather a lot further, in fact). After extolling the more obvious virtues of the weapon, Bartlet had suggested that

> at festivall times, a Bull (instead of baytng him with dogges) were tyed to a stake conveniently placed upon a Common, or other spacious place; men might then make triall with their fire-shafts (a brave and manlike sport) where happely the madding of the enraged beast (besides inuring men to conflict) would teach some profitable stratagem for warre.

While English bowyery was to some extent now in decay (a phrase the bowyers themselves used with increasing frequency), Scottish bowyers were apparently in the ascendant, since during the seventeenth century, no fewer than 64 of that trade are noticed in Edinburgh alone.[35] From an examination of contemporary paintings, the profile of the seventeenth-century Scottish longbow appears to have differed from the English pattern; and although there is some circumstantial evidence that might suggest otherwise, it may have been characterized by the recurved shape of its limb ends. Its distinctive profile was achieved by direct or indirect heat through steaming, and it was known by some as the "MacNaughton bow."

In fact, the Scottish longbow, or at least those used by the gentry, seems broadly to have followed the shape of a Continental weapon (the Burgundian bow), and this perhaps illustrates an influence that Continental Europe may have had upon professional Scottish bow making. Side by side with these commercially produced bows, however, were others of a more rural nature used by Highland clansmen. They are exemplified in poems by Alisdair Mac Mhaighstir Alasdair written between the late seventeenth and eighteenth centuries. Originally in Gaelic, the anglicized translation is as follows:

May God bless our swords
Our bows handsome of yew,
That would be braced in the face
of battle
And the arrows of birch that
splinter not,
In their quivers of badger
gloomy.

Traditionally, the best of native Highland war bows were made of yew from Esagaran (near Loch Treig) with bowstrings of hemp. Arrows of birch were fletched with feathers from the eagles of Loch Treig and armed with arrowheads forged by the smith MacPhedran.

To Scotland fell the dubious honor of the last recorded use of the longbow (albeit the Scottish weapon) in national warfare. In 1644, James Graham, Marquis of Montrose

A woodcut from *A New Invention of Shooting Fire-shafts in Long Bowes*, 1628. Published by John Bartlet, who was called "a true patriot for the common good of his native country of England." Combustible material was contained within sacking and set alight by a slow-burning fuse.

(himself an archer who had competed for the Musselburgh Silver Arrow), had with Alasdair MacColla MacDonald's Irishmen and the Atholl Highlanders—armed with bows, arrows, and broadswords—fought and won engagements against Covenanter armies of superior strength at Tippermuir (outside Perth), Aberdeen, and Iverlochy.[36] It has been said disparagingly that Montrose was armed with inferior weapons, but this is to belittle the bow; and Montrose was fully familiar with its properties, as he had two bows made for his personal use in 1628 by James Pett of Edinburgh.

The Scottish war bow was also employed in a great clan battle that took place in 1688 at Mulroy in Lochaber between the Macdonalds of Keppoch and the Mackintoshes of Moy, and this is considered by many to be the last use of the longbow in organized warfare. So there we will leave this simple weapon at the nadir of its career, for it is now time to consider its cousin, the recreational longbow.

7 / The Rise of the Recreational Longbow

It is arguable that recreation has always played its part in the use and development of the longbow. Shooting at butts or roving, while excellent training for the uncertain distances encountered in warfare, is by its very nature both recreational and competitive. The formal archery tournament so vividly described in the "Lyttel Geste of Robyn Hode" will serve as introduction.[1]

> Lysten gentil men, and herken what I shall say,
> How the proud sheryfe of Notyngham, dyde crye a full fayre play . . .
> That all the best archers of the north, sholde come upon a day,
> And they that sho[o]teth allther best, the game shall bear away . . .
> He that sho[o]teth allther best, furthest fayre and lowe,
> At a pair of fynly buttes, under the grenewode shawe [thicket] . . .
> A ryght good arowe he shall have, the shaft of sylver whyte,
> The hede and the feders of ryche rede golde, in England is none lyke.

The butts were "fayre and longe" but, predictably, Robin "always slist [sliced] the wand [stick target]."

The geste is believed to be a compilation of earlier tales assembled by an unknown person during the first part of the fifteenth century. The outlaw tales themselves are believed by at least one knowledgeable authority to date from the fourteenth century or even earlier and are thus among the earliest vernacular accounts of certain aspects of English social life at that time.[2] The awarding of silver arrows for skill with the bow and arrow was a feature of archery tournaments throughout succeeding centuries—and the practice is ongoing.

If butt shooting was formal and competitive, then shooting at "hoyles" was casual—although also competitive.[3] "Hoyles"—a northern English dialect word descriptive of small humps, bumps, and prominences in the ground such as mole hills and the like—was often a way of passing time on a long walk into the local village or even to church. A popular form of the more formal roving and shot for a wager of pence, it was conducted at much shorter distances of no more than between 15 or 20 yards.

The third form of contest, while essentially competitive, has certain features that suggest formal training for hunting and woodcraft. It is "shooting under the lyne," and again we turn to Robin Hood and the geste.[4] In this tale, he and the king shoot together.

> *On every* [each] *syde a rose garlonde, they shot under the lyne,*
> *Who so fayleth of the rose garlonde, sayd Robyn, his takyll* [gear] *he shall tyne* [forfeit] . . .
> *And bere a buffet on his hede. . . .*

Robin then shoots, and twice he splits the wand. Little John and Will Scarlet follow him but fail, and accordingly they receive a buffet. Robin then shoots his third arrow but, this time, fails to hit the wand. He duly hands his arrow over to his opponent who gives him such a box on the ears that it knocks him over. The skill in shooting "under the line," or beneath overhanging tree branches, is to aim low enough to miss them but with sufficient elevation to reach the mark. The "buffet" around the head and the forfeiting of one's arrow appears to suggest some form of quasi-official training, related perhaps to hunting. But for the account of an unrelated but very similar activity in France during the fifteenth century, the appearance of this exercise in a popular ballad, particularly one involving Robin Hood, might suggest a fertile imagination and some doubt about how authentic it was.

However, in the ninth chapter of an anonymous French treatise, *L'art d'archerie*, we read of shooting at butts "under the screen" and the virtue of this when perfecting technique. The recommended method was to erect a screen (a gantry) across the range, positioning two butts at equal distances from this. The screen had to be one foot high for every ten paces between the butts, and with the suggested distance between the butts being 100 paces, ten feet in height was necessary. The bottom edge of the screen had bells hanging from it so that if an arrow even brushed it in passing, it would be heard.

The skill of shooting under the screen, as with shooting beneath the "lyne" was to achieve a hit on the target without forfeiting an arrow. The two techniques—one English, the other French, and separated by as much as a century—are united in their common purpose, which was to improve the quality of archery.

During the bow's period as a primary weapon, it would have been virtually impossible to separate recreation from practice for warfare. Nevertheless, a little bit of sugar helps the medicine go down, and this was so with compulsory practice. Many fifteenth- and sixteenth-century English villages had active guilds to which the villagers belonged. Closely related to the Church and the focus for most of the villagers' social activity, these guilds held festivals; and Church ales, as they were called, provided occasions for revelry and enjoyment. The money raised formed much of the revenue for the Church and was used for the maintenance of lights (wax candles) at various side altars and for certain other village necessities.

In the village of Croscombe in the English county of Somerset during the fifteenth century were groupings typical of these guilds.[5] The village had seven: the Young Men (or "yonglyngs"), the Maidens, the Webbers (weavers), the Tuckers (fullers), the Archers (personated by those calling themselves Robin Hood and Little John), the Hogglers (probably the agricultural laborers), and the Wives (an early version of the mothers union or perhaps the women's institute?).

We are told that each guild brought money to the church wardens; in the case of the Archers, this came from the "Robin Hood exhibition at the village butts." One can visualize the men of the village, whose archery practice was compulsory, demonstrating their prowess with a bow to an audience of admiring maidens and male critics too old or infirm now to take part. One can imagine the satisfaction with which their tutors, masquerading as forest heroes, watched their charges show off their strength and skill.

As an aside, it is tempting to see these guilds as the forerunners of organizations with which today we are well familiar in England. The Young Men and the Maidens have a modern counterpart in the Young Men's, and Young Women's, Christian Association—the YMCA and YWCA.

The Weavers would have served apprenticeships, and the Tuckers, likewise. Their guilds, ancient even then, would have been associated with "parental organizations" located at the guildhall of a nearby large town or city. Thus, the Weavers Company, oldest of the City of London livery companies, had been formed prior to 1150.

Arising perhaps from their fraternal guild association, it was the Hogglers who formed the first trade union at Tolpuddle in Dorsetshire and who were transported for their pains, while the guild of Archers was surely an archery club in all but name! Indeed, if the claim of a certain Scottish archery society, The Ancient Society of Kilwinning Archers, to have been formed in 1483 is valid, then this may have had its origins in a village guild, thereby exemplifying the transition from guild to formal society. Before leaving the Kilwinning archers and passing on, we ought to consider their unique form of recreational archery, the "papingo"—an archaic relic from the past, reflective of earlier times, and unique by today's standards, but enjoyed by all. "Papingo" (or "popinjay") shooting was once the subject of a festival, held on the first Sunday in May, when the figure of a parrot (originally a live bird) was suspended from a pole

A sixteenth-century engraving of butt shooting.

and shot at.[6] He who cut the string and brought the figure to earth was called Captain of the Popinjay and accorded a triumphal journey home. The patent of Henry VIII concerning the Guild or Fraternity of Saint George specifically included permission to shoot at the popinjay.[7]

In Scotland, in addition to shooting at their 30-yard butts at ground level, the Kilwinning archers suspend the figure of a winged dove from the tower of the town church and shoot at it from immediately below. The act of bringing down the figure is called in Scots "dinging doon the doo," and the "dinger" is duly rewarded. Although it may be a rustic activity on the periphery of archery, the Scottish papingo shoot is paralleled by the more sophisticated and once intensely competitive Continental archery activity, *tir a la perche*.[8]

While archery practice was required by statute across the country, despite threat and reward, it tended to be honored more in the breach than in the observance. We have read how Edward III issued an edict to his sheriffs around the time of Crécy to forbid those "strong in body" to apply themselves to any recreation except the art of shooting, under penalty of imprisonment.

Not everyone had to be pressured into shooting however. It was a recognized form of relaxation and one indulged in by many during their leisure time.

An example of this comes from Calais, where expatriate Englishmen were busily engaged in peaceful trade during the year 1478. A challenge was issued by the married men of the Staple to their bachelor colleagues to shoot a match "for a dyner or a super, price xijd [7 pence] a man." The challenge is nicely worded and addressed to "owre welbelufed good Brodyr Thomas Wryght and all other Bacheleres beyng fremen of the Staple be thes delyuered." There follow twelve names, a number of which are still to be found in English traditional archery circles today. The result of the match is not recorded, but one may be sure that when the archery was over, they all sat down to a good meal in jovial accord, as indeed do their remote descendants after shooting today.

Londoners who exercised the art of shooting had for many years used the fields on the outskirts of the City, although at times these were far from ideal. Moorfields, for example, a principal venue for the City's archers, was at one time the City's latrine, an arrangement scarcely conducive to either pleasure or profit. Matters were slow to change, but a century or so later in 1497, a field of around 12 acres was prepared "for archers and other military citizens to shoot in." Later on, this area was expanded by an additional five acres. Although Moorfields was probably the earlier site, it was Finsbury Fields that became the more notable, since it was here that the annual competitions for shooting were held and prizes awarded for distances shot.

Henry VIII, the archer king, was instrumental in establishing these contests, and the first seems to have taken place in 1521 when the first day of the wrestling was adopted for "Games of Shotyng."[9] The new arrangements were published, probably by written proclamation, although since many of the potential participants would have been illiterate, the announcement might well have been read in its entirety. In this event, one can readily understand the interest with which it was undoubtedly greeted. However, they were not to be let off lightly. King Henry was well aware of the failings of his subjects, and he had preceded the carrot of prizes with a well-directed homily.

The principal of the event was designated master of the game, and to him would have fallen responsibility for delivering both homily and prize list. In our imagination we may picture him, fully conscious of regal majesty at his back as he gathers himself to his full height and clearing his throat, addresses the eager crowd on his king's behalf.

> My Lord Maier and my Maisters the Aldermen of the Citie of London callyng to their remembraunce the manyfold benfitts and comodities that have comen to this Realme by the feat of Archery and Shotyng in the long bowe wherby, God be thanked, this said Realme hath ever in tyme hertofore passed been

defended ageynst the cruell malice and daunger of the awkeward enemyes and so from hensforth God willyng shalbe for ever whiche said feat of shotyng every good true Inglysshman is naturally bound to maynteigne, supporte and upholde to the best of his powere.

One may imagine a certain shuffling of feet at this barbed thrust, and perhaps he paused for a moment here to glance over his spectacles to let the import of that remark be absorbed before passing on.

And to the intent that the saide Feate of Archerie should be the better maynteigned and upheld, to encorage the King's Subjetts more and more to use and exercyse the same, my said Lord and Maisters have appoynted and fully concluded that on Sonday cume vij [7] nights whiche shalbe the ffirst day of September next comyng shalbe a severall game of Shotyng in the ffeld called *ffynesbury feld* at ij [2] of the clok at afternone.

And who will come thether and take a long bowe in hys hand havyng the Standard therein therefor appoynted, and ffayrest draweth, clenlyest delyvereth and fardest of ground shoteth shall have for hys best game a Crowne of Gold of the value of xxs, or xxs in money therfore. . . .

The master of the game's work was not yet over however. The Tudor Englishman was as alien to management at important events as are present-day football hooligans, and authority laid down the law unequivocally. On behalf of the king, every man present at the game of shooting was charged to "kepe the Kyng's peace in his owne persone, upon the payne of Imprisonament and farther to make ffyne (be fined)." Finally, with thought for the personal safety of his subjects, the king declared that "no persone be so hardy to stand within xxti [20] yards of any of the Stakes appoynted for a Marke upon the perill that wil fall therefof." In order that no one should be in any doubt of the imminence of danger, a trumpet was sounded before each and every shot.

We can speculate about the arrows used and indeed we should, since there is some conjecture necessary when the standard arrow and the bearing arrow are considered. The standard presents no great difficulty. It was almost certainly a war arrow—a sheaf, or a livery arrow, such as would have been habitually used in battle. The event was directly related to training for warfare, and the use of a battle shaft is entirely consistent with this purpose. The bearing arrow is something of a puzzle however. There was no difference in the monetary prize or in the precious metal awarded for the game or prize. Perhaps a little less material went into the arrow than the crown, but who knows? Thomas Roberts, writing two and a half centuries later, defines a bearing arrow as one with steady flight.[10] This implies selection, or even personalizing, of an arrow chosen for its ability to fly well and true. Nothing wrong with that, you say, and rightly so. If the archer had the time before battle to check and personalize his shafts, then his shots would be the surer and his worth the greater. Equally, however, he should be able to make his shots count with whatever came to hand, and sheaf arrows were not always the best tackle.

It is the flight arrow that is perhaps the most curious, since this was shot principally for distance. By its nature it would have been light—and being light, it would have had limited effect upon its target. Ascham is not precise in his remarks

King Henry VIII portrayed shooting with the longbow at the Field of the Cloth of Gold, 1520, where he impressed King Francis I with the power of English archery and his own considerable prowess as an archer.

about flight or distance shooting; his advice, which is excellent as one would expect, falls rather in the general area of suitability for purpose. We must turn to his predecessor, the anonymous fifteenth-century author of the French treatise *L'art d'archerie* for some specific comment upon flight shooting and flight shafts.[11] There is nothing in Ascham's book to suggest that he knew of this particular work, but as we will discover in a later chapter, he was well acquainted with (and derided) certain methods of French stance and styles of shooting and their foibles, although he does not identify them as French.

Concerning the flight bow, the anonymous Frenchman quotes from the book of *Roi Modus*. The bow should ideally be the length of two arrows and one hand's breadth. Later in his book, he mentions that an archer should draw ten hands' breadths. If a hand's breadth is taken as 3 1/2 inches, then a 35-inch shaft is indicated. Assuming this length and adding a hand's breadth of 3 1/2 inches, this would seem to indicate a 73- or 74-inch weapon. This does seem overlong for distance work; however, flight arrows are traditionally shorter than a standard shaft, and a shorter arrow (and thus a shorter bow) might be indicated! The point is open. The flight arrow, the French author writes, should be of light but stiff wood. He goes on to say that the French flight arrows are not as good as those from England, because England has access to lighter and stiffer wood. There is no flight arrow as good as the English! Flight arrows should be fletched with pigeon's or duck's primary feathers. Rather surprisingly, although three fletches seem to have been the norm in this country, in France, things were ordered differently. Some French flight arrows had six and others nine fletches. One is not unduly surprised that English arrows flew better and further! Heads might be of either horn or iron. However, there was one particular trick of the trade to which certain Finsbury contestants might have been wise. It was the practice of the cognoscenti to drill out a shaft to within two inches of the shaftment and fill it with either lead or quicksilver. The additional stiffness and weight made these arrows the most advantageous.

Shooting for games or rewards took place periodically from 1521 until at least 1596 despite the demotion of the bow as a weapon of war. Sir Thomas Elyot, author of *The Boke Named The Governour*, an advisory tome on acceptable conduct published in 1531, is fulsomely explicit in his praise of the advantage derived from shooting.

> In myn oppinion none may be compared with shooting in the longe bowe and that for sondry utilities that come thereof, wherein it incomparably excelleth all other exercise. For in drawyng of a bowe easie and congruent to his strength he that shoteth bothe moderately exercise his armes and the over (upper) part of his body . . . . In shootynge at buttes or brode arowe markes is a mediocrite of exercise of the lower partes of the body and legges . . . .

Sir Thomas has kindly words to say about tennis, taken in small doses, and reserves his judgment on bowling. However, he is vitriolic about the English national game.

> To be utterly abjected of al noble men is foot balle wherein is nothinge but beastly furie and extreme violence whereof procedeth hurte and consequently rancour and malice do remaine with them that be wounded wherfore it is to be put in perpetuall silence.

There has been more than one occasion to prove that this sagacious knight hit the nail squarely on the head.

The practice of archery with the longbow was indeed thought a most desirable activity for the gentry and the author of *The Institucion of a Gentleman*, published in 1555, also praised its virtue. After a xenophobic paragraph or two outlining past deeds of the English bowman, he extols the activity.

> Therefore it shall become all Gentlemen to use this, our English pastime of shooting for their greatest game and disport. This pastime hath in it two singular points which in no other game as yet could ever be found: that it is serveth for a pastime and a defence in the wars.

By Henry VIII's statute of 1515, all men, with certain exceptions, were required to possess a bow and arrows; and if they had boys or were responsible for them, had to teach them to shoot. Instruction started at seven years of age and continued until 17, when they were considered old enough to join the men. Roger Ascham exemplifies the process in the preamble to his book when he eulogizes Sir Humphrey Wingfield, the benefactor responsible for his education.[12] When Sir Humphrey returned to school from London, he brought with him bows and arrows. When the lads went out to shoot with these, he accompanied them. Those that shot well, he praised, and to them he gave the best bows. Those that shot badly were mocked until they shot better!

Poignant direct evidence for archery practice by the young comes from a coroner's inquest in Nottingham. At Newark on June 10, 1534, while shooting at small targets with other lads for recreation, eight-year-old Francis Spayning hit and killed young Thomas Riche who ran between them. It is unlikely that Thomas was unique in succumbing to unsupervised shooting. From a coroner's report in June 1550 there is further evidence of a lack of discipline.

> Thomas Lamont the younger, and other honest men asssembled together at Upton (Nottinghamshire) were shooting at "garden buttes." As soon as Thomas had shot, Richard Allott suddenly and unexpectedly ran between the butts, and Thomas' arrow worth one penny struck the left side of his (Richard's) head, giving him a wound 1 inch deep and 1/2 inch wide of which he languished from 29th June to 1st July when he died thereof. Thus Thomas in shooting his arrow at said buttes and by Richard's unexpected running, slew Richard by misadventure.

While it was a parent's statutory responsibility to provide a bow and to teach his youngster to shoot it, his success—or otherwise—was also monitored periodically.[13] We have a glimpse of the arrangements for this from a poem by Richard Robinson, a minor Elizabethan man of letters whose family home was Newark, in Nottinghamshire.[14]

> *Myself remembered of a childe in Contreye native mine;*
> *A May game was of Robyn-hode and of this traine that time,*

To traine up young men, stripplings and eche other younger childe
In shooting, yearely this with solemne feast was by the Guylde
And Brotherhood of Townsmen done, with sport, with joy, and love
To proffet which in present tyme, and afterward did prove.

The arrangements are reminiscent of those at Croscombe in Somerset mentioned earlier.

Quite fortuitously, we know something of the bows that youngsters of that time were using, for an archaeological excavation at Acton Court near Bristol in the late 1980s recovered from the moat two child's longbows dating from the 1540s.[15] One can readily appreciate their use by young members of the family of Sir Nicholas Poynz (the owner) as they shot at garden butts or longer-flight distances in the nearby park. Although suffering from some mechanical damage, each is in comparatively good condition; and since they differ one from the other, comparison is interesting and fruitful.[16]

The first bow is made probably of yew; the length of this bow is 40 1/4 inches. Of ogival cross section, the back shows evidence of sapwood. The limbs taper evenly to the the tips. Although both tips are damaged, they are coned, an indication that horn nocks were originally fitted. The point of balance is 15 millimeters distant from the mathematical center, suggesting a distinction between upper and lower limbs.

The second bow is made probably of yew; being damaged at one end, it is slightly shorter at 38 inches and of a cambered (D-shaped) section. The remaining tip has been carefully coned. The point of balance is 25 millimeters from the center, but this will have been affected by the absence of the tip.

While the variance between cross sections may have resulted from a whim, there is some evidence of reasoned separate purpose for each. The French manuscript *L'art d'archerie* of circa 1500 advises the use of a round section for flight or distance shooting and a square section with straight sides and broad back for butt shooting. It may be that these bows were used for instruction in both forms of archery.[17] It is speculative of course by whom they were made, although there is evidence for professionalism. However, the names of contemporary local bowyers are known; and it is not a flight of fancy to suggest that if one was commissioned to supply Nicholas Poyntz with these juvenile weapons, then we are looking at the work of either John Phillips, John Powell, Robert Jordan, or Robert Vickeris from the city of Bristow (Bristol).[18]

In another part of the country, a small and insignificant piece of leatherwork recovered from an archaeological excavation in 1949 has recently been recognized for what it was: a juvenile's archery tab, or finger protection.[19] Let us leave hard uncompromising fact for a little and indulge a flight of fancy.

We are in Coventry. It is 1500, and a new century has dawned. To celebrate, the city guild of Robin Hood is busily preparing Barker Butts for the May fair. Stalls are set out in readiness; the guild of Housewives has jars of jam and patties spread out on muslin cloths. Tempting jars of candied elecampane delight young eyes, and excitement is palpable. Watching closely is young Jenkyn Pritchard. By his side is a bow made for him by his father; in his belt are two arrows. On his fingers is a three-finger pigskin leather tab.

The beadle calls all to order, and as the cathedral bell rings loud and clear, the fun begins. For Jenkyn it must be the archery. Towering above him is the guild master attired as Robin. By his side is a man of equal size, John Little. It is Jenkyn's turn. He is left handed. His father has roughly cut a finger tab for him, and he wears it on his left hand in readiness. But Robin will have none of this. If Jenkyn is to be of use in war, he is to shoot as a right-handed archer. He must wear his new-cut tab on his right hand. With trepidation he changes hands, takes stance awkwardly, and shoots his shafts. They miss the mark, and he walks away dejected. He trudges home through Palmer Lane and in despair he throws this useless tab away. He will never make an archer!

We are in Coventry. It is 1949. An amateur archaeologist is digging in Palmer Lane. Among his many finds—an archer's tab. Could it be? The material is so far unidentified but may be pigskin. The size of the finger holes indicate use by a juvenile. The smooth side is cut conventionally for a sinistral, although it is the rough side that bears the marks of string crease.

To hone skill, garden archery (or garden butts) was an activity enjoyed by old and young alike, and there is little doubt that the original owner of that discarded pigskin tab would have shot regularly with his fellows. No less a person than Andrew Boorde, Henry VIII's physician, remarked that "a payre of Butts be a good thing about a mansyon place," and there is little doubt that the younger element took full advantage of them, since with a heady combination of statute law and Henry's benign patronage, recreational archery blossomed. An astute soldier and a leader who understood the nature of his subjects, he recognized the advantage of the carrot of privilege as well as the stick. To him must be attributed creation of the first recognizable archery society for gentlemen when in 1537 he granted the archers of London a charter of incorporation under the title of the Fraternity or Guild of St. George, extending the scope of what may have been its original narrowly confined membership nationwide, for at least one country gentleman from Wiltshire was subsequently inducted to its ranks.

Although there is some circumstantial evidence for the guild's earlier existence, the charter set its future organization and parameters firmly in place. Three overseers were appointed to arrange matters, and beneath them were four masters who were directed to "begin, guard and establish a perpetual Fraternity to develop the Science of Artillerie," by which was meant longbows, crossbows, and handguns. The masters had authority to "choose and admit all manner of honest persons whatever," including, rather curiously perhaps, "foreigners." One trusts that the masters were properly selective in exercising this right, since in Henry's Tudor England,

A medieval juvenile's crude three-finger shooting tab for the protection of fingers. Recovered from an excavation in Coventry, Warwickshire. Photo courtesy of Coventry City Museum, Godiva Collection.

the presence of foreigners was regarded with an often-justified suspicion.

While the fraternity was established essentially as a recreational body, it had a clearly defined secondary purpose; indeed, there is little doubt that Henry saw that purpose as of primary significance, since the charter specified that "for the better increase of the defense of the realm and maintaining the science of shooting" the members of the fraternity were granted license "for their disport and pastime at all manner of Marks and Butts . . . both in London, and suburbs, and all other parts of the realm of England." As might be expected, the royal parks and forests were excepted. Even Henry was not that magnanimous!

Apart from the freedom to shoot at almost anything, either moving or not, the fraternity enjoyed other privileges. The masters and rulers, and their successors, were exempted from jury service; and in an age where strict dress codes applied, they were permitted to wear embroidery of silver wire on their jackets, gowns, coats, and doublets. With the exception of purple and scarlet, appropriate only for royalty, they were allowed to wear whatever color of silk, velvet, satin, or damask might please them. In short, membership of the Fraternity, or Guild, of St. George was an achievement of some considerable advantage if one wished to be noticed.

One other important prerogative fell to the masters and rulers of the guild. No other fraternity or guild could be formed in any part of the realm unless specifically licensed by them. This proscription is of some interest in the context of a second fifteenth-century archery society, Prince Arthur's Knights. Although there is some circumstantial evidence for its origin, contributed by the minor Elizabethan man of letters Richard Robinson, which purports to set out its history, we actually know very little of the beginnings of this curiously named society. The matter is enigmatic, and like all good enigmas, it fuels speculation.

We will try to draw together the various threads. The ultimate originator of the society's title may have been Henry VII's son and heir to the throne, Prince Arthur. Although young, he practiced archery assiduously; and popular history records that until his premature death in 1502, he was an excellent shot. He was so good a shot, in fact, that other excellent London archers were likened to him, and it was said that they shot like Prince Arthur. However, we learn from a book published by Robinson that

> by Patent of his princely prerogative, (Henry VIII) ordained, granted, and confirmed unto this Honourable City of London, free election of a Chieftaine and of citizens representing the memory of that magnificent King Arthur and the knights of the same Order, which should for the maintenance of shooting only, meet together once a year, with solemn and friendly celebration thereof.[20]

In 1583, Robinson published a second book and included the following: "And furthermore for the maintenance of the same laudable exercise (shooting) in this honourable City of London by his gracious Charter confirmed unto the worshipful Citizens of the same, this your now famous Order of Knights of Prince Arthur's Round Table."[21]

The charter of patent cannot now be traced, and thus the year that this society was actually formed is uncertain. However, there is some circumstantial evidence for 1542–1543, since that was the millennium of the year(s) in which it was believed that the legendary King Arthur died. Robinson draws our attention to two possible individuals, each of whom has some claim to be the first chieftain of whom Henry's charter of patent apparently speaks.

The first, Sir William Bowyer, was mayor in 1543; and the second, Sir Martin Bowes, was mayor in 1544–1545. Sir Martin was a man of great eminence and a member of the powerful Goldsmiths Company, which played an influential part in archery matters later during the century. He owned land at Moorfields and, significantly perhaps, also at Mile-end. Each was directly concerned with archery; but the latter was the shooting ground frequented by archers from the east of the City and the stamping ground for the later, reformed society. Beyond the belief commonly held that King Henry visited Mile-end occasionally to watch the shooting, plus the exhortation to citizens to meet there annually for formal contest, nothing has survived of the form such contests took. Stowe, in his *Survey of London*, mentions that

> in the time of Henry VIII the citizens of London exercised their part of shoot-ing at Mile-end Green and that the chief of their archers was called "Prince Arthur". The rest of the archers were called his "knights." the exercise was so manly, that as the king used it himself, he disdained not to sometimes come to Mile-end to see and commend it.[22]

What form of shooting he watched can only be guessed, but speculation suggests a game similar to that shot at Finsbury, Moorfields, or Hoxton fields, although there is some later circumstantial evidence for roving. Certain road names in the area are similar to the names of marks on Finsbury Fields and suggest the existence of a number of marks similar to those known to have been there. A casual reference to a costly stake set up by a "Baron Stirrop" in the 1580s confirms the existence of at least one such.[23]

Sir William Wood, compiler of the sixteenth-century *Bowman's Glory* records, "he (King Henry) being one day at Mile-end when Prince Arthur and his Knights were shooting did greatly commend the Game and allowed there-of, lauding them to their encouragement." And so it goes.

The original Prince Arthur's Knights may not have survived as a society much beyond Henry's death in 1547, although a period of just three years seems little enough time for citizens to tire of the privilege accorded them by the monarch. Be that as it may, however, we know for certainty that they were reformed in 1578 by persons of consequence within the City of London. The title Prince Arthur was assumed by Thomas Smith, the chief farmer of customs of Queen Elizabeth I, with Alderman Hugh Offley designated as Sir Lancelot. Closely associated with the society was Lord Grey of Wilton, who, with Smith, was deeply involved in contemporary Irish affairs, and there is some reason to think that he too was actually a knight of the society. Offley was a close friend of Richard Mulcaster, seemingly a knight of the company, although he is not identifiable as such, and first master of the Merchant Taylor's School in London. Mulcaster refers to the society, with which he was evidently delight-ed, in an aside within his *Positions*, a work published in 1581.

> In praising of archerie as a principall exercise to the preserving of health how can I but praise them who professe it thoroughly, and maintain it

nobly,—the friendly and frank fellowship of Prince Arthure's knights in and about the Citie of London which of late years have so revived the exercise. . . .

While a prime tenet of the society and its knights was the recreational pleasure of archery, it seems apparent that it had a second and equally important purpose: the training of Londoners in the use of the bow. Although the weapon was by now obsolete and was shortly to become so as a primary arm, skill in its use was still required by statute law. This requirement was observed reluctantly by London's citizens and with concern by the makers of the weapon and its arrows, the bowyers and fletchers who were seriously affected by this lack of interest and naturally welcomed anything that boosted sales and lifted men off the bread line. Mulcaster's enthusiasm for the longbow shines through his work, and it would seem that by 1581, there had been a resurgence of interest in the old weapon—primarily for pleasure perhaps, but with the added advantage of enhanced skills in time of war.

It was in September 1583 that perhaps the best known of archery displays took place; and we are indebted to Sir William Wood, marshal to the Regiment of Archers, for publishing in 1682 an account of this "Worthy Show and Shooting by the Duke of Shoreditch and his Associates the Worshipful Citizens of London."[24] The name "Duke of Shoreditch" was the perpetuation by a prominent citizen of one of many quasi-titles given to members of his archer guard by Henry VIII in recognition of skill while shooting with them. He is not identified but may have been connected with the Worshipful Company of Goldsmiths and might possibly have been their master then.

The procession and shooting took place on September 17, although there seems no particular reason for the choice of date. The archers assembled in Smithfield at Merchant-Taylors Hall under their captains and moved off in full panoply, with ensigns flying and trumpets and drums sounding, stopping on the way for various activities, including, among other things, a mock fight between enthusiastic archers and handgunners, which, from the lively account, may have got a little out of hand.

It is possible, even likely, that the so-called Duke of Shoreditch was the leader of an organization similar to Prince Arthur's Knights, since his associates included marquesses and earls and the curiously named Black Train led by the Black Prince of Portugal. This body of men was seemingly, from other references, a martial column of handgunners and bowmen drawn from one or more of the City's wards, forming part of the City's recently established trained band. The procession wound around the streets of the City, its way cleared by the oddly named "whifflers," men armed with wooden swords who walked ahead and by its side to keep an undisciplined crowd, eager for the spectacle, under some semblance of control.

Eventually all concerned reached Shoreditch Church and turned into Hoxton Fields, where a tent had been erected for the Duke of Shoreditch and chief citizens. Immediately in front was the shooting line from which the archers would aim at a butt specially erected for the occasion set up at seven score and eight yards. This distance seems an arbitrary one and unrelated to what would later be standard lengths based upon the linear rood. Incredibly, we are told that 3,000 archers shot that day; and to continue the statistics, a grand total of 4,400 persons paraded, 942 of whom wore chains of gold to denote their rank.

Sir William Wood, Captain of the Finsbury Archers, whose rules the company has observed from their introduction in 1687. From a painting in the possession of the Royal Toxophilite Society.

Preparations for the shooting got under way, with ensigns bringing their contingents of archers to the line. To the sound of trumpets, heralds proclaimed the safety proscription first defined by Henry VIII: "Every man shall avoid Forty foot from each side of the Butt; otherwise to stand to their own perils." We are not told when shooting began or, for that matter, how many arrows were shot, although it would be surprising if men shot more than one each. By three o'clock, after the ensigns' archers had shot, a ripple of excitement passed through the crowd. Prince Arthur's Knights were approaching the field mounted on stately palfreys, each with ten pages in attendance and Irish lackeys (servants) running alongside armed with darts. Accompanying them were 200 archers on foot, half in front and half behind the knights. Once arrived at the duke's tent, a messenger clad in a jacket of black velvet, with a black velvet cap and a green satin doublet, addressed the duke on Prince Arthur's behalf.

The gist of his lengthy oration concerned the repute in which Prince Arthur and his court held the longbow and in whose honor, through this troop of his knights, the prince was presenting five bows of gold and five silver arrows "requiring your Nobleness to bestow them on five of the most valiant, active, and most expert of your train, in shooting in the Long Bow, requesting friendly we may presently see the delivery of them to those persons most worthy."

The duke received the gifts with good grace, but at this point, all the excitement got too much for the crowds who broke through the barriers and swarmed around both the duke and the knights. Sadly, a sumptuous banquet that had been prepared could not be served "by reason of the unruliness and throng of the people." One can only imagine the mutterings of the chef!

With the departure of the knights, shooting recommenced and went on until nightfall when it was stopped by the duke to be completed the following day, Wednesday. Besides the bows and arrows of gold and silver, money prizes, or games, were on offer, and these were substantial. The first was 53 shillings 4 pence, the second was five nobles (33 shillings 4 pence), the third was four nobles (26 shillings 8 pence), the fourth was 20 shillings, and the fifth was 10 shillings.[25] From the account, it would seem that many, if not most, of those taking part were apprentices, and the winners were feted both by their masters and parents.

To close the proceedings, the Duke of Shoreditch was escorted home by men-at-arms. An associated troop of harquebussers arrived at the duke's residence in a state of barely suppressed excitement, and with many hurrahs and shouts of joy, discharged their pieces enthusiastically into the air "to the honour of the Duke, and the good liking of them all," causing the duke's window glass to fall out and shatter. After two exhausting days and a lost luncheon, one suspects that the duke may have felt a certain ambivalence toward this display of bonhomie!

Despite valiant attempts made during the early seventeenth century to persuade a reluctant council to reinstate the longbow as a warlike weapon—attempts that in fact, resulted in a modest revival of its military role—it was clear that the time had now come for men to set aside its martial image and welcome it simply as a means for social pleasure. We will meet it as such in the next chapter.

8 | *Archery, the Social Dimension*

As the seventeenth century opened, lip service was still paid to statute law, for archery practice was required of all able-bodied men. However, those few who shot did so largely because they found it enjoyable; for despite the activities of ill-disposed landowners, it was still possible to rove and shoot at the marks on Finsbury Fields and elsewhere, and this freedom would continue for the remainder of the century.

The Society of Finsbury Archers, earliest of the formal archery societies and increasingly prominent as the century progressed, is of uncertain origin; however, there is reference in January of 1570 to a letter concerning a prospective fort at Bunhill that would be "a great security to the Archers of Finsbury."[1] While this suggests some form of organized activity, it seems unlikely that a formal society was constituted much before 1600.

The booklet *Ayme for Finsburie Archers*, an alphabetical table of the names of every mark within the fields, with their true distances measured by line and shown on a map, was published in 1601 "for the ease of the skilfull, and behoose (assistance) of the yong beginners in the famous exercise of Archerie."[2] This replaced another less accurate version published in 1594, although whether archery had been formalized by then is open to some doubt.

The earliest record of a formal society connected specifically to Finsbury Fields, which may or may not have been the Society of Finsbury Archers, is contained within the history of the Honourable Artillery Company —the military body charged with oversight of the shooting grounds.[3] The account of Kielway Guidott, Steward of the Company of Archers, dated February 25, 1636, was submitted to the company by reason of the death of his partner

Thomas Naylor and is circumstantial evidence for an earlier existence than the usually accepted date of 1652.

We will return to these Finsbury bowmen, but first we will make a foray into fiction, albeit fiction founded perhaps on practice. Once more we open the pages of the Robin Hood ballads, that repository of arcane archery lore, and turn to "Robin Hood and Queen Katherine," since this is a stylized account of an archery contest on Finsbury Fields.

As with many broadside ballads, it is difficult to date; but circumstantial evidence suggests a printing during the first quarter of the seventeenth century, with an oral rendering perhaps earlier still. There are two principal accounts; the earlier and shorter version was recorded by Joseph Ritson,[4] and the longer was recorded in the Forresters Manuscript, edited by Stephen Knight. It is this latter with which we are concerned, for although tantalizing in its paucity, it provides some detail of both the event and the equipment used.

We are told that Robin's bow is of yew, but with a silken string. Silk was not brought into England in any quantity prior to the sixteenth century, although its use for bowstrings is noticed earlier. Here it serves to emphasize the quality of Robin's equipment. Silk was seemingly recommended for distance shooting because of its inherent elasticity (although current experiment may yet prove us wrong, we would question this logic today when inert strings are considered more effective). Made of yew, however, and with a superior string, Robin's bow was set up for maximum cast.

His arrows were of "silver cheste," and here is a minor puzzle. If "sugar chest" is intended, then the author flies in the face of Roger Ascham, who regarded it as making "dead, heavy, lumpish and hobbling shafts." If "silver birch" is meant, however, then the choice is right by Ascham, being "strong enough to stand in a bow and light enough to fly far."[5]

The king seeks to measure out the mark with a line, thus enabling an exact distance to be known (as were the distances between the contemporary permanent marks). Robin will have none of this though. He prefers the challenge of an unknown length. "Measure no Marks for us my liege, we'll shoot at sun and moon."

For all that, the marks are set eventually at 15 score (300 yards) or possibly 300 paces if a line was used, and the tournament commences. Evidently lulling the opposition into a sense of false security, Robin and his two companions allow the king's men to take the first three arrows, theirs being closest to the mark. Seemingly badly placed to win, and having extracted substantial wagers against their chances, Robin, Much, and Will Scarlet then pull back to equal scores.

The game now stands at three and three. Excitement grips the ladies of the court who are gathered round to watch. They cry, "Woodcock beware thine eye," a potentially puzzling reference that warrants explanation. A "woodcock" described a simple or gullible person and suggests that the queen and her ladies, having guessed what is about to happen, are mocking the king's archers. Predictably, they are right. Tempest, the king's bow bearer, shoots first, followed by Robin, who splits his arrow into three pieces, and Much, whose arrow strikes within one finger of the prick (peg). A yeoman of the crown is then said to shoot "underhand"—an expression that can have two meanings. To shoot underhand is to elevate the bow so as to see the mark or target from below the wrist. An underhand shaft, however, also describes the profile of a shaft known variously as "rush-grown" or "bobtailed," having a profile that tapers from pile to nock. As Ascham would say, "small breasted and large toward the head."

To answer this shot, Clifton (the alias of Little John) shoots either a "bearded" (Forresters Manuscript) or a "bearing" (Ritson version) arrow. Here we have another choice, for again, each is a valid archery expression. The former is the vernacular for a broadheaded military, or hunting, shaft, and the latter is for an arrow with a steady flight. Accepting the accusation of partiality, we will opt for bearing, particularly since the arrow hit and split the wand. Clifton then claims the upshot, or the deciding shot, and the match is over in Robin's favor.

As depicted, the contest itself does not entirely fit the known rules for formal archery on Finsbury Fields during either the sixteenth or the seventeenth centuries and is thus enigmatic. Arrows were seemingly shot individually and not in pairs as was then the practice. However, personal variations certainly existed, and what is described would have been familiar enough to an audience. Fifteen score yards was not an unusually long distance between marks, for many in the fields exceeded this.

An irrelevant coincidence, included for its curiosity, concerns the term "woodcock." Henry Wodcocke, a London bowyer, received the royal writ in 1556, a year in which the ballad was seemingly current. Could it be that here is a topical throwaway comment on an eccentric bowyer?

While recreational activity generally was severely curtailed during the Puritan commonwealth, and the morally degenerate watched their backs carefully as they indulged in forbidden pastimes, there is little doubt that archery continued to be practiced to some degree. It was not until the restoration of the monarchy, however, that it bloomed fully once more. Charles II had enjoyed the sport while in exile on the Continent and was congenially disposed to the pastime.

Knowing of his interest, and to celebrate re-establishment of the old order, the London Court of Aldermen arranged an archery show on St. Bartholomew's Day (August 21) in 1663 to display the "truly ENGLISH and Manly Exercises of Wrestling, Archery, and Sword and Dagger," an important occasion that included laudatory speeches by Mr. William Smee, Clerk of the (Smithfield) Market and master of the game *pro hoc vice* (for the time) from whom we learn that there had been a lapse of 24 years since the last such occasion.[6] The shooting arrangements closely followed those set down in the preceding century, which were hallowed by time. Mr. Smee, addressing the lord mayor and other dignitaries present, told them that "the Bow And Arrow you will presently Honour with your view are all remaining Trophies of our French Conquests and the best Testimonies of our ENGLISH Valour, and are authentique testimonies thereof." This seems to indicate that war bows and arrows, and not the recreational bow, were used at least on this occasion and suggests that the transition from war bow profile to recreational style, lighter draw weight, and shorter length had yet to happen. Accepting this, we can reasonably infer that the very respectable winning flight distance of 22 score (440 yards) achieved by Mr. Lancelot Girlington and personally measured by Mr. Smee was made with a bow of not less than 100 pounds draw weight.

Of evident satisfaction to the court of aldermen was the defrayment of costs by the Honourable Artillery Company "who were nobly pleased to beare all the charges of the severall feats." It would seem from various sources that shooting the Pound Arrow (a battle shaft) as the event became known, in the presence of the lord mayor, was practiced well into the next century, providing one last tenuous link with the ancient weapon.[7]

Those who habitually used the Finsbury Fields were accustomed and expected to shoot for distance between marks, and it is instructive to compare the availability of marks set at the major length of 18 score (360 yards) across the years. In 1601, when the war bow was still in some evidence, these numbered 204; however, in 1628, a generation later, the number had dropped substantially to 123.[8] Since the marks were positioned with the authority of the stake master, it might seem that he had bowed to pressure from those who were now either using lighter draw weight recreational bows; could see no virtue, or purpose, in shooting (and walking) long distances; or were prevented by enclosures from doing so. The reason is arguable, but the circumstance exists to be explained. For comparison, in 1727, of 25 marks then existing, just one exceeded 15 score (300 yards), most being no more than 200 yards apart.

Let us return to the Society of Finsbury Archers. In 1652, two stewards were appointed for the year to make the necessary arrangements for the shooting and for the important dinners associated with it. Although the Great Fire of 1666 put an end to their activities for three years, in 1668, they were back once more and were to continue without further interruption until 1757, at which time encroachment caused by the expansion of the City made shooting too difficult to continue. The society was to remained moribund until 1781, when the few surviving members joined the newly formed Toxophilite Society, bringing their principal awards with them.

Awards were formalized around 1670, but the tradition of silver arrows continued, since Sir Reginald Foster, Baronet, and Warwick Ledgingham, Esq., the

A Finsbury archer of the seventeenth century. From half of a ticket of entry to a bow meeting. Notice his four arrows, his bow with its recurved tips, and his measuring pole.

two stewards for the year, gave two of these (each of 11 ounces 5 pennyweight) to be shot for by members. One of these arrows having been lost, Mr. Ellis, a steward in 1672, replaced it with another weighing 12 ounces 5 pennyweight. The circumstance of the lost arrow is interesting and will be the subject of conjecture to be considered later in this chapter.

On Monday, August 14, 1671, the society's meeting was held in the artillery garden of the Honourable Artillery Company, when 30 members attended. The form this meeting took is not recorded, but if it followed normal practice, then a target would be set up and shooting for a silver arrow, or "spoons" would begin at eight score (160 yards), the length being reduced by ten yards after each of three rounds until all prizes had been won. Although it seems likely that they were a select, and possibly a selective, society, whether 30 was a true reflection of their then strength is debatable, since much larger gatherings of archers took place at that time. A company of 350, for instance, turned out to march past the monarch and the lord mayor in 1676, with the officers wearing green scarves and each man a green riband; while in May of the following year, over 1,000 shot whistling arrows to entertain the king.[9] In 1681, an unspecified number marched in procession from London to Hampton Court to shoot for

30 pieces of silver plate worth £30. Shooting was conducted at 160 yards, a distance that seems to have been normal for the time, the target being placed upon a butt erected for the purpose. We are not told of the style of target face, but in the fashion of a slightly later time, it may have been a paper measuring in diameter one inch for every ten yards set out as a number of concentric circles—much the same as today's targets.

The king, we are told, was pleased with the shooting and permitted as many as wished to kiss his hand. Sadly, with the inevitability that attends important occasions in England, it rained; and after seeing six of the 30 prizes won, an increasingly damp king was obliged to retire—perhaps to refresh his ardor with the congenial comforts of Nell Gwynn.

In April of 1682, it all happened again. At least 1,000 archers gathered to shoot, loosing three showers of whistling arrows as a preliminary to the occasion. Sir William Wood, who recorded this gathering comments, "for now Gentlemen begin to be pleased with the Divertissement and pleased with this Manly recreation." It is a throwaway remark but significant in the context of longbow archery, since modern recreational shooting might be said to stem from this time. Quite what part the personal interest in archery shown by the restored monarch played in this development is open to question, for Charles was known to approve the sport; but the opportunity to demonstrate one's ability in front of one's monarch and to receive his favors in return must have been an attractive proposition, and perhaps outweighed the more remote chance of a share in the prizes.

There is some suggestion that Charles II's wife, Catherine, showed interest in the activity, for in 1676, the Finsbury Archers (with, one assumes, the queen's permission) gave themselves the additional title of Queen Catherine's Archers, perhaps to counter the interest shown by others in her husband. A substantial and ornate badge known as the Catherine of Braganza Shield was bought by subscription, and this was held in the custody of the society's marshal, Sir William Wood. This shield was brought with the rump of the Finsbury Archers when the Toxophilite Society was formed and today is a treasured possession of the Royal Toxophilite Society, held safely for them in the London Victoria and Albert Museum.

Sadly, Charles died in 1685, and in consequence, the gentry's newly discovered interest in archery as a recreation slumped to some extent. However, the pattern had been set, and societies had begun to be formed in both England and Scotland. Roving at fixed marks on Finsbury Fields continued unabated, extolled by Robert Shotterel and Thomas Durfey, members of the Finsbury society in their poem "Archerie Reviv'd or the Bow-Man's Excellence"—a lengthy paean of praise for the longbow.[10] Rural butts, now used for pleasure by villagers and small boys, were still to be found in certain areas, but target shooting was growing in popularity and would eventually become the more widely accepted form of archery.

Shooting at targets took two forms: either at portable "basts," or bosses, placed in pairs 160 yards (eight score) apart or at fixed butts set so as to give distances of 120 yards, 90 yards, 60 yards, and 30 yards, these distances being determined by the archaic "rood" measurement of 7 1/2 yards. From butt shooting came the alternative expression "shooting the roods," particularly common in the next century.

At least two other formally organized societies devoted to the recreational longbow now joined the Finsbury archers. In 1673, the Society of Archers at Scorton in Yorkshire was formed,[11] and three years later in Scotland, gentlemen members of the King's Company of Archers first shot together.[12]

There are mysteries associated with each, and it is proper that in a book devoted to the longbow these are explained. We will consider the Scorton society first. Formed by a group of Yorkshire gentlemen, its principal award is an ancient silver arrow, and herein lies the first mystery: the origin of the arrow. The story goes that Henry Calverley, a founder of the society, sought permission of the family of John Wastell to use an old silver arrow in their possession as the award. This was given on the strict understanding that its origin should not be divulged. The condition of the arrow in its early days is not known, but it is now in two halves: a stele and a fletched shaftment, conjoined by a ferrule. A report obtained from the assay master at the Birmingham assay office indicates a date of about 1670, although the stele is believed to be older than the shaftment.

There are various suggestions about the arrow's earlier life, some more fanciful than others. One that appeals to me, however, with some supporting circumstantial evidence, is for an origin from the Society of Finsbury Archers. It is known that two silver arrows were gifted to the society in 1670, and one being subsequently lost, it was replaced in 1672. Could that lost arrow be the one that arrived at Scorton? Supporting the suggestion of a connection are the Scorton society's earliest rules. A comparison between these and the regulations set down for the administration of the Finsbury archers reveals so many similarities of style, phrasing, and wording that it is difficult to avoid the conclusion of a common origin.[13] However, there is a difficulty here; the Finsbury rules were set down by Sir William Wood, their marshal, in 1687, 14 years after the formation of the Scorton society. If one dismisses the suggestion that William Wood drew on the young Scorton society for his regulations but accepts that he revised those already existing within his society rather than creating new, then were the 1673 Scorton rules those to which the Finsbury archers originally shot (which, being associated with the arrow, were an obvious choice)? The matter will never be truly resolved and remains an archery enigma.

The second mystery concerns the Scottish club and its origins. Although formally established in 1676, there is hearsay evidence of the destruction of earlier records by fire toward the end of the sixteenth century and a strong tradition that its predecessors had at one time formed a guard for Scottish kings—those who were with James IV at Flodden dying around his body. It was with the bodyguard aspect firmly in mind that in 1703, the company sought royal recognition from Queen Anne; and it seems appropriate that she, as last of the ruling Stuart monarchs, accorded them this honor. Thus, the Royal Company, now the sovereign's ceremonial bodyguard for Scotland, has attended Britain's monarchs while in that country for over 300 years.

From the respective rules of both the Finsbury and the Scorton societies we know something both of the target faces used and of the rewards for good shooting. If we assume a connection between these respective regulations, we know that prior to 1687, target faces consisted of four concentric circles, only the innermost being specifically distinguished by the color "gilded," or yellow. From 1687, however, target faces were drawn with five concentric circles, all of which were accorded a specific color: gilded and red for the first two, followed by inner white, black, and outer white.

While on the field, seventeenth-century shooting arrangements were quite precise. The order in which archers addressed the target was decided by the drawing of lots, and everyone shot in pairs, loosing two arrows each. At Finsbury and at Scorton, three rounds were shot at 160 yards, the archers then moved in by increments of ten yards until all awards were won. While at Finsbury no minimum distance was stipulated—"the Captain with the consent of the major part of the Company, upon the drawing on of the evening shall have liberty to approach somewhat nearer upon a removal to hasten down the shooting of the game before night"—at Scorton, however, matters were arranged differently; the minimum distance was 60 yards and no closer. "Their approach to the target be never nearer than sixty yards at which they must stand and shoot them out, if not won before." We know a little of the bows that these target archers used, gathered from reading of the method by which they were constructed. This, together with a reasonable presumption that draw weights would have been commensurate with the distances then shot and the technique then in use, provides us with as thorough a picture of seventeenth-century English longbow design as, lacking examples, we can reasonably expect.

We are fortunate to have a comparatively detailed account of the stages of bow making, for the broad sequence of seventeenth-century bow manufacture has been set down for us in a seventeenth-century treatise on armorials.[14] It included cleaving the staffs, which were the bow staffs at their first cleft; hewing them with a hatchet; pointing them (tapering is seemingly intended); planing them; setting them to the right or straightening them if bent; horning them; nicking (nocking) the horns; planing them for a second time; stringing them to whether they come right, one place as well as another (we would term this "tillering"); rasping them to make them in a little shape (we would call this bringing them round in compass); polishing them to make them smooth; and rubbing them with a boar's tooth and an oilcloth to shine them and set a gloss upon them.

With these details, we glean also that the practice of including "belly wedges," or cork noches, as they were termed, "to keep the arrow from sticking in the bowe if it be drawn throw" was common; and although eventually dropped by English bow makers, this continued to be a feature of professionally made Scottish bows for the next century and a half.

Shooting requires both bow and arrow, and in the matter of arrows, we strike an even richer vein, for the sequence of manufacture of seventeenth-century arrows is known in full. It is as follows: cleaving a staff out of timber to make the shaft; pointing it out, or cutting it round first with a knife out of the rough; ripping it to give it the first round; shaving it, or rounding with a hollow shave (plane); smoothing it by polishing with a fish skin; slitting it to put in the horn (piece) for the nick (nock); cross slitting to make the nick (nock) of the arrow; fitting the head by shaping the end to put on the pile, or head; and heading the arrow by gluing it on.

Drawing the feathers involved cutting, or stripping, the feathers of their quills; paring the feathers by cutting them back to make them lie close; ribbing by cutting the side skirts away; cutting them of a length to their shapes and breadth; pressing the feathers by putting them in a wet cloth to keep them even and straight; polishing, glazing, or varnishing the arrow with glue, rubbing it in as far as the feathers go (the shaftment) before they are set on; feathering the arrow by gluing on the feathers; paring, or cutting them down, by cutting the feathers evenly and all of a similar length and breadth; poising the arrows to know whether the arrows are of equal weight as they are of length; and turning them by giving them a twirl in one's hand to see if they are straight.

In passing, it is of interest to record that as late as 1765, apprentice fletchers were still being indentured.[15] In this year, Edward Frost was bound to William Jeffery, a fletcher of the City of London. The indentures of another, Uriah Streater, apprenticed in 1758, are held with the Worshipful Company of Fletchers' records at the guildhall in London. While target archery, or its close associate, butt shooting, seems to have occupied the seventeenth-century English societies, matters were arranged differently in Scotland. Distance shooting was very much the order of the day, and the numerous silver arrows shot for as prizes, some of which survive today, were seldom contested at less than 180 yards. By far the oldest arrow, still shot for by the Royal Company of Archers, is the Musselburgh Arrow; a conservative date for its origin is the cusp of the late sixteenth, early seventeenth century, and it is the oldest British archery award.

Scarcely less ancient is the Peebles Arrow, dating from at least 1628, followed in age by the Selkirk Arrow, 1660; the Aberdeen Grammar School Arrow of 1664; and the Stirling Arrow, first shot for in 1678.[16] Clearly, the Scots were more careful of their silver arrows than were their English neighbors.

The death of Charles II had some considerable effect upon the practice of recreational archery, and it may be presumed that the number of men taking part fell away sharply from the thousand and more who regularly turned up to shoot in the royal presence. The impetus still remained, however; and it is incorrect to believe, as some do, that a revival of the longbow was delayed until the last quarter of the eighteenth century. It can be amply demonstrated that archery with the recreational weapon was a feature of genteel social life during the whole of the century.

We are now joining a period when the earliest extant recreational longbows are available for scrutiny, and we will take full advantage of their presence. The first and earliest example is in a particular way the more interesting and certainly the most unusual of three bows that are representative of the period, since it is hinged. Bows that could be taken apart for carriage purposes were not uncommon a century later, but a hinged carriage bow dating from the first quarter of the eighteenth century is a rare piece indeed. From the nature, shape, and decoration of the hinge straps, it has been dated to between 1720 and 1740; and the appearance of the brass, with the patina and degradation of the wood, confirms its great age.

Since the bow evidently predates the hinge, it follows that it is older still and is thus among the earliest of the English sporting recreational weapons still in existence. While its actual purpose is something of a mystery, modification

An early hinged self-yew longbow whose decorated hinge strap has been dated to the first quarter of the eighteenth century. Notice the upper nock which although not original dates from the turn of the nineteenth century and is carved to represent a ram's horn. Maker unknown. Author's collection. Photos by Tony Lockwood.

was evidently carefully considered and performed, moreover, by a competent smith.

It is made of yew, though whether this was native or from the Continent cannot be determined. Before conversion to a hinged bow, it was a little over 6 feet long, with limbs of equal length. The hinge straps are 5 1/8 and 5 1/2 inches long, respectively, and the upper limb hinge has a shaped brass strap on the belly. On the back is a shaped and polished wrought-iron strap with some slight evidence for simple decoration. Age has taken its toll on each; that on the back of the lower limb is purely functional and badly rusted, since it was at one time overlaid by a damp hessian handle covering. On the belly of the lower limb, cut crudely into the wood, is a longitudinal slot housing the metal strip activating the locking catch.

There is evidence to suggest that the present handle covering is not original, and it may be that an earlier cover of leather was fitted before the hinge conversion. There is no mark on the weapon to indicate provenance or maker. Its girth of 4 1/4 inches at its center compares with the 3 1/2 inches of a later eighteenth-century longbow and the 4 5/8 inches of a typical Tudor war bow. From this and its overall length, a draw weight in excess of 80 pounds is deduced. There is no evidence of a handle riser, and therefore it would have worked in the hand as nearly all old bows did.

It is tempting to speculate on the life of such a weapon before it was converted. Could it perhaps once have been a roving bow such as would have been seen on the Finsbury Fields in the heyday of the late seventeenth century? Was is a well-loved object subsequently converted for ease of carriage, ending its days as a butt, or target, bow? We will never know. Whatever its purpose, the hinge has failed and is badly cracked, while the limbs show some string follow—and this speaks for much use either before or after conversion.

Unlike their predecessor, Charles II, neither the following Stuart monarchs nor the stolid early Hanoverians showed any special interest in archery; and without the stimulus of royal support, interest among a certain class waned. The longbow was still in evidence, it is true, but was used now by diehard archers for whom the patronizing Charles and his sycophants had been largely a transient irrelevance. It would regain its prominence when in the 1780s, the Prince of Wales, later George IV, involved himself. By how much the activity had declined nationally we cannot know; the archers of Yorkshire continued to meet annually to contest the silver arrow at Scorton, and it is questionable that they should have met just once a year. While it is true that we know of no other meetings, it seems likely that they gathered together on an informal, if irregular, basis to shoot and enjoy each other's company, and this was the probable

Typical of a late eighteenth-century bow meeting. Notice the drummer, rear center, who marked the completion of each round of shooting, after which all archers would march to the target.

habit of other groups across the country. A short-lived society was formed at Aycliffe in County Durham during 1758, while nearby, in the same year, The Gentlemen Archers of Darlington formed themselves into a club that was to shoot regularly until 1851.[17]

Early eighteenth-century archery societies were exclusively male affairs, and for the young bucks who formed them, the pleasures of wine, food, music, and other elegant entertainment were very much a feature of their shooting days.

While these societies of gentlemen catered to adults, archery was a required activity at certain British schools. Prominent among these were Harrow School in England and Aberdeen Grammar School in Scotland, the latter succumbing to the advance of progress as the eighteenth century drew to a close. Shooting for a silver arrow continued at Harrow for much of the century, however, ending in 1771 after a particularly rowdy meeting when spectators from London disrupted the occasion. Some worm-eaten bows and arrows from that period are still held at the school, and one of the arrows is displayed with other more modern examples in a case at the hall of the Worshipful Company of Fletchers in London.

Although as a social recreation, archery with the longbow was confined to the leisured classes, tradition concerns an event that took place annually at

Alderley Edge in Cheshire at Easter time, when nominated retainers from the many armigerous families in the area took part in a public spectacle together with representatives from local towns and villages. After selection by lots, or in some other way, these bowmen were paired against each other and the results recorded in a curious piece of doggerel verse. Here is a brief excerpt from one such, which is believed to date to the late eighteenth or early nineteenth century.

> *The bird and babby so 'tis said, did shoot away an asses head.*
> *And Saracen with nodding plume, did victory over thief assume.*
> *The unicorn, its head had bored in vain against the chequer board.*
> *The labouring man, with mighty flail three noble wheatsheafs did assail,*
> *And rams head proved itself too slick for tricks of monkey on a stick.*
> *And savage men with lion's claws, did seize three arrows in their claws.*[18]

The eagle-and-child crest of the Stanley family was known colloquially as the "bird and babby," while the ass's head identified the Mainwarings. The Saracen's head was the device of the Warburtons, and the thief's neck belonged to the Davenport family. The lion and birch tree of the town of Swettenham was known irreverently as the monkey on a stick! And thus did the verse identify the protagonists and their allegiance.

The form that this event at Alderley Edge took is not recorded, but it would have been consistent with eighteenth-century practice for there to have been a contest at 120 yards (or 16 roods) shot at butts, with scoring at inches, each contestant shooting either one or two arrows.[19] In this form of archery, the diameter of the target was determined by the distance shot—1 inch for every rood.

In the early eighteenth century, three forms of recreational archery were practiced. Butt shooting involved four small circles of 16 inches, 12 inches, 8 inches, and 4 inches drawn on papers set on four butts, each size commensurate with a multiple of the distance shot (roods). Target rounds were shot between two targets set at a suitable distance apart, furnished with concentric circles (usually five), each having a particular value. Lastly, where space allowed, roving involved shooting at marks placed at varying distances from one another.

Scoring arrangements and their associated rewards varied between clubs until formalized during the nineteenth century. In target archery, silver plate (often in the form of silver spoons) was purchased with subscriptions, and this was apportioned by individual value to the target's rings. Thus, the central, or captain's, ring attracted the greater value. When eventually target archery predominated, values of 9, 7, 5, 3, and 1 were accorded to the rings. Although scoring (or "numbers" as the practice was known) now attracted prizes, for many years, awards for hits rather than numbers took precedence. This arrangement is still in place within the British Long-Bow Society. In roving, the arrow nearest the mark took precedence and won that round. Seven wins usually concluded the game, although arrangements varied between societies.

As all those connected with the organization of events know well, the presence of a celebrity will usually ensure a successful occasion. As

A medallion associated with the Robin Hood Society of London, a late eighteenth-century archery society. One of two bearing the same name. The second was based in Gloucestershire, shooting at the Hunters Hall Inn, Kingscote. From the author's collection. Photo by Tony Lockwood.

the eighteenth century rolled on, one such luminary appeared on the horizon in the person of George, Prince of Wales, the dissipated dilettante son of King George III, later to become Prince Regent, and later still, King George IV. A man of extravagant and occasionally unpleasant habits, intensely occupied with himself, he nevertheless enjoyed the company of archers and the simplicity of shooting and was the catalyst for a fresh burgeoning of interest in the longbow among sycophantic gentry and minor nobility of the period.

Principal among the archery societies that he favored was the Royal Kentish Bowmen, formed in 1785, whose title he distinguished and with whom he often shot at their ground on Dartford Heath, London, presenting them with awards from time to time. A fine silver bugle horn given to the society in 1794 and won by Edward Hussey is still extant.

In keeping with the tradition of the period, much time was spent in the enjoyment of food and drink; and with these social essentials came song, a feature of organized late eighteenth-century archery being the ballad. Those sung at the Kentish Bowmen's meetings were gathered together by a member, William Dodd, and being published long after the demise of the society, recalled both the boisterous nature of the gatherings and their more tender side as they contemplated the females who were never very far away.

Although the societies of the time were almost exclusively male affairs, there were two that were equally open to women. Principal among these was the perhaps inappropriately named Royal British Bowmen, a title advertising patronage by the Prince Regent.[20] Its formation in 1787 provides another of those elusive enigmas that bejewel archery. Nominally founded by Sir Foster Cunliffe, a society song composed by Mr. Hayman, a musically literate member about the society's origin (one of very many composed for and sung at their meetings) had it that

> In tracing the Society I find it first began,
> Like Paradise of old, with a woman and a man.
> And contented they did go.
> This woman was a Lady fair, & likewise wondrous civil
> And to her came another man who prov'd a very Devil.
> And a walking they did go.
> He spoke to her of shafts and darts—and numerous stories told
> Of colours 'white', & 'black', and 'red', & then he talks of Gold.
> And a-tempting he did go.
> He swore if she'd adopt his plan he'd much exalt her name
> And what was more her dear good man sh'd not think her to blame
> And a-thinking she did go.[21]

This woman was none other than Lady Cunliffe, and the song goes on at length to describe how, after a display of shooting, she became fascinated by archery—but had to overcome the initial reluctance of her husband, Sir Foster Cunliffe.

She persuaded him to lay out an archery ground at their house, Acton Park, in north Wales, and this he did after canvassing the owners of great houses in the immediate area. All agreed that a society devoted to archery would be a worthy addition to the social round, and with the principle settled, the Prince of Wales was at once invited to become its patron and just as readily accepted. So, despite the tribute paid to Sir Foster for his vision, the true founder of the Royal British Bowmen was seemingly his wife. But here is the puzzle. Who was the "very Devil" who planted the seed? No one knows for certain, but curiosity is kindled and we have a clue, for the first man given freedom of the society was that doyen of the longbow, the "reviver of archery," Sir Ashton Lever.

And if it was Sir Ashton Lever, then this would be very much in keeping with his activities on behalf of the bow; for it was this gentleman who (with his friend, bow maker Thomas Waring) had shared responsibility for the creation in 1781 of the Toxophilite Society (today's Royal Toxophilite Society and

Sir Ashton Lever (d. 1788), founder of the Toxophilite Society, demonstrates his technique. Notice the arrows placed within a pouch suspended from his belt. Thomas Waring the Elder is suggested as the figure pointing in the background. From a print in the possession of the Royal Toxophilite Society.

England's present premier archery club). As with other contemporary societies, there was a fine balance between social interplay, with its flirtatious dancing and witty conversation, and quasi-competitive archery. Distances shot were nominally the rood lengths of 60 yards for the ladies and 90 yards for the men, but these seem to have varied at a whim. On September 16, 1791, ladies shot 50 arrows at 70 yards and gentlemen shot 40 at 120 yards. Prizes were awarded to the first lady for 16 hits with 54 scored and to the first gentleman with 8 hits and 40 scored, an indication perhaps of the quality of shooting at the time. Arrows were shot in pairs: "a tandem of arrows" was a contemporary expression. Forty arrows would thus have involved 20 "ends" of two, or ten rounds of "down and back" and about 1 1/2 miles of walking.

With the onset of the Napoleonic troubles culminating in war, the society became dormant, recommencing activity in 1803. Although a few meetings were held, the revival fizzled out, and it was not until 1818 that matters were begun in earnest again, the Prince Regent once more offering his patronage.

The ethos of the society was communion with nature. Archery had ever been regarded as a "worthy game, a wholesome kind of exercise, and one commended in physic"—an activity that took place in the open air where everyone could see what was going on. During the eighteenth century, shooting with a bow was perceived to be a pastime concomitant with natural things; and to mark the point, male members of the society dressed in hunters' garb of green and buff: green trowsers (sic) and buff waistcoats. With some understandable initial reluctance, the lady members wore gowns of "stuff," a coarse woolen cloth, and gave up the use of cosmetics; while to emphasize the bucolic nature of the day and to satisfy appetites stimulated by the exercise of shooting and walking, the food served at the meetings consisted of vegetables, accompanied by a substantial helping of bacon and beans.

> *With one accord the dishes all, in single ranks and circle fall*
> *And vegetables hot withal, for the Royal British Bowmen.*
> *While beans and bacon always hot, exempted from the common lot,*
> *Come reeking out of boiling pot, for the Royal British Bowmen.*

Luncheon and the shooting having ended, the company would then have retired to the marquee for dancing and social concourse. In this regard, however, after a strenuous day's shooting and a hearty meal of pork and beans, the atmosphere in this crowded environment might be best left unremarked!

In the later eighteenth century, archery was now but a sanitized shadow of its former self. Rugged hard-swearing English and Welsh longbowmen, victors at Crécy, Agincourt, and Poitiers, were supplanted by Regency beaux and belles. Seventeenth-century distance shooting "at sun and moon" was now replaced by butt, or target, shooting at measured distances, and the rough war weapons of self-yew were displaced by recreational bows crafted from exotic woods by those bowyers who remained.

And these were few and far between. In London, perhaps the odd one or two survived, while in Manchester, the Kelsall family kept the craft alive. Others there would have been, scattered across the country, who eked out a living with other work. As luck would have it, however, and quite by chance, a certain Thomas Waring had met old Mr. Kelsall in his younger days and had been shown the art of bow making, knowledge that he fortunately retained.

With the resurgence of shooting, this knowledge proved invaluable; and before long, Waring was acknowledged as the best of the then-contemporary makers of bows. Few of his early weapons survive, but from those that do, he is shown to have been an innovator. Not having undergone a formal apprenticeship, he gave his ideas free rein; and while working conventionally in yew, he also branched out into the more exotic woods. A particular favorite was ruby wood (*Pterocarpus santalinus*), also known as red sandalwood; backed with hickory, it was recognized as a good compression wood. A specimen in my possession made by Waring is marked at 69, and is the heaviest marked bow in my extensive collection.

Among Waring's more unusual innovations was one bow, the belly of which was formed of a piece of dark wood that may be ebony, flanked by quadrants

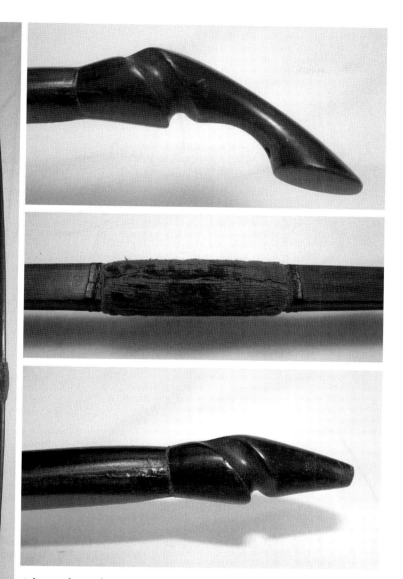

A late eighteenth-century or early nineteenth-century recreational long-bow of heavy draw weight (69 pounds). Made in ruby wood, backed by hickory, by Thomas Waring the Elder of London. Waring died prematurely in 1805 and was followed by his 17-year-old son Thomas the Younger, who carried on the business until 1842. From the author's collection. Photos by Tony Lockwood.

of lancewood, the whole backed by a strip of hickory: a lamination copied in the United States in 1878 by the firm of Conroy, Bissett, and Malleson (who substituted bamboo for ebony). How successfully this performed is unknown, both Waring's bow and the United States example survive, but neither is in shootable condition.

A little more is known of Scottish than English bow makers and their skills (or in some cases, lack of skills) in the eighteenth century. The Royal Company kept meticulous records, and we know that in the matter of bowyery, things were not always to the company's liking.[22] Although for many years they had been served exceptionally well by George Neilson, his successor and ex-apprentice, George Comb, had evidently not benefited from his master's teaching and was soon dismissed for neglect of duty and general bad conduct. Comb was replaced by Andrew Donaldson, whose work was so poor that the company found it necessary to instigate an arrangement whereby only bows of his make that had been examined and stamped with the company's mark "R.C. ARCHERS" might be sold to company members. Fortunately for both parties, Donaldson enlisted as a soldier, and the company turned to James Campbell and John Macintosh for its bows. Although their work was acceptable, their time was short, and the century ended with William Buchanan and George Lindsay-Rae in post.

Running like a silver thread through the indifferent workmanship of the company's bow makers was Thomas Grant of Edinburgh. Apprenticed to bower Robert Jack in 1716, he survived the century as perhaps the most respected of eighteenth-century Scottish bow makers. Although never a company bowyer, his work was prized nevertheless, and one example is said to have been of such virtue that the Earl of Aylesford offered the company the enormous sum (at the time) of 50 guineas for it. The offer was turned down, however, and it resides now in a glass case at Archers Hall in Edinburgh (the company's headquarters), its nocks having been removed to prevent it from ever being drawn up.

An example of Grant's work dating from about 1765 was for many years at Blair Atholl Castle, where it hung on the wall. Removed from its resting place during work on the castle, someone unknown endeavored to string its 200-year-old limbs, splintering the lower one. Happily, it is now repaired and safely in my possession. Of self-lancewood, it is fitted with the almost ubiquitous Scottish belly wedge and has side nocks and a handle covering liberally adorned with silver wire. No draw weight is marked, but it is evident from the girth of 3 1/2 inches that it was a heavy bow to draw and evidently used for distance shooting. A second contemporary Edinburgh bower, recorded in 1794,

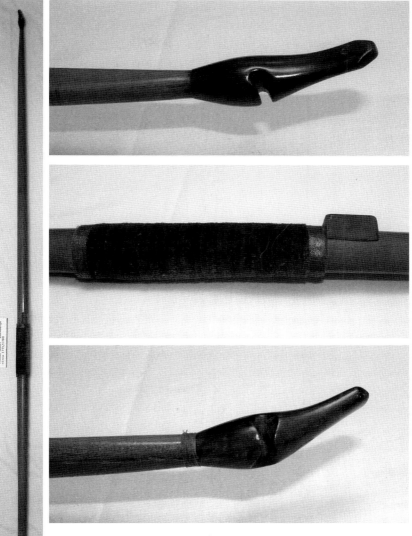

An eighteenth-century Scottish bow in self-lancewood by Thomas Grant of Edinburgh. Notice the presence of side-nocked grooves for ease of stringing and a belly wedge to prevent drawing an arrow inside the bow. The cloth handle covering is secured at each end by bands of silver wire. From the author's collection. Photos by Tony Lockwood.

was William Phin. Coupling the construction of fishing rods with that of bows, he survived well into the nineteenth century. Although no stamped work attributable to him survives, it is possible that an unmarked bow in my collection believed to be of Scottish make may be his. This weapon is of self-lancewood and has a flat back, a built-up grip covered in fine velvet or velveteen, with thin lace edging, and was originally fitted with a belly wedge. The horn nocks with their crude grooves do not conform to the accepted Scottish "spoon" style, however, and doubt about its origins must therefore remain.

While the Royal Company of Archers—their role in earlier times occasionally disputed but now by tacit agreement the sovereign's bodyguard—strutted its stuff in Edinburgh, by 1784, the newly fledged Toxophilite Society in London was faced with problems concerning its shooting ground. Having a historic connection with the Honourable Artillery Company, it was natural to seek help from that quarter, and permission was given for shooting to take place in the company's garden at Finsbury. This was to mark an even closer association between the two bodies, for the members agreed to form a flank division of the company with a captain, a lieutenant, and two sergeants. The archer's division formed part of the company for 20 years, and for much of that time, it paraded as a quasi-military body, turning out for drilling, parading, and occasional (one assumes) guard duty when the company was called to restore order during the civil unrest that marked late eighteenth-century London. The division was stood down in 1803.

The orders of the archer's division are explicit in every sense. Item 3 concerns their apparel.

> The Uniform of the Division shall consist of a green cloth coat, with fall down collar, and Artois sleeve; waistcoat and breeches of white cloth or kerseymere; buttons of yellow metal, with the Prince of Wales Feather, and such other devices as the present Captain shall direct, black round hat, with a uniform button, green feather, gold loop, and a cockade. And that each Member of the Division shall, when on Duty wear a bayonet and gaiters.

With the imminence of serious trouble from Napoleonic France, national institutions were stirring to rumbustious defiance—none more so than the archery societies, many of whose younger members had joined the country's volunteer yeomanry regiments in a flush of patriotic enthusiasm. Toasts to "John Bull" were made, and jingoistic songs were sung to stiffen sinews and summon up the blood. Typical of these was one prepared for the Robin Hood society of Gloucestershire by composer Hayman Florio. Called "The Zodiac," its verses are explicit of national feelings.

Of the stern British LEO, his rays scorched the mane,
And he bade him be true to JOHN BULL.
"Who's afraid," growled he, rousing, and lay down again,
"Whilst my Archers have quivers brimful."

It is at this time that the last attempt to introduce the bow into British military service proper was recorded. A few decades earlier the American colonists contemplated using the longbow out of necessity while preparing to fight for independence. In 1776, anxious about a serious shortfall in gunpowder, Benjamin Franklin wrote to General Charles Lee extolling the virtues of the longbow and giving six reasons for its use. At one time the General seriously considered arming his continental troops with the simpler weapon but the timely arrival of powder relieved his anxiety and such plans as had been made were shelved. In 1798, as Napoleonic jitters were exercising the English nation, Richard Oswald Mason (although not an archer) in association with Thomas Waring (who for reasons of his own, kept in the background) produced his book *Pro Aris et Focis* addressed to "His Majesty's Ministers for the Defence of The Country."[23] This set out in explicit detail the exercise of bow and pike, not conjoined as William Neade had required but worked together as a unit. The bow was to be of 60 pounds or more, and the pike (which could be viewed conveniently at "Mr. Waring's Manufactory") had a neatly built-in arrangement to allow it to be rested on the ground independently of the archer who was thus able to concentrate upon his weapon. Although dismissed as anachronistic and unworkable, the combination would probably have had as much chance of success as the coupling idea successfully steered past King Charles by William Neade.

The patriotic Richard was thanked for his interest in the well-being of the nation and invited to join the Toxophilite Society (where he learned to shoot); and with his carefully thought-through invention conveniently forgotten, the century drew to a close.

9 | *The Fellowship of the Bow*

The nineteenth century opened with England embroiled in the turmoil of Napoleonic crisis. With many of its menfolk in military service, thoughts were naturally elsewhere than on the archery field, and inevitably, societies had dwindled numerically. Of the premier clubs, while the Royal British Bowman had succumbed to circumstance—temporarily as it happened—the Woodmen of Arden, the Royal Company of Archers, and the Toxophilite Society, with a few others, survived and flourished.

Sadly, besides affecting late eighteenth-century societies generally, Napoleon's activities had ended those national archery meetings that had taken place annually since 1792 on Blackheath near London. Although matters were slowly to improve, it would be some years before archery regained its previous hold on the social scene and over 40 before national meetings were to recommence.

Club competition was very much the order of the day, although conducted in fraternal harmony with proper regard for the social niceties of the time. A healthy discipline pervaded the meetings, with target captains on hand to ensure that protocol was properly followed. A military band was often present to add "oompa" to the occasion, and this invariably included a bugler with very specific duties.

Two-way shooting was virtually universal with four men allotted to a target.[1] Accepted practice was for the first to move left from behind the boss toward its front, assuming a marked position on the aiming line. When he had shot his arrow, or arrows, at the far target, he would return to his place by moving to the right. Meanwhile, the second archer, having braced his bow and nocked his arrow, would follow him to the line. While he was shooting, the third archer would have braced his bow in readiness, and so on until all four had shot. When the line was clear of archers, the bugler would sound his instrument, the band would strike up a suitably martial air, and all would then march in line abreast toward the other end. It was the duty of the captain of the target, his position distinguished by a colored sash, to call for hits and numbers (scores) to be recorded, and these were verified by his lieutenant. At important meetings, scorers were provided.[2] One feels that Napoleon, had he been present, would have been suitably impressed!

Unlike today, it was tacitly assumed that all shooters were right handed. No account was taken of left-handed archers, and in at least one society, they were banned from the line. At best, sinistrals were regarded as disruptive of established shooting protocol; and by some, such as George Agar Hansard, a Gwent Bowman and author of *The Book of Archery*, they were seen with forthright animosity.[3] His unequivocal view is there for all to see and know.

> A bowman left-handed is undoubtedly the most ungainly of monsters to whom the recommendation of even so grave an authority as Plato fails to reconcile us. The Greek philosopher considered that children should be taught to use both hands with equal dexterity, and attributes it to the imprudence of mothers and nurses that there is any difference; for among the Scythians, he says, men drew the bow equally with both hands. I repeat however that it has a very contemptible appearance, and is unpardonable, because anyone may cure himself of the bad habit in a week.

We will leave Mr. Hansard to his prejudice and be thankful that two centuries later, there is a more enlightened approach to this entirely natural phenomenon.

As we have seen earlier, it was the practice of the existing societies and clubs to hold meetings to compete for silver plate, and the Woodmen of Arden were (and indeed still are) no exception. One of their two principal awards is a fine silver arrow presented to the society by the Countess of Aylesford in 1788 and shot for at a specified minimum distance of nine score (180 yards).[4] In 1802, this arrow was contested for and won by William Palmer of Coleshill in Warwickshire. By great good fortune, the pair of arrows with which he achieved this feat is still with us. Each measures 27 inches from top of nock to point of pile, is parallel in profile, and is of indigenous wood, probably birch. Each weighs exactly 370 grains. Each is footed (two point) and has a self-nock with a slender 1 3/4-inch nockpiece fitted. Piles are parallel with bullet point and brazed. Fletchings are of goose, 4 inches in length, and their profile is low triangular. The maker is not identified, and so we are left to speculate. Perhaps these are shafts by Thomas Waring the Elder (his life had still a little way to run) or perhaps they are by the Thompson family member who served the Woodmen of Arden as bowyer and chief marker at that time. We will never know.

The resurgence of interest in the old weapon was fueled to some extent by enthusiastic compilers of archaic archery history. Leading the field by a decade was Mr. Daines Barrington with his 1783 essay in *Archaeologia*. He was followed by Henry Oldfield, who published his *Anecdotes of Archery* in 1791, beating Eli Hargrove and his similarly entitled book to the tape by just one year. Walter Michael Moseley's erudite "Essay on Archery" was also published in 1792. With the century scarcely turned, in 1801, Thomas Roberts, a dedicated Toxophilite, produced *The English Bowman*, a most valuable book full of historical fact and common sense advice, much of which is valid today.

It was a pleasant practice in those far-off days for societies to offer reciprocal shooting arrangements to one another, and one such agreement concerned the Woodmen of Arden and the Toxophilite Society. Making full use of this facility was Thomas Roberts himself, a most enthusiastic member of that society. His personal copy of *The English Bowman* has recently come to light, and there inscribed among the pages, interwoven with interesting anecdotes and much contemporary archery lore, we find his private shooting record at the Woodmen's Forest Hall grounds.

From one of his anecdotes, we learn that a Woodman, the Reverend William Dilke, was in the habit of attaching a small length of knotted string to the little finger of his bow hand when shooting at the nine-score yards. There was a purpose to this curious practice, for he found that by dangling this cord so that the end aligned with the clout target, he obtained an accurate shot. Indeed, his recorded successes prove the virtue of this arrangement, for the reverend gentleman, a founder member of the Woodmen of Arden, won principal awards in 1786, 1787, 1788, 1791, and 1796. It is a practice that some of today's archers who shoot unsuccessfully at clout might usefully emulate.

Many of Roberts' penciled notes refer to the niceties of bow making and their application.

> Old bows were generally taped whenever a Fret or Pin appeared. The taping was either of a single twine or consisted of fine hemp. . . . A remarkably neat and ingenious way of Lapping, said to have been the invention of an old bowyer named GLOVER and known to few has of late been practised which for neatness and for efficacy also far exceeds anything of the kind hitherto practised. It consists of a spiral direction of a single thread of silk completely

covering that part of the bow where a fret appears. This lapping is frequently moistened with hot isinglass glue. If when that is perfectly dry a coat of the Copal oil varnish is laid upon it no wet will affect it.

The turn of the eighteenth century was very much the era of the "backed" bow. Roberts was particularly taken with backed bows and extolled their virtues. "A Backed Bow will cast an arrow well which would be too sluggish in a self-one if not very springy." He contrasts a self-bow with a backed bow.

In its first quality a self-bow is deemed to hold a decided preference. Its superior steadiness arises from its nature, as it yields more to the string than the backed bow and does not sink (let down, or follow the string). The certainty of a backed bow will be more or less according to its curvature backwards which is the cause of its great velocity, and that velocity has the effect of diminishing cast.

Cast in this sense means the operation, or "springiness," of the bow. The comments that Roberts makes and the conclusions that he draws are interesting. Unless it is steamed, a self-bow is by its nature largely straight; if it is curved, then this is because the bowyer has followed the grain. A backed bow is better only if it has a deflexed profile. Modern bows are invariably backed but seldom deflexed. Perhaps there is a lesson to be learned. "Backed Bows very much reflexed shoot best with a high bend (bracing height). This kind of bow if braced very low is apt to reflex itself (turn inside out)."

As was the practice of the time, Roberts personalized his favorite bows by naming them, and he meticulously records their capabilities.

NAVARETTA shot 214 yards, wind gentle but in favour of the cross, and 197 yards against it. FLODDEN shot 212 yards with wind being gentle and a cross wind. I gained 40 yards with a 6s. 4d. (weight against silver coin) lancewood arrow.

He was unhappy with the bow named "Poitiers," however, calling it "unpliable and very hard and strong." He found it impossible to draw this bow more than 26 inches. It is therefore not surprising that he eventually donated it to the Woodmen as a prize on the understanding that whoever won it would have shot over 12 score with it.[5] Such a feat, having been duly achieved, gained the bow in question for the Reverend E. Finch on August 12, 1818.

Besides his own bows, Roberts shot with those of other archers. Mr. Anderson's "Cupid" seems to have attracted him, although after shooting 270 yards with it, he managed to crack its lower limb. Somewhat predictably perhaps, he struggled with a weapon named "Sampson" made by Thomas Waring.

With this he managed just 196 yards, having noted that its cast was disproportionate to the strength needed to draw it.

In other ways, Waring did not confine himself to conventional bowyery. With an eye perhaps to the construction of the Japanese bow (known as *yumi*), he employed a T-bar method, using a lateral strip of wood fastened to the inside back of the bow, having glued a quadrant of another wood on either side to form a D section. This system, using bamboo as the central strip, was actually patented in America during 1878 by the firm of Conroy, Bisset, and Mallison.

Waring the Elder was prominent in the bow-making scene from the 1780s, and his bows were largely used by members of the Royal Kentish Bowmen, the Hainault Foresters, Loyal Archers, Robin Hood's Bowmen, Southampton Archers, the Toxophilites, and other southern English clubs and societies. We should not think of archery as a practice confined largely to the south of the country, however, for much also took place in the north. Cheshire may have been a powerhouse for bow making at that time, with Samuel Stanway of Northwich, Ashton of Wigan, and Joseph Wrigley and Edward and John Kelsall of Manchester providing equipment for northern enthusiasts.

Sadly, Thomas Waring died from a stroke in 1806, leaving his thriving bow-and-arrow warehouse and business to his young son, also Thomas, aged then just 17. Despite his youth, Waring the Younger made a success of this daunting challenge and maintained the business until 1840 when he retired. Following his father, he also used exotic woods on the bellies of his bows, becoming well thought of as both a bowyer and a fletcher.

Bow making was to some extent still in the experimental stage. Self-staves of yew were in perpetual demand, but supplies from Europe were yet to reach their later peak. Other woods were regularly used (we have noticed Waring's employment of ruby wood), but we will now examine an unusual bow made by a northern contemporary, marked J. A. W. and believed to have been made by Joseph Wrigley of Manchester.

Dating from the turn of the century, Wrigley's bow design differs in two fundamental respects from that of Waring, first, because it is made from six separate pieces of wood, off-cuts perhaps from some other process, but second, and more importantly, because these piece are scarfed together and not fishtail spliced as was more usual at the time. The method used to construct this type of weapon is interesting and one that has earned the finished products the name of "tea-caddy" bows because of their manufacture from odd off-cuts of wood normally thrown into tea chests as waste. In its construction, the hickory

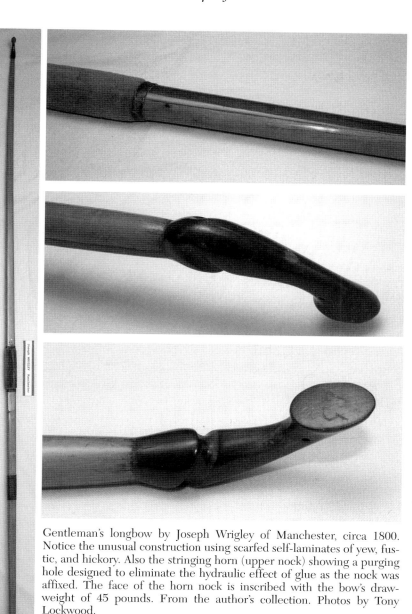

Gentleman's longbow by Joseph Wrigley of Manchester, circa 1800. Notice the unusual construction using scarfed self-laminates of yew, fustic, and hickory. Also the stringing horn (upper nock) showing a purging hole designed to eliminate the hydraulic effect of glue as the nock was affixed. The face of the horn nock is inscribed with the bow's draw-weight of 45 pounds. From the author's collection. Photos by Tony Lockwood.

back of Wrigley's bow was first laid down and deflexed slightly. On it were glued the two separate strips of fustic (*Chlorophia tinctania*) that when scarfed together, formed the core of the upper limb. This strip tapered to just beyond the handle. To this was then scarfed the fustic core forming the lower limb, the taper extending 3 inches beyond the handle section into the upper limb. Finally, two pieces of wood were scarfed together to form the belly. These six pieces combined to make one bow. Stamped 45 to indicate its draw weight, how it performed one may only guess. The stringing horn on this bow exhibits a purging hole, common to bows of the time and indicating that it was bespoken to the bow. The lower horn is believed not to be original.

With the country returned to peace after Napoleonic violence, archery was once more firmly on the social scene, and bows were in constant demand. Unlike Scotland, where the bowyer's skill had been kept alive by the Royal Company, in England it was still a period of experiment. Old skills, virtually forgotten, were relearned, and weapons reflected this. Bow makers were still in short supply, particularly in the provinces, although numbers slowly increased, aided by Henry Bown of Leamington and John Hughes of Derby who began to supply archery tackle during 1820.

In London, John Calvert competed with Thomas Waring the Younger for trade; while in the West Country, John Spreat of Bath, a West Country ivory turner and entrepreneur whose main activity was to make "fancy ware," satisfied the requirements of the minor nobility and gentry who visited the city during the season. Spreat, who was partnered in business by his nephew, another John, also led the field in instruction, offering his daughter, Bessie, to initiate ladies in the use of the bow. Spreat's weapons merit some attention, since he devised and used an elliptical section that was almost unique to him.

Working in self-lancewood (*Duguetia quitarensis* or *Oxandra lanceolata*), he also exploited a niche in the market for bows that could be carried without damage either to them or the general public, producing and marketing the Abbey-Green Jointed Bow "for travelling; when put together which may be done in one minute are warranted to be as firm and elastic, as if of a single piece: and will pack with a Quiver of a dozen Arrows, Belt, Brace &c. &c in a small flat Case, half the length of the Bow and about five inches wide."

We are not told what form the joint took, and to my knowledge, no examples survive; but the arrangement was perhaps of the plug-and-socket variety, a system that had the advantage of stiffening the handle section, thus avoiding the bow working in the hand.

Although yew, hickory, and lemonwood had their followers, and most later bowyer's rang the changes around them, lancewood—the preferred material of

Spreat and many others since his time—had something of a dual personality. Extolled by some as having a cast that was almost perfection, but condemned by others as being brittle and susceptible to chrysalling, it nevertheless remained a staple of bow making during the whole of the nineteenth century and well into the twentieth.

In Scotland, bow making was developing independently, as one might expect. Apprentices were regularly taken on by Royal Company bowyers, or "bowers" as they were locally known, and invariably, they eventually took the place of their masters. Tradition was therefore passed on without the trial-and-error experiment that accompanied the bow making of Waring and other English makers.

John Spreat of Bath, Somerset. An innovative Georgian bowyer and archer whose bows were unusual for their elliptical section. Spreat's daughter Bess is advertised in 1837 as "initiating ladies in the use of the bow." The original drawing is held by Miss Heaps, a direct descendant.

In the Scottish capital of Edinburgh, the century opened with George Lindsay Rae in post as provider of the Royal Company of Archers; and it seems likely that it was he who made a bow that Sir Nathaniel Spens, captain general of the company, presented in 1810 to be shot for in commemoration of his sixtieth year as an archer. Since I now own this bow, a description may be of interest. It is of self-yew, believed native, 68 inches in length between nocks (the upper limb is 33 inches, the lower, 30 inches). A belly wedge was originally fitted but has since been removed. String grooves are frontal and partial in the Scottish style. The stringing (upper) horn is also of Scottish style and has a purging hole. Limb section are evenly tapered, with flat back, square sides, and convex belly. It may be fairly taken as representative of good Scottish bowery at the commencement of the century. Above the handle is a silver plate recording its winning by James Millar, Advocate.[6]

Lindsay Rae was succeeded by John Brand as bower to the company, although shortly afterward, having fallen ill, he was replaced by Peter Muir, a man who was to become a legend for the excellence of his work and his prowess as an archer (he was national champion three times).[7] Many of Muir's

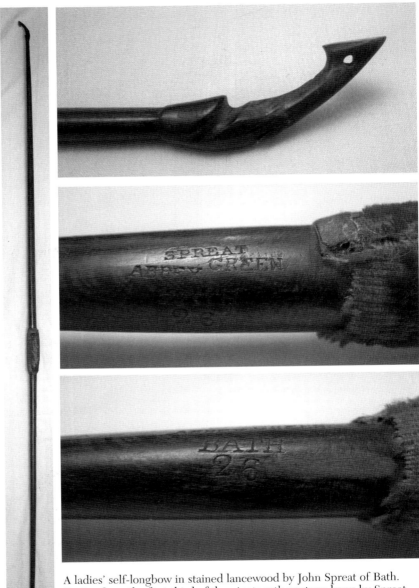

A ladies' self-longbow in stained lancewood by John Spreat of Bath. Dating from the first third of the nineteenth century, bows by Spreat are unusual for his use of an elliptical section in rather than the more usual plano-convex (D) section of that time. Notice the draw-weight 26 incised on the bow limb. From the author's collection. Photos by Tony Lockwood.

bows survive, and each is evidence of his mastery of bow making. He remained the company's bower until 1878 when he retired. He died in 1886.

The magic of the bow had now extended beyond Britain to America, and in September 1828, five young men formed an archery club that they called the United Bowman of Philadelphia; the first American archery society, which, being still very much alive, is the doyen of the activity today.[8] Equipment proved a problem in those far-off days, so an order was sent to Thomas Waring for a set. This duly arrived and comprised a backed lemonwood bow, 12 arrows, bracer, tassel, shooting glove, grease box, spare strings, target faces, and Waring's *Treatise on Archery*. With shipping fees, etc., the whole cost was 12 pounds 6 pence (or, at the exchange rate then current, about $53.35), a substantial sum in those days. But, with the Waring bow as an example from which to fashion their own, others were soon made to his pattern, and archery in America was up and running.

Back in England, equipment was undergoing change, for mixed clubs with male and female membership were now increasingly the vogue, and equipment reflected this. Where a man's bow was often purely functional, a lady's recreational bow enjoyed the distinction of superior finish, with silk handle coverings edged with silver wire and arrow passes in mother of pearl to elevate it above the basic weapon. Core laminates in exotic woods, sometimes with elaborately carved stringing horns further illustrated the quality of its owner.

As the 1820s drew on, archery was rapidly becoming a suitable, even a necessary, social pastime. Major Wingfield and his lawn tennis was a generation away, and disporting with the bow and arrow provided a healthy and acceptable way of meeting with the opposite sex. Moreover, it offered predatory mothers the opportunity to cast a practiced eye over eligible bachelors, potential catches for their numbers of unmarried daughters. Many a nineteenth-century marriage owed its existence to the archery field.

Target archery was now largely the preferred style, certainly by female club members. The day of distance shooting, as enjoyed by the Royal Company of Archers, the Woodmen of Arden, and, among others, the persistent Mr. Roberts, was now ending, and with it the need for powerful bows. True, men still shot the roods at the Royal Toxophilite Society's grounds, and that involved six score (120) yards, while some still enjoyed shooting for length—but they were becoming fewer. Although women occasionally shot at 70 yards, their habitual distances were 60 yards and 50 yards, and their bows correspondingly lighter. Draw weights were now largely commensurate with the distances shot; men's weights stabilized at around 50 pounds and women's at around 30

The United Bowmen of Philadelphia, a senior North American archery society founded in 1828. An 1834 charcoal sketch by Felix Darley, believed to be in the possession of the society.

pounds; although a serious archeress might carry two bows, one for 60 yards and a lighter example for 50-yard shooting.

With Queen Victoria on the throne, many societies came to accept women, even if they did not actually welcome them. However, the male ego dominated still; this was the era of the forester societies, where the image of Robin Hood prevailed. Typical of these was the Selwood Foresters, one of the largest of the time and based at Stourhead in Wiltshire, residence of Sir Richard Colt Hoare. Here they shot on terraces below a tower dedicated to Alfred the Great, king of England, and from whose summit their patron's banner, a silver crescent moon inscribed *crescat*, streamed on meeting days.

We are not told at what distances these forester archers habitually shot, but on one recorded occasion, shooting took place at 100 paces, or about 85 yards. At that time, the gentlemen's first prize was an embroidered cap, worked, we are informed through the local newspaper, by the "hands of seven young maidens"—a formula reminiscent of some ancient Celtic spell! The lady's award was a superior Scottish thistle, "bedewed and glittering in its native gems," a rather prickly prize that she may have regarded with some ambivalence.

The growth of social archery can be measured to some degree by the proliferation of bow makers during the 1830s and 1840s. Although it is true that Muir (whose reputation was second to none) and Thompson, bowyer to the Woodmen of Arden, took a share of the market, until that time, the London Manufactory of Thomas Waring the Younger, supported by those of John Calvert (1818–1840) and John Willis (1823–1848), provided much of the equipment for those clubs and societies that had survived the Napoleonic campaign. In the provinces, the situation was much the same. Henry Bown of Leamington had begun his bow making in 1820 after instruction from Dick Thompson of Meriden, and by 1828, John Hughes of Derby had advertised himself as a "manufacturer of bows, arrows and every other article connected with archery." Further north, William Ainsworth of Preston was considered to be a superior bowyer by no less a person than Sir Foster Cunliffe, president of the Royal British Bowmen, a commendation that did William's reputation no harm at all.

Ainsworth is said to have made over 100 bows and 800 arrows; he was notable for his promise to replace a bow if it failed within one year—in marked contrast to Thomas Waring, whose guarantee extended for just one fortnight! With an ancient bow by Ainsworth at hand, let us examine it and record its construction before advancing further into the misty world of nineteenth-century archery.

This bow by Ainsworth consists of back and belly with two core laminates. It would seem that construction began with a self-hickory back, to which was glued a strip of fustic also believed to be "self" (without removing the handle cover, there is no way to tell). Glued beneath this were two pieces of greenheart (*Nectandra rodiaie*) scarfed together and tapering away 6 inches from each limb end. Finally, a belly of two pieces of yew, also scarfed together, was added. Insufficient examples exist for us to know how standard the practice of scarfing rather than fishtail splicing was at that time. The draw weight of this bow is marked at 51 pounds, and it is fitted with a rectangular arrow pass in mother of pearl. The section used by Ainsworth is similar to that utilized by Joseph Wrigley on his weapon described earlier, although that of Ainsworth has cambered sides. Of incidental interest is a later bow in self-yew by this maker that follows convention in both section and material, and it is difficult to appreciate that both have come from the same "stable."

If any feature is common to earlier nineteenth-century bows, it is the use of fustic and other exotic woods in their construction. John Hughes of Derby was seemingly no exception. Of the four bows by this maker in my possession, three have a single core laminate in this material and just one is of self-lancewood. However, all are ladies' bows with light draw weights in the middle twenties, and fustic may not have been a feature of his heavier bows for men.

By the 1830s, archery was now a social necessity, and clubs had become more numerous. The new queen, Victoria, took a modest interest in the pastime, accepting patronage of the St. Leonards Archery Society in Sussex and dubbing it royal. Bow making was now commercially profitable, and London bowyer's were in serious competition with each other, with at least ten existing between 1830 and 1846. Of these, one or two stand out, if not for the excellence of their work, then for their eccentricity. In London, bowyer Charles Gomez, who seems to have been of South American extraction, advertised an archery match between himself and "a celebrated archer" in 1831.[9] The prize was 50 guineas, and tickets cost 2 shillings 6 pence (50 cents) with half an hour's archery practice thrown in for good measure. After the match, we are told that Gomez "will exhibit the use of the javelin (which he taught) and also the method of catching a wild horse by lasso on horseback or on foot, whilst dressed in the costume of a South American." The spectators truly got their 50 cents' worth from Mr. Gomez!

Further afield in the provinces, the family of Thompson at Meriden in Warwickshire combined grave digging and coffin making with bowyery and marking for the Woodmen of Arden; while Pilkington, the Broughton Bowyer of Manchester, kept a steel bow of 125 pounds draw weight in his workshop and, with no perceivable purpose, challenged his male customers to draw it. Predictably, few did, but then as one or two may have muttered when offered the artifact, who would want to? (Odysseus?)

The increase in bow making during the middle years of the century reflected the number of archers now taking part in the activity. One hundred and seventy-seven separate clubs and societies spanned the length and breadth of the country (including those in Ireland).[10] With many clubs exceeding 100 and sometimes 200 members, the opportunities for an aspirant bow maker were never better. Some of those who took advantage of the shoals of newcomers were themselves quite new to bow making—a fact that did nothing to stifle their enthusiasm. If the number of weapons that have survived is a guide, then many seem to have concentrated upon the lighter ladies' bows, where the need to reach just 60 yards placed fewer demands upon the quality of their work. Although recognizably of longbow shape, many of the bows made for women utilized a far flatter section than those made for men and this, combined with their shorter draw length and coupled with innate female care for personal property, is reason perhaps for their survival in some numbers, for as numerous existing examples demonstrate, ladies' bows tended to outlast those of their male companions.

When Thomas Waring the Younger retired from bow making in 1842, he and his father had between them been at the forefront of the expansion of archery as a recreational pastime for over 60 years, from those eighteenth-century beginnings in a garden in London's Leicester House, where a tiny band of Toxophilites met to shoot, to the multiplicity of archery grounds across the land where thousands met in pleasant concourse, drawn together by their love of the bow.

Thomas Waring the Younger was succeeded by Robert Hamm, who continued the business until 1863 and published the last edition of his predecessor's *Treatise on Archery*. Hamm seems to have followed his own path, however, in the matter of material and section—or so the one bow in my possession appears to show.[11] Distinctive features of Waring's weapons—the light, close-grained hickory, the exotic belly of ruby wood, and apple-red handle coverings—are perhaps things of the past.

Around 1846, a partnership was formed that was to remain at the forefront of bow making for the remainder of the century and beyond, for it was then that a partnership of Thomas Aldred and Joseph Ainge and James Buchanan purchased a bow-making business from John and David Freeman.[12] Neither Aldred nor Ainge, however, appear to have been bowyer's, and certainly Aldred was initially a sleeping partner in the firm. The workshop was run by Buchanan (a man whose antecedents may have included William Buchanan, bowyer to the Royal Company between 1793 and 1802) and helped, it is thought, by Ainge. It was predictable perhaps that this arrangement would not continue, for Buchanan soon decided to break free to start his own business. Ainge may then have run the workshop alone for some time, before Aldred, having now to give up his own profession, joined him. Although bows and arrows exist bearing the stamp of Ainge and Aldred, it would seem that the former also departed before long, leaving Aldred by himself in direct competition with Buchanan, his erstwhile partner. This made a friendly rivalry that was to continue into the next century when, both having long since died, their firms were finally absorbed into that of F(rederick) H(enry) Ayres, Ltd.[13]

As those knowledgeable in the matter are aware, it is possible to identify a Buchanan bow by reference to its stringing, or upper, horn nock, since it is invariably grooved on the upper forward edge. A minor mystery surrounds this feature, however, since a bow by the Freeman brothers exhibits a similar groove. Rather than creating this identifying characteristic, did Buchanan perhaps just adopt an existing Freeman feature? This is of little consequence in the overall scheme of things but is one of the many small enigmas littering the corridor of antiquarian archery.

Both Buchanan and Aldred had their adherents, the faithful who chose only to use bows made by their favored bowyer. It has been said that Horace Alfred Ford, 12 times national archery champion, preferred Buchanan bows above all others, and his choice was wise. A Buchanan bow that is allegedly linked to him is a superb example of its day. Made of self-Spanish yew with a length between the nocks of 71 1/2 inches and a draw weight of 56 pounds, its provenance rests on the letters H. A. F. in ancient green ink inscribed below the handle. Of 16 examples of Buchanan's work in my collection, 12 are of self-yew, one is yew backed with yew, and another is yew backed with hickory. It would seem that James Buchanan preferred to work in this medium. Of the remaining two, one is of lancewood backed with hickory and the other a sandwich of hickory back and yew belly with a core of fustic, perhaps an early example of his work.

Although James Buchanan and Thomas Aldred were in business for the same period exactly, it seems that more of the latter's bows may survive. This is a curious fact and another minor mystery, yet one supported by comparative numbers in collections. In contrast to just 16 examples of Buchanan's work, I also possess 37 by Aldred, and we will now look at these in a little depth.

Despite Aldred's known preference for Spanish yew, just 15 are exclusively of this wood; while a further five have yew bellies, four are backed by yew, and one by hickory. Of the remainder, three are of stained self-lancewood, three are of beefwood backed by hickory, five are of lancewood, or lemonwood, backed by hickory (the texture makes it difficult to determine which), one is of hickory-backed ruby wood, and one—the only one—has a yew belly and a hickory back sandwiching a fustic core. In addition, a bow by Ainge and Aldred, made before Joseph Ainge left the business, is of ruby wood backed by hickory.

As was customary between nineteenth-century commercial rivals, there was the sensitive matter of precedence. One obvious ploy was to obtain royal patronage, and as was common with other bowyer's in contemporary London, both James Buchanan and Thomas Aldred claimed to be supported by royalty. Buchanan certainly received the royal warrant, and to an already imposing list of the great and good, he added the emperor of Russia, the emperor of Brazil, the king of Portugal, and the principal courts of Europe. Conceding Buchanan's impressive royal warrant, but not to be outdone, Aldred claimed the Prince and Princess of Wales for himself, adding, for good measure, the king of the Belgians and the king of Denmark while trumping Buchanan's king of Portugal with that country's queen. To clinch matters, he then threw in the sultan of Turkey and the khedive of Egypt before playing his ace, Napoleon III, who had once personally presented him with a gold snuff box. In the matter of precedence, the honors, he must have felt, were now even.

In an earlier chapter, we briefly examined the process of fashioning a seventeenth-century longbow. It is now time to look closely at nineteenth-century

A man's self-yew longbow by Thomas Aldred of London. One of three previously owned by Colonel "Mad Jack" Churchill, a British Army officer whose many exploits during the Second World War included the despatch of an enemy soldier with longbow and arrow during the British retreat to Dunkirk in 1940. From the author's collection. Photos by Tony Lockwood.

procedure as performed within the workshops of Thomas Aldred, a typical
London bow maker specializing in yew.[14] After selecting suitable trees from the
slopes of the Spanish Pyrenees, a primary source for the best of bow woods,
they were stored in the log for a year. After this time, they were cut into lengths
of approximately 7 feet 6 inches (90 inches) and sawn into as many sections as
the experienced bowyer thought would make bows. These sections, with bark
intact, were then left for a further year to season. During the third year, the
bark was removed and the sections roughly trimmed and cut into lengths suitable for limbs. If the section was good throughout its length, then it was cut
into equal halves; but if a knot or a shake was present in a section, then only
one limb would be obtained. When this was done, the limbs were put aside for
a further year, after which they were carefully examined, paired, and tied
together. These selected limbs were trimmed into the square, with any remaining knots cut out, and then carefully coupled by means of a double fishtail joint.
This coupling was chosen to give a maximum surface for gluing, the best hide
glue being used. Where practicable, this operation was always performed in the
spring, since the temperature then was neither too hot nor too cold, thus allowing the glue to set properly. The limbs were set to one side for a further year
to allow the glue to mature, after which the center of the bow was bound with
hemp strongly glued into position to further strengthen the splice and to provide a foundation for the handle riser. The bow was then shaped to the correct
section, and any remaining knots and pins were raised for strength. During the
fifth year, the horns were added, and the bow was tillered to bring it around in
compass. It was then weighed, and the weight was marked. Handle braid was
put on, the arrow pass was added, the bow was polished, and it was finally ready
to be sold.

There were criteria that we are given to understand were followed concerning the length of the bow. A weapon made to accommodate a 28-inch arrow
should not be less than 72 inches between nocks. Curious to see whether
bowyer Aldred applied this rule of thumb to himself, I examined 17 men's bows
from Aldred's workshop. Of these, ten are between 71 and 72 inches and would
pass muster. Five are between 70 and 71 inches, one is 69 inches, and one is 67
1/2 inches. Of the two shorter bows, one belonged to National Champion C. J.
Longman and the other to Colonel "Mad Jack" Churchill, a charismatic com-
mando leader who carried longbows with him during the Second World War.
As a matter of passing interest, Scottish bows made by Peter Muir and used
with 28-inch arrows seem seldom to have exceeded 69 1/2 inches. Clearly
Aldred's criteria were there only for the guidance of the wise!

Members of the Royal Toxophilite Society at practice on their grounds at Bayswater, London, in 1830. Notice the insubstantial target and stand. From a picture by R. Cruikshank, belonging to C. J. Longman, now in the possession of the society.

During the late eighteenth and early nineteenth centuries, archery was largely a sanitized social occasion, an excuse for like-minded gentlefolk with time on their hands to gather together in pleasant commune and ping away at targets during long summer days and evenings. They took tea, prepared for them by servants, in marquees erected on immaculate lawns in front of great houses, then changed for the customary ball where "galops" and "quadrilles" sapped what energy remained after an exacting afternoon drawing the bow.

While for some years, with household matters occupying their time, ladies were largely immune to the subtler attractions of competitive archery, their menfolk were not; and money was contributed for the purchase of silver plate, often spoons, to be awarded as prizes to those skillful or fortunate enough to hit particular scoring rings. Following the practice of their predecessors, the Finsbury Archers, the Toxophilite Society perpetuated a similar arrangement until 1794—although with a somewhat different twist: it was hard cash provided from the society's funds, and not just spoons, that changed hands. However, with accuracy increasing, the society's wealth was depleting rapidly; and in 1794, after the annual, or summer target day, the balance had been reduced by 57 pounds 9 shillings 6 pence, a significant sum in those days. Each hit in the gold had netted the archer 2 shillings 6 pence. A hit in the red gained him 2 shillings, one in the inner white (later the blue) resulted in 1 shilling 6 pence, one in the black produced 1 shilling, and one in the outer white earned the archer 6 pence. Predictably perhaps, on the advice of an anxious treasurer, the committee put a stop to this get-rich-quick practice.

For all the hedonistic flummery that surrounded these early archery occasions—the *fêtes champêtre* and picnics on the lawn—many archers were keen to improve their personal performances. Club events were held at which competition was encouraged, with prizes of varying value offered, some of which would today seem either ostentatious or just odd. Thus, while a contestant at one tournament carried off a mahogany writing desk, elsewhere, another winner received a jar of pickles. Perhaps the strangest award went to the winning team in a Devon tournament, which returned home with the marquee! Conscious of the need to draw in top names, the organizers sought for variety of prizes, and particularly favored for 1865 was the "reconnoiterer glass," which from the advertising copy seems to have been a sort of telescope.[15] Marketed as the "Toxophilite's Favourite" with an "adaptability to uses in which protracted and minute observation of arrows entering various ranges at different distances is absolutely necessary, as in archery matches, renders the Reconnoiterer one of the best aids to visual power ever placed at the command of toxophilites." It no doubt graced the back pocket of many an aspirant champion. Those who practice traditional longbow archery today will be aware that such sighting aids are expressly forbidden.

Competitive public archery meetings had been held since the days of the Society of Finsbury Archers, and true annual national meetings had taken place from 1789. Had archery not been severely curtailed by the Napoleonic campaign, it is probable that these popular meetings would have continued; but overriding circumstance dictated their end, and they ceased in 1795. The will and wish was still there, however; and so it was that in May of 1844, a general gathering of archers took place at the Black Swan Hotel, York, at which the decision was taken to hold the Grand National Meeting of the archers of Great Britain at York during that summer. The tournament—at which 74 archers entered and during which 69 actually shot—duly took place on August 1 and 2. Inevitably, the weather intervened in this prestigious event; for in keeping with what has happened at important English archery occasions since Agincourt, torrential rain interrupted the first day.

The round shot (six dozen arrows at 100 yards, four dozen at 80 yards, and two dozen at 60 yards) was the one that the West Berkshire Archery Club had used for many years and the one that is now known simply as the York. A demanding round, it serves to decide the British National Championship—despite foreign interference in target archery and the Continentally inspired metric round. In spite of the inclement weather, the national meeting was declared a resounding success, and a committee was formed then and there to decide the arrangements for a second. At this, it was agreed that ladies should be allowed to take part, and 11 hardy souls subsequently shot eight dozen arrows at 60 yards. No ladies shot at the third meeting, and just six participated at the fourth, again shooting eight dozen arrows at 60 yards. At the fifth meeting, five ladies shot six dozen arrows at 60 yards and six dozen at 50 yards. It was not until the sixth meeting, held at Derby, that the ladies' national round of four dozen arrows at 60 yards and two dozen at 50 yards (shot twice and therefore known as a double) was instituted, and this became their championship round. It is a matter of some incidental curiosity that while the men's round adopted the title "York" from the place of its inception, the ladies' round is not known as the Derby round from the place where it was first shot.

The first gentleman champion of this second series of national meetings was the Reverend J. Higginson, a principal founder of the tournament, with 221 scored and 53 hits—and to him went the vase costing £55. Some way below was a doggedly determined Mr. Robinson of Richmond Archers (Yorkshire) who scored just eight, with two hits at 60 yards. To him went the wooden spoon and a place in posterity! In those early days of serious competition, while scores were never high, they were consistent with the techniques used. Arrows were drawn to the eye or the cheek; the effect of an arrow bending around a bow on release had yet to be understood, and despite the advice freely available in Roger Ascham's *Toxophilus*, the five points "whereof cometh good shotinge" were often honored more in the breech than in the observance. Matters were about to change, however, for a chance meeting between two gentlemen in Brighton on England's south coast in 1845 was to alter the course of competitive English archery.

Horace Ford was introduced to the pastime that he was eventually to dominate by Edward Maitland, a talented member of Queens Park Archery Society, and Ford learned his archery on the club's ground at Brighton in Sussex. Maitland was himself an archer of considerable renown, being British national champion in 1848; but just 12 months later, his gifted pupil was to begin a so-far unbeaten 11-year sequence of championships. Ford was a scientific archer. He studied the bow and the arrow and how they interrelated. He realized that the traditional draw of arrow to the eye was not conducive to accuracy and relocated it beneath the chin. This had two significant effects. First, with the eye now over the arrow, there was a direct association between eye, arrow point, and target, with an immediate improvement in accuracy. Second, because the nock was lower in relation to the eye, the point of aim could also be lower, with closer reference to the target. Although he may not have absolutely understood the "archer's paradox," Ford recognized that as an arrow moved forward across the bow limb, it might be expected to be deflected and change direction relative to the point at which it had been aimed. An arrow that was sufficiently flexible would bend to compensate for this and would, as we today say, "paradoxically," travel toward its original point.

Anxious that anyone who wished to improve his or her technique might benefit from his practical researches, in 1859 Ford wrote a book, *Archery, its Theory and Practice*, in which he set out his findings in meticulous detail.[16] It is a measure of the great man's wisdom that his book is still in print and sought today by those concerned with the finer points of traditional longbow shooting. Ford paid great attention to stance, and although in his latter days, his loose was unconventional (because of problems with his flexors), his technique did not deviate. He has had his detractors, it is true; and were he to have lived a full span, he would surely have been saddened by those who impugned the accuracy of his scores. He died prematurely at the age of 58 in 1880, and his remains lie today in peace within a recently refurbished grave at Locksbrook Cemetery in Bath, Somerset.

While archery remained a popular activity, in 1874, a challenge had been mounted by Major Wingfield, who patented a game that he originally named "sphairistike" but that quickly evolved into lawn tennis. Unlike croquet, which predated it by some 20 years, its appeal was immediate; and although by that year there were still 120 archery clubs and societies in being, many of the younger members added tennis to their activities, some even deserting archery for this new pastime. Certain clubs embraced tennis as an additional, or in certain cases, a principal, attraction; and at least one all-tennis club, the Society of Wiltshire Archers, today bears evidence of its origin in its name.

Archery has long been a family activity, and the nineteenth century certainly reflected this. Well-made bows by reputable bowyers, with arrows suited to them, were available for both juveniles and the older child. They were highly desirable as presents but evidently often played with until damaged beyond repair, since few remain for examination. Evidence of the hard wear they suffered comes from a charming diary kept by ten-year-old Emily Pepys in 1844. The daughter of a clergyman, she and her brother Herbert had been given bows and arrows by their Papa. Herbert, however, had broken his, and while it was at Worcester being repaired, Emily lent him hers. She records

> I lent Herbert my bow for a little while but no sooner did he begin shooting than he broke one of my arrows. . . . Then after that Herbert laid my bow under the target thinking it would be a safe place (naughty, naughty Herbert!) but the first shot of (cousin) Henry's went underneath and chipped a piece clean out. so that my bow is hardly fit for use , but I daresay it will last a little longer.

While most juvenile archery took place informally and, from evidence at coroners' inquests, not always with adequate supervision, there are occasional references to tournaments for young archers. An early example is of one that it seems took place on Durdham Down in Clifton, Bristol, in the 1790s; and we are indebted to Miss Maria Edgeworth, a prolific compiler of "moral tales," for what few details there are.

The meeting, described in her tale "Two Strings to Your Bow," was for boys only and took place after a tournament for ladies—itself an event of some interest for the time. The meeting was preceded by a parade of adult archers, behind

Horace Alfred Ford (d. 1880), National British Champion twelve times. Interred at Locksbrook Cemetery, Bath, England. Author's collection.

which the lads followed, led by Lady Diana Sweepstakes, the organizer, on a horse (a person, incidentally, of whom the moral Miss Edgeworth heartily disapproved, since she gambled!). At the contest, three arrows were shot in sequence by each archer, the best to count, an arrangement seemingly contrary to what was then normal practice for adults. The target distance is not given, but speculatively it would have been at 30 yards, the shortest of the rood distances. Before Ben, the hero of the tale, shoots, he is told that there is an arrow within one inch of the mark. Having shot two arrows, his bowstring breaks, but undeterred, he replaces it with the piece of parcel cord he has thoughtfully kept in his pocket. Predictably, he wins the prize, a "very handsome bow and arrow." The moral, "waste not, want not," is made effectively; and with this brief vignette of "public" archery over two centuries ago, Miss Edgeworth has left us with a tantalizingly unslaked thirst for more!

While juvenile archery clubs seem to have existed in the nineteenth century, none is recorded in the archer's registers. One such, although perhaps a transient affair, was the impressively named Royal Glamorgan Juvenile Archery

A garden archery scene from August, 1865, Kiddington Rectory. Author's collection.

Club, based at Merthyr Mawr in south Wales, which held a Grand Extra Birthday Bow-Meeting on September 19, 1873. The 12 contestants were divided equally into those over and those under 14 years of age, and all seem to have shot the ladies' national round at 60 and 50 yards. It is to the credit of these young folk that they hit at all at 60 yards with the light bows available to them—only one young archer made double figures. Things improved somewhat at the shorter distance, however, and apart from a Miss Lloyd, who avoided the target altogether at both distances, everyone seems to have been competent at the closer range.

As the last quarter of the century drew on, there were archery stirrings across the Atlantic. Although there were those dedicated to the pastime, archery had not been particularly favored in the United States. As Maurice Thompson had observed, there was a prejudice against it, although why he did not explain. Despite major problems with equipment—much of which had to be imported from the United Kingdom to supplement the very limited home-produced material—American clubs had struggled gamely on, to receive a welcome boost when their national organization decided to hold an inaugural grand meeting of archers at Chicago in 1879. It was a resounding success, and with prejudice fading fast, archery became a growth activity.

The reason for this important change in attitude may lie with the personal example of the brothers Thompson—Maurice, the writer, and Will, the successful archer and (in 1878) president of the newly formed National Archery Association of America. Their circumstances are a reflection of triumph over adversity and the stuff of which archery legend is made. These bear recounting.

Whereas the six young men who formed the United Bowmen of Philadelphia in 1826 did so for recreation and, with others who shot from that time, were concerned largely with butts and targets, a more practical purpose for archery followed the conclusion of the American Civil War in 1865. Confederate soldiers Will and Maurice Thompson may justifiably claim to have been among the first white American archers to experience, through painful necessity, the pleasures of hunting with the bow.

Both Thompsons had learned their craft during the 1850s among the backwoods bordering their father's plantation in the Cherokee lands of North Georgia and were taught their skills by Thomas Williams, a solitary ancient hermit who lived by the bow. The lore passed to the boys by this old man was later to stand them in good stead, for having lost the war, as disbanded Confederate troops, they were expressly forbidden the use of the gun for any purpose. However, with their archery skills honed and now put to practical use, the Thompson brothers and their families did not go hungry; and as time passed, their hunting for food became an exercise for pleasure. Maurice Thompson's 1877 account of its fascination, first in the magazine *Scribner's Monthly* and then in his book *The Witchery of Archery*, made compulsive reading for that growing number who enjoyed pitting their wits against nature.[17]

Besides the use of the bow to provide for the table and the pleasures of hunting, both Will and Maurice enjoyed target shooting and roving. Their local club, the Wabash Merrie Bowmen, became a focus for this social activity. As Will in particular quickly grew adept at target archery, he went on to take the American championship five times between 1879 and 1908, shooting the double York round.

Through their interests in all forms of the activity—hunting, target, and roving—in a very real way, the brothers Thompson exemplified the broad appeal of archery, and here we may interject a modern thought. Sadly, with today's mainstream emphasis on excellence at all costs, an either-or attitude prevails. One is either a hunter or a target shooter, a field archer or (occasionally) a rover. The witchery of archery written of so lucidly by author Maurice Thompson, which doubtless played its part in overcoming initial prejudice, has been exorcised and replaced with an all-consuming gravity of purpose! Surely those who do not explore beyond their habitual use of the bow are the losers.

A scene from the first tournament of the National Archery Association in Chicago, 1879, at which Will Thompson (center foreground) became the first North American National Champion.

While Thomas Aldred, Frederick H. Ayres, James Buchanan, Peter Muir, and Philip Highfield continued to supply the market with their wares, American firms now devoted more resources to satisfying the clubs and societies proliferating across the country, and an illuminating example of this rapid rise comes from contrasts in advertising copy. In their little booklet, published in 1878, Peck & Snyder, archery stockists, included the following eulogy by Maurice Thompson. "No bows in this country can equal those beautiful weapons made by Philip Highfield, of London." A year later, having been persuaded otherwise by American manufacturer Horsman, Mr. Thompson's opinions changed, however, and he now wrote, "The best bows I have ever seen are now being made by Mr. E. H. Horsman of New York. . . . They stand better than any English bows of the same Class . . . They just will not break." One should not be unduly cynical about this change of heart. Horsman's bows were certainly well made. In fact, when one compares an example with one by Highfield, the only discernible difference is in the cross section. Highfield used sloping sides and a ridged belly, while Horsman favored a more conventional, rounded section.

Since American manufacturers were not yet inhibited by the adherence to status quo imposed on British manufacturers by a conservative archery public suspicious of change, the United States Patent Office was to receive and deal with a number of curious deviations from the normal shape and construction of longbows. Among the more acceptable of these was a weapon by archery

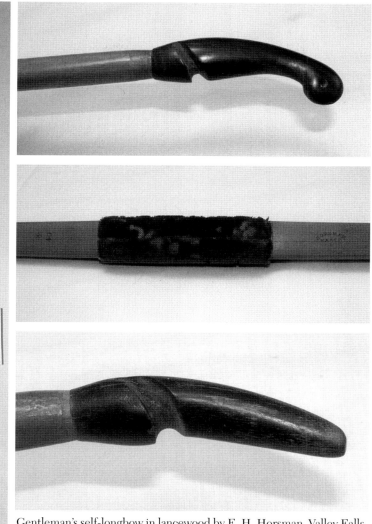

Gentleman's self-longbow in lancewood by E. H. Horsman, Valley Falls, Rhode Island, United States. Bows by Horsman directly replaced those previously supplied by Philip Highfield of London and were heartily endorsed by both Will and Maurice Thompson. Using one, Will Thompson took first place at the inaugural National Archery Tournament in 1879. From the author's collection. Photos by Tony Lockwood.

Components of the ferrous metal Royal Archer center-shot bow constructed to a patent obtained by Wright & Thorne in 1878 and marketed commercially by Perry Mason & Co. of Temple Place, Boston, USA. Notice the metal nocks. From the author's collection. Photo by Tony Lockwood.

makers Conroy, Bisset, and Malleson that embodied bamboo in its construction. This was sandwiched between two quadrants also of bamboo and glued to a backing of hickory—a principle that mirrored a similar arrangement by Thomas Waring the Elder some 78 years previously.

Made by makers Perry Mason & Co. of Boston, there was also the Royal Archer center-shot bow.[18] This curiosity incorporated a metal handle, 7 1/2 inches long, in the center of which was a hole 1 1/2 inches in diameter furnished with four equally spaced wings set so as to allow a 5/16-inch shaft to pass easily through. Arrows were provided, with fletchings of hair cloth. Bow nocks were of cast iron, and arrows were fitted with brass nocks and piles. A number of these oddities were sold and presumably shot, although to what effect is not recorded. Advanced as this center-shot design undoubtedly was, the accompanying instruction booklet was outdated in its information, referring, as it did, to the "inner white," a color that had been replaced by blue some 30 years earlier. This then was the scene of change in Britain and America as the nineteenth century closed and archers with their longbows prepared to meet the challenge of the new. As we will see in the final chapter of this brief history, change was not long in coming.

10   *Resurgam*

The twentieth century opened with scarcely a cloud in the archery sky. While a protracted war in South Africa against the Boers had siphoned away some young men, their departure had not radically affected clubs. It is true that the number of societies had significantly diminished since the heyday of the mid-nineteenth century—a mere 68 compared with the 150 of earlier days—but this reflected the diversity of recreational activity then available. Archery catered for those who sought the calm discipline of social and friendly competitive exercise rather than team activity and, more especially, the rough and tumble of contact sport.

The bows they used had long since stabilized in both section and profile, and with yew still accessible and good wood available for arrows, the ten or so major suppliers of equipment (all of whom drew their principal profit from the manufacture of other sporting products) had little difficulty in satisfying demand. Despite the loss of Thomas Aldred and James Buchanan, whose deaths in the 1880s were within two years of each other, their respective firms continued to thrive, led on the one hand by James Izzard, grandson of Aldred, and on the other by the redoubtable Jimmy Duff, ex-apprentice bowyer and author of some renown shortly to try his fortune in the United States.[1] Longbows bearing the stamps of Izzard and Duff were now being made and sold. Some export to America continued, although this had inevitably diminished with the growing number of indigenous makers. Meanwhile, the eccentric American designs patented in the 1870s and 1880s, having enjoyed their brief moments of fame, had disappeared into the woodshed of history. In short, all was tranquility on the archery lawns of England and America.

Vastly improved communication, coupled with close friendships and family connections, now allowed fraternal exchanges between Continental and English archers. So it was that in 1904, the first experimental international archery meeting ever held was planned for July at Le Touquet (Paris Plage) in France. Duly held, it was deemed a great success, and proved to be the forerunner of a further five— until the rolling clouds of European war put an end to this fragile expression of archery fellowship.[2]

The arrangements for the meeting were presided over by Baron Pierre de Coubertin, president of the infant Olympic movement, while the committee included archery dignitaries from the national societies of England, France, Belgium, and Switzerland.

This event took place at the grounds of Le Touquet Société des Sports during the annual archery festival of Le Grande Prix Provinciale and resulted in the first ever international success by an Englishwoman, Mrs. Lewis Weedon of the West Kent Archery Society. Her silvered medallion, which must be one of the earliest existing international sporting medals, is inscribed *Concours de tir a l'arc: Le touquet: 1er prix*: National round: Juillet 1904. On the obverse, medieval archers are depicted against the backdrop of a mast for *tir a la perche*, or as we would say in England, the "popinjay."

The medal won by Mrs. Lewis Weedon in 1904, first international award won by a lady archer using the longbow. Author's collection. Photo by Tony Lockwood.

Le Grande Prix Provinciale (or Le Bouquet as it is alternatively called, after the floral symbol of the meeting, which is accorded a place of honor) is generally celebrated during May and is a gathering of *chevaliers d'arc* and *demoiselles* in their companies who attend from towns and villages in the surrounding countryside. A solemn occasion with much ancient ritual, it is preceded by a grand mass dedicated to St. Sebastian, historic patron of French archery. This, then, was the prestigious backdrop to the first-ever international archery occasion.[3]

In 1904, shooting connected with Le Grande Prix Provinciale took place in the local *jardin de l'arc* at butts formed of packed straw. Targets were as usual of cardboard, 30 inches square, with various concentric rings, and a central black bull's-eye 1 inch in diameter. A pair of butts had been placed in covered shelters, each side of the range having been planted with trees, with wooden screens providing an additional protection for the public. The shooting was at 50 meters, and as each company of chevaliers took part, the whole affair often lasted for two months or more. Bows used were the French and Belgian equivalents of the English longbow, take-down weapons of conventional length, section and taper, differing only in having an arrangement for an arrow shelf.

During July of 1908, the third (modern) Olympic games, a major international event and one that included an archery competition, was held in England. Overseas opposition was notably conspicuous by its absence, with a small French contingent and just one American man shooting; the meeting was nevertheless declared a success, although, rather predictably, the major awards were all secured by English competitors.[4] There is a curious ambiguity when one examines the women's target list, for although Alice B. Legh, 18 times national champion, received an invitation to shoot, she declined the offer. Inevitably, there has been speculation as to why this was so, and there seem several possible reasons. First, since the national championships were to be held just two days later, and she was defending her title, she might not have wished to risk her position by taking part in another demanding tournament so soon before this premier archery event. The Olympic movement had yet to find its niche in both the public imagination and among archers, many of whom were just not interested in either taking part or, indeed, in even watching. In addition, the weather prospects were not good. Second, Alice may perhaps have felt threatened by fellow Cheltenham archeress, Sybil "Queenie" Newall, her protégée, and did not wish to risk the chance of being beaten. Subsequently, Queenie, an excellent archeress, twice interrupted Alice's run of national championship honors. Third, and perhaps least likely, predicting that Queenie would do well, she may have stood aside to let her take the glory.

As history records, Queenie did win and took the gold medal; the first—indeed, the only—gold medal in archery won by a British woman at the Olympic games. Queenie was 53 years old at the time, and she remains the oldest female gold medal winner in Olympic history in any sport. The men's gold medal was won by Mr. Willie Dod of Welford Park Archers in Surrey, and the silver, by Mr. Richard Brooks-King of Somerset. It is on record that some few years ago, this latter medal was entrusted to the Olympic movement for safekeeping, and some might feel it to be a sad indictment of this prestigious organization that it cannot now be found. Fortunately, the others are more securely kept!

There is little doubt that in different circumstances, archery, both social and competitive, national and international, would have been more widely practiced. However, the clouds of war were slowly gathering over Europe, and 1914 saw the end of these fledgling encounters. As the conflict dragged on, and year by year casualties mounted, those clubs that still remained viable were run largely by female members. Others closed for the duration of hostilities, and a significant proportion of these did not restart. A cursory examination of club records as late as 1922 show women archers to outnumber men by nearly ten to one.[5] Archery had become an activity dominated by women.

Queenie Newall, Olympic champion archer, 1908, and international competitor. Author's collection.

Besides its more obvious wide effect on nations, the Great War had induced a feeling of camaraderie irrespective of rank among those engaged in fighting. Now largely gone was the old order of things; the flower of English aristocracy lay dead in Flanders mud, and the firm grip of a leisured class upon society had been badly shaken. Hitherto rigid social barriers were breaking down, and emerging slowly in their place was a country increasingly conscious of the equality of all men and women under God. Despite this, however, England was still a class-conscious nation, and archery continued to be an activity indulged in largely by those with leisure to take part.

Although protocol and proper behavior remained an immutable tenet of membership, clubs and societies that a generation earlier would not have tolerated persons from other than the genteel class now accepted them, if not gratefully, then with fortitude, in order to survive. Other activities formerly exclusively the province of the gentry were soon to be opened to those who, ten short years before, had "known their place" and, moreover, kept to it.

It should not be thought that ordinary folk were denied shooting with a bow. Far from it; there had always been some opportunities for the working-class archer to practice. During the nineteenth century, there were public archeries in London and other cities and large towns where bows and arrows might be hired for a small sum (with the invariable proviso that breakages should be paid for). In Bath Spa, John Spreat and his nephew, whom we noticed in the preceding chapter, were closely associated with just such a short-lived venture.[6] Events open to the public—we would call them taster sessions—took place regularly on Blackheath in London during the first decade of the twentieth century, and at these meetings, targets and mannequins were set up at which to shoot. The bows provided were rather basic in style, with their tips crudely carved and blackened to simulate horn, but they were effective nonetheless and well suited to their purpose. One such example from my collection is 72 inches from tip to tip, dating perhaps from the first decade of the twentieth century. It is of lancewood stained to represent yew and has a red plush handle. It has no bow weight marked and no maker's name to identify it.

Willy Dod, Olympic champion archer, 1908. Notice the unusual form of draw using two fingers below the arrow. Author's collection.

During the preceding century, before the establishment of the Grand National Archery Society and the creation of regulations governing the occasion, public meetings, including the national meeting, were nominally open to all; and study of target lists does show the occasional individual with no apparent allegiance to a particular club or society, who has perhaps joined in "on spec." One lady in particular merits comment, for she was an instructor to members of the fledgling Cheltenham Archery Club. Justifying her qualification to teach, Mrs. J. Dunton entered the grand national archery meetings in 1856 and 1857 as a private individual, taking awards in each.[7]

However, the experience of the young working-class men of an artisan's club, Ye Grene Companye, who entered and won principal awards at the Scorton meeting during the early years of the twentieth century, would have typified entrenched attitudes. Patronized by some archers and rudely ignored by others, despite the excellence of their shooting, it was many years before they were accepted as equals on the archery field. It is to their credit that they persevered, despite continued positive discrimination against them by some and a general lack of encouragement from others.

Although a minor revolution in bow material and design was to affect the place of the longbow in traditional archery, during the decades before the Second World War, the organization and activities of British archery clubs and societies really changed very little. Egalitarian now to some degree, although still primarily the province of those with leisure, their members attended private practice during the week, in readiness for their club's grand days and what were now five public meetings. To the long-established national, northern counties, Leamington, midland counties, and western regional meetings had now been added a southern counties annual tournament.

What change did occur was not confined to clubs. The bowyery scene was also to alter. In London, bowyers Philip Highfield and Joseph Feltham finished trading in 1910. The lucrative American market that they had serviced for so long had now gone, replaced by a two-way flow, as American bowyers found interest in their wares developing abroad. After surviving without their founders for nearly 30 years, the businesses of James Buchanan and Thomas Aldred merged in 1918 with that of Frederick Henry Ayres, son of the founder of the firm, F. H. Ayres, and two names that had been synonymous with first-class bowyery ceased to appear on bow limbs. The 1920s had seen a slow return to stability by British clubs after the horror of war, a process greatly helped by the production of a magazine in replacement of the defunct *Archer's Register*, an annual publication that had served as a record, a reference, and a forum for archers from 1864 to 1914. The new publication, entitled *Archery News*, was the brainchild of Miss Christina Philips, a dedicated archeress who had recognized the value of the old registers in motivating clubs and individuals by summarizing their achievements while offering them the opportunity to exchange views. Miss Philips was to continue as editor for 26 years from 1922 until 1948, during which time her magazine reflected both important and minor changes in the archery world.

The 1930s were notable both for the emergence of an organization designed to encourage international competition and cooperation and for the development and marketing of the steel bow, a weapon that within a few years was to replace the longbow on both club and tournament shooting line. Another innovation of this period was that creation of controversy, the bow sight—of which more will be said later.

While the social element remained strong, there was now an increasingly competitive edge to archery that was not to the liking of all within clubs, as archers for whom competition with accomplishment was their raison d'être joined with those who had no such aspirations toward excellence beyond the wish to shoot moderately well and enjoy the company of their fellow archers.

Of natural interest to these competitive spirits was the first international congress of nations, held in Lwow, Poland, on September 4, 1931, for it was at this that the Federation International de Tir a l'Arc (FITA) was formed; and with four nations participating, the archery world championships were initiated.[8] From the beginning, it was apparent and recognized that with a number of countries involved, there was the probability, almost the certainty, of disparate types of bow eventually meeting in competition, with one performing better than another. Such indeed was to be the case, sadly to the detriment of the traditional English longbow, whose decline may be linked to the inception of the international federation.

Magazine cover for *Archery News*, May 1934. Published between 1922 and 1948. The founder and editor was Christina Phillips.

A sticking point for certain die-hard archers wedded to the status quo were the new international rounds initiated by the federation, which were shot at metric distances. Those in favor saw them as progressive, while archers who opposed did so largely because they feared that the traditional English rounds, whose distances had been measured in yards since time immemorial, would be isolated and become redundant. However, the novelty of metric shooting was to largely overcome xenophobic prejudice, and a new breed of international archer was shortly to appear on the scene.

Let us now move from changes in archery organization and consider the steel bow, a weapon that was directly to replace the traditional longbow. With hostilities over and advances in metallurgy resulting from wartime necessity available, weapons were metaphorically returning to plowshares. Techniques developed to keep abreast of rival armorers could now be devoted to peaceful purpose, and one minor target was the development of a weapon for recreational archery that gave better cast for less draw weight, was generally more reliable, and, importantly, was unaffected by weather. The viable steel bow was about to arrive.

Although the German firm WUM had toyed with metallic bows composed of nickel-steel springs held together by clamps (rather like car springs are formed) and had marketed them under the brand name of CHIC, these were largely playthings.[9] There is little evidence to suggest that they had found any favor with club archers, and the associated claim for a 60-meter range might best be taken with a liberal pinch of salt. Germany was not a member of the federation, however, and whatever appeal the CHIC bow may have had among the German archery fraternity, it was not destined to be a player on the international scene.

In America, there had been patents issued in 1872 to Ephraim S. Morton and again in 1880 to George A. Badger for metal bows.[10] While this latter showed some promise with its concave-convex cross section, neither was progressed commercially, and the longbow remained unchallenged by technology. It is to 1928 that we must turn, and to a brief note in the magazine *Ye Sylvan Archer* for March that mentions "a recent invention of interest to archers is a metal backed bow. Ernest C. Austin of Hollywood, California is the inventor. Mr. Austin reports his best scores for the YORK Round as 98 Hits, with 496 scored, and for the American Round 88 Hits, 572 scored." For all its claimed success, I can find no further reference to this weapon or indeed to Mr. Austin himself, since there is no sign of him in the national tournaments.

In Sweden, matters were making steady progress, however, for in the early 1930s, the firm of See Fabriks Aktiebolag of Sandvigen had investigated uses for flexible tubular steel; and since this proved suited to the construction of bows, a number were duly made and tested. These proved successful, and in 1934, the international Swedish ladies team marshaled on the shooting line largely equipped with SEEFAB (as they became known) bows. The performance of these objects was carefully observed, and although the team was beaten into second place by one from Poland using conventional longbows, their scores were sufficiently outstanding for aspiring champions to note. Though faint at first, the writing on the wall was beginning to be seen for the traditional longbow.

While in England, international competitors and club archers alike continued to remain faithful to the old weapon, by 1938, there may have been some transfer of affection. Although the national champion for that year, Mrs. Lindner, seemingly used her self-yew longbow of 30 pounds draw weight made by Aldred (I have this in my collection), at least one other member in the team photograph holds what looks suspiciously like a SEEFAB metal bow. Along with SEEFAB bows came steel arrows and, for a time at least, steel bracers together with the ultimate horror, steel strings!

Meanwhile, during the 1930s, across the Atlantic, two eminent engineering physicists, Clarence N. Hickman and Paul E. Klopsteg, turned their attention to the physical aspects of the bow and arrow in a series of erudite articles that were published in the American archery publications *Sylvan Archer* and *Archery Review*.[11] Each article was an important contribution to the scientific study of the bow and its physical properties, and among those with most impact was Klopsteg's 1932 discussion of fiber stresses in bow limbs. In this he discussed the most suitable cross section for a bow through determination of what he described as its neutral axis, the assumed center of gravity of the limbs, drawing attention to the failure of a longbow's traditional D section to cater for the disparity between the tensile and compressive properties of wood. To overcome this, Klopsteg argued that the neutral axis separating tension and compression should lie either parallel with the geometric axis or ideally toward the belly, thus reducing strain upon an area least likely to bear it. He considered that improved performance would result by arranging for the belly of the bow to be shaped accordingly. To achieve this, he suggested a reversed cross section that he called trapezoidal but followed this later in 1932 by advancing a wide, flat, and thin rectangular limb section as offering the best combination of each property.

The essence of Klopsteg's argument was that to correct the disparity between tension and compression capability resulting from conventional longbow sections, such sections should be wider and narrower in the belly than in the back, with the lesser mass to the rear of its neutral axis. To demonstrate this, he suggested laying out the shape of a proposed section on a heavy piece of cardboard, cutting it out, and drawing a line from back to belly, bisecting this to find the geometric center, or medial axis, then balancing the section conveniently along this line marking the point of balance. This, said Klopsteg, is the neutral plane, or axis, and the assumed center of gravity of the bow. By noting the relative positions of each, it can be readily seen how much mass will be to the rear of the neutral axis, and the proposed section may be adjusted to the maker's wish.

Led by Klopsteg, Hickman, Nagler, and others, the 1930s were an era of much practical experiment. Now that the old longbow had been taken apart and its construction found wanting, manufacturers sought to modify the traditional profile and section. American makers Philip Rownsevelle and Harold Rohm created a bow embodying a flat back combined with low-cambered sides and belly (a conventional plano-convex section) but with a profile broadening from the handle for some 6 inches before tapering evenly to the limb end. This new shaping was an early stage in the transition from the recognized longbow shape and D section to the profile and flat section that were to become standardized as a flat-bow convention. In addition, the Rounsevelle Rohm bow was provided with those self-nocks now so characteristic of the wooden flat bow. A similar experimental section, but with heavily recurved, nonworking ears, was created by English bowyer and top-flight archer, Frank Bilson. This weapon, although it did have applied nocks, again illustrates a departure from tradition. In June 1935, Hickman took matters further by designing and patenting a bow with reflexed limbs. The Russ Wilcox duoflex bow illustrates the principal admirably.[12]

Despite fast-developing threats to its existence from both Sweden and America, the longbow still held sway in England. The 1939 international championships were dominated by the threat of hostilities, and perhaps with an eye to war clouds on the horizon, the British team was led into the arena by Jack Churchill, a dyed-in-the-wool eccentric, kilted and playing the bagpipes. What evidence there is suggests that some competitors at least carried their longbows proudly. Certainly Churchill used his, and I am delighted to have that bow in my possession.

With the war over, in 1946, national and international competition was resumed. Among other heroic achievements by fellow archers who had served their country, the martial exploits of Colonel Jack Churchill—now known as "Mad Jack" for the very best of reasons—had been duly recorded, including his dispatch of a German soldier with a longbow and hunting arrow during the retreat to Dunkirk.

In clubs and societies, although the traditional weapon was still in regular use, new challengers were in the arena; while emerging from the shadows was another and potentially the most serious opponent yet—the flat-sectioned bow with its recurved limbs developed from Hickman's theoretical design.

Fully conscious of the impact of SEEFAB steel bows on the scene, Accles & Pollock, a major English producer of flexible steel tubing, now decided to market a steel bow not dissimilar to that sold by the Swedish firm, but trademarked Apollo; while simultaneously, the long-established archery firm of Jaques offered a steel bow to complement their Golden Arrow range. *The British Archer* magazine, first published in 1949, carried advertisements for Apollo steel bows in its inaugural edition, and a combination of curiosity and aggressive marketing resulted in significant numbers being sold to club archers. Despite advances in technology and the replacement of natural materials by metal, shooting with the longbow remained relatively unsophisticated. Unlike the crossbow and the handgun, each of which had developed crude aids to aiming, the twentieth-century longbow was shot in a manner differing little from that of prehistoric times.

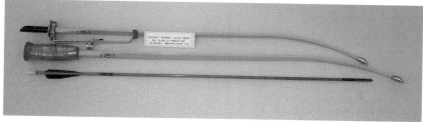

Steel bows and arrows by See Fabriks Aktiebolg of Sweden, marketed as *SEEFAB* (top) and Accles and Pollock, England, marketed as *Apollo* (middle). Notice the metal sights fitted to each bow. Earlier examples were not so fitted. Author's collection. Photos by Tony Lockwood.

Enter the bow sight, and matters were set to change. But first, a glance at the past is in order. In Tudor times and earlier, men shot largely by instinct, from knowledge gained over many years of practice. But this was seemingly not always so, for Roger Ascham records a colleague who habitually left his quiver and other tackle some way up the shooting range. He tells us that others supposed it was for reasons of security; Roger's astute observation was that a more probable reason for its placing was in order for it to be used as an aiming mark.[13] Several hundred years later, in the late nineteenth century, James

Spedding, an archer well ahead of his time, devised an arrangement whereby a pin was pushed into material fixed to the back of his bow. By moving the pin, he was able to align it with an aiming mark. He used this—without comment from authority—to some effect at national meetings, and by so doing, improved his scores. He is recorded as remarking that he wished someone would complain about this rudimentary sight, because he would then know that there was something to it![14]

In nineteenth-century America, it had been fashionable for a time to add a small ring to the bowstring at eye level; while later still, in England, it was popular to add small knots of silk to bowstrings, so that when at full draw, they might similarly be aligned with points of aim to form a back sight. It is to the United States, however, that we must go to examine two of the first true archery sights, both of which were prior to 1927, some years before the commercial emergence of the steel bow. The first, a simple device, was invented and used by Abner Shepardson of Melrose, Massachusetts. Shepardson had made the longbow with which Dr. Paul W. Crouch gained the championship of the United States in 1925 and 1927, and Dr. Crouch believed his bow sight to have helped on those occasions. The Shepardson bow sight consisted of a heavy brass ring that clamped snugly around the bow above the handle.[15] Secured to this was a metal rod, attached to which was a movable horizontal bar projecting to the left or right (dependent upon handedness), terminating in a peephole, and able to be slid up and down. There was no facility for windage, or side-to-side variation, however.

The Lambert bow sight was of similar vintage and operated on much the same principle, although it was rather more sophisticated in that there was adjustment for windage.[16] Amid reasoned arguments for its use, the inventor, Arthur W. Lambert, claimed, rather curiously, that with the sight mounted above the handle, it could also be used for underhand shooting; that is, with the bow hand elevated above the target. To achieve this, he positioned a sighting pin, suitably bent, to the right of the bow limb, aligning this to some suitable feature while positioning the arrow point toward the target. This he called indirect aiming and claimed it to have been successful.

In 1932, Paul Klopsteg set his seal of approval on bow sights in an article comparing these with points of aim, and it then became acceptable to use one. Improvements in scoring quickly followed. Subsequently, Heber Butts devoted a chapter to the principle in his 1938 book, *Archery Shooting Techniques*.

Despite the apparent advantage of the new system, point-of-aim shooting was still taught to those beginning archery. However, in 1936, respected coaches Dave and Cia Craft conducted a questionnaire that showed that of the top 80 archers in the United States and Canada, 39 percent now used bow sights; and taking their lead from this statistic, the Crafts recommended that novices now be introduced to them.[17] Whether these top archers included Russell Hoogerhyde, the reigning national champion, is debatable; for in his 1933 book, *Archery*, written with colleague Carl Thompson, Russell extols the range stick, a calibrated, handheld gadget that aided point-of-aim shooting, and this seems to have been his personal preference. Indeed, he indicates as much in an article on shooting technique within Robert Rhode's 1963 compilation of championship shooting styles.[18]

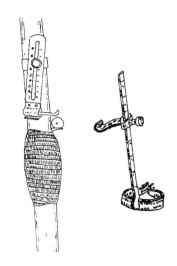

Two early North American bow sights, the Lambert (left), circa 1928 and the Shepardson, circa 1925. The Shepardson was instrumental in helping Dr. Paul W. Crouch win the American National Championship in 1925. From *Modern Archery* (New York: 1932). With acknowledgements to Arthur W. Lambert.

While now legitimate and thus acceptable at national events, for aspirant international archers, all this was to no avail. Bow sights of all descriptions were banned by the international federation until the 1950s—although the governing body for British archery specifically permitted them. Within the 1950 GNAS shooting regulations, which applied as much to longbows as to other bow types, guidance on FITA rules was explicit.

> Under the Rules of the International Federation, the center of the target is set 1.30 meters from the ground, and only three arrows are shot at each end. The only other major difference from the G.N.A.S. Regulations is that no projecting sight is allowed on the bow.

Permitted by the federation, however, and allowed by GNAS was the facility for "an attachment on the string, not exceeding one centimeter in diameter." This latter gave rise to some ambiguity, since the facial position to which it should be drawn was not initially defined; and until standardized as touching the lips or the nose, this attachment occasionally found its way up the string to be used as a back sight.

It is to the credit of the British Long-Bow Society, formed in 1951 to protect traditions associated with the weapon, that from its inception, the founding fathers banned sights altogether on longbows, permitting just an elastic band or marks on the bow limb—a practice that was followed by the Grand National Archery Society itself within its own longbow rules.

Although in the immediate postwar years, there was still some interest in the old longbow, good bow wood was now much more difficult to come by; quality yew was in particularly short supply, and self-lemonwood, although acceptable, was no real substitute.

In May 1945, Philip Purle advertised "very soon now a new and interesting type of bow and arrow will be available," adding that it would be a "short, flat type, with a novel take-apart handle." It was not until 1947, however, that the monopoly of advertising enjoyed by the SEEFAB bow was challenged by both F. H. Ayres and Lillywhites of London, who offered flat bows and longbows as alternatives to the ubiquitous steel bows. Nonetheless, under the onslaught of steel bows and flat bows, the number of traditionally sectioned and profiled longbows on club shooting lines was now rapidly diminishing, a situation that was neatly summed up by the firm of Slazenger/Ayres in an advertisement appearing within the first of The British Archer magazines when they began publication in 1949.

> The men who today make F. H. Ayres archery equipment draw heavily upon more than 100 years experience of the craft. But like archery itself they are always ready to take advantage of new methods and new materials.

Another early edition of *The British Archer* carried a short poetic epitaph, poignant in its message. Entitled "Progress" (with apologies to whomsoever needs them) by A. G. Banks, it summed up the situation in which erstwhile loyal adherents of the longbow found themselves.

In White and Green, sad White and Green,
And woeful scattered height and line,
Tho' peerless wrought in beef and pine,
And matched , they say, in weight and spine,
Are shamefully (and always mine),
Those wooden arrows seen.
Hand me that sissy bow of Tin,
With thirty paltry pounds therein
And by St. Hubert! 'ere this day be past

Tho' Apollo rule it be my last,
I swear that Gold, and Red, and Blue,
Shall now be piercéd through and through,
By shafts duralumin.
Oh! fair Diane and all ye gods
Preserve me now if Merlin nods,
From Whites and Greens dropped in the sods,
Speed straight these bright metallic rods.
But shades of Muir, Buchanan, Ford!
That puny little bows of Tin,
Should now be Kings, where yew was Lord,
And shafts Duralumin.

Mention of Apollo, Diana, and Merlin are references to the model names of some steel bows, but Duralumin? This was a trade name for the aluminum alloy tubing from which arrows were made; it replaced earlier steel shafts marketed by SEEFAB and Apollo. Although light and capable of accuracy, alloy tubing had its limitations. Unlike steel shafts that could be barreled—and occasionally were—for better stability in flight, Duralumin could only be manufactured to a parallel profile. Wooden arrows continued to be made, however, particularly those tapered, or breasted, for clout shooting; and as the poem suggests, these were matched for weight (still against silver coinage) and also for spine, or whippiness. Horn nocks had not entirely disappeared and were occasionally to be seen on these wooden arrows, although the aluminum slip-over design introduced by the firm of Aldred—who patented the process in the early years of the twentieth century—had by now lost their early image as string cutters and were in almost universal use.[19]

But for all its proven ability and its ousting of the longbow from club and national meetings, the days of the steel bow were numbered. Word from America was of new bows that were both sweet to draw and loose and, weight for weight, faster than both the steel bow and the longbow; for manufacture of the recurved bow had been perfected, and this was to dominate the archery scene for a generation.

First outshot and now outclassed, the old longbow was reeling from two body blows, but aid was on its way. In May of 1951, Mr. Kenneth Ryall Webb, a respected senior archer, proposed the formation of an organization to save the ancient weapon from ending its day as a forgotten relic in some dusty museum.[20] Sufficient numbers of old-timers expressed interest, and in September of that year, supported by the Royal Toxophilite Society, the

Woodmen of Arden, the Royal Company of Archers, and other influential members of the archery establishment, the British Long-Bow Society was formed, to shoot two way in the old manner with recreational longbows modeled on those of the nineteenth and early twentieth centuries.

For nearly 30 years, the old bow gathered strength behind these formidable ramparts, its qualities steadfastly defended by a slowly growing number of men and women for whom tradition and comradeship were worthier aims than accuracy at all costs until in 1984, a new generation nurtured on recurved composite weapons rediscovered the traditional longbow and its pain and pleasure. Under new leadership, the British Long-Bow Society encouraged and developed this latent interest. Longbows began to be seen once more on the shooting lines of clubs, few at first, but in increasing numbers as converts were gained. Target and clout tournaments offering English rounds shot in traditional style and using the old weapon began to be held once more across the country; while the presence of the longbow, always a strong contender for awards, continued to grow at field events.

Field archery had been introduced from America where, administered by the National Field Archery Association since 1939, it had served to maintain skills during the close seasons. Here in Britain, this branch of archery expanded in scope and popularity, proving a worthy alternative to the sport of bow hunting, an activity over which the old longbow had historically presided. However, in 1963, legislation was passed that might in earlier times have had a devastating effect upon the sporting community at large (if anyone had had the inclination or the temerity to introduce it). The Deer Act now banned hunting with all weapons, including the bow and arrow—an event that proved of more historic concern than practical effect, since within the archery fraternity, there had been a good deal of internecine controversy and some confrontation over the practice.[21]

While hunting camps had sometimes been held on private land, and the occasional deer met its doom to provide roast venison over a camp fire, the use of the bow for blood sport had never enjoyed much popularity in Britain during modern times; field shooting at target faces (on which an animal was portrayed) was more and more seen as a fully satisfying alternative. Despite the seemingly low level of interest, short and powerful hunting bows and arrows in wood with hunting points had been readily available from Ayres and Jaques since well before the Second World War, while examples in Duralumin continued to be made by Purle virtually until legislation banned hunting.[22] One event that caused some unseemly mirth among those opposed to the practice concerned an aspirant bow hunter who, while crouching too close to a fox's earth for its comfort, was bitten by the creature in a painful place and retired discomfited for a tetanus injection.

With the recovery of the Tudor warship *Mary Rose* in 1982 and the many longbows and arrows salvaged from it, a latent interest in the war bow quickly developed; and with technical drawings for guidance, one or two bowyers created replicas to be shot for test purposes. Necessary restrictions placed upon the dissemination of information prior to the publication of an archaeological report prevented this information from reaching a wider public, however, and this inevitably caused frustration among

Mark Stretton at full draw with a 200 pound replica English war bow in the course of his attempt to set a world record in August 2004. Author's collection

those who, rightly or wrongly, considered themselves competent to construct examples. Through the dedication of such as Lieutenant Commander W. F. Paterson, RN, and Dr. T. S. R. Hardy, CBE, MA, who devoted much time to the subject, knowledge of the Tudor war bow's capabilities was slowly garnered; and in 1987, the British Long-Bow Society inaugurated an event at which replicas were shot for distance, using a version of the Tudor arrow, 32 inches in length and armed with a broadhead, or bodkin, point. Seventeen years later, shooting the Standard Arrow has become popular among traditional archers, and modern examples of the great English war bow fashioned from yew once more loft their battle shafts to full bow shot of 12 score yards, delivered by the powerful arms of English archers.

With those who shoot with the recreational bow numbering now in their thousands and a buoyant society to safeguard their well-being, and with bowyers, fletchers, stringmakers, and arrowsmiths supported by a vibrant craft guild (endorsed by the ancient London livery companies of bowyers and fletchers) to make their equipment, the longbow has truly returned to both dominate and tantalize. The steel bow, the weapon that once supplanted it, is but a distant memory, a lost chapter in the long history of recreational archery, its very existence virtually unknown to archers of today. Such is the wayward path of fate!

Modern longbowmen shooting the traditional English war bow. Author's collection.

What of the future? It would be a foolish person who predicted this with certainty. We who use the longbow and administer its shooting recognize the vulnerability of our position. Where our forbears grasped the opportunities for achievement offered by new technology and discarded the old for the new, we have consciously discarded the new for the old. It is for us to hold in check an inclination to disturb what we have ourselves decided is the status quo. As yew and other conventional bow woods become increasingly difficult to obtain and bowyers face an almost insatiable demand for longbows, some may turn more and more to exotic woods and multilaminates with which to create their wares. Others may make even greater use of bamboo, and split-cane bows might become commonplace. To make full use of a scarce commodity, scarfing could reappear alongside fishtail splicing. We who steward the old weapon must not fail it again. On the broader scene, the signs are that archery will polarize to form two factions: one dedicated to forcing personal excellence through the medium of ever more sophisticated technical advance, its governing body subordinate to a national program, the other sidelined and dismissed as irrelevant to the deity of commerce, left in peace to enjoy its unending tussle with simple stick and string.

Epilogue

In one sense, the recreational longbow with its attendant arrow is secure, accepted by today's generation of archers as integral to the archery scene, but the context in which it is at present countenanced differs significantly from earlier days. Where once it was pre-eminent, now it is an anachronism, a weapon inferior in purpose, dependent upon a sentimental affection for bygone days; charismatic, and with power to influence its own destiny, it has trodden the path to the abyss, but has been turned back at the brink. Those who keep faith with it cannot shut their minds to advances in technology and practice; the pages of this history have amply demonstrated that. Today's composite and compound bows exist and cannot be denied. Modern glues allow the creation of a bow in days rather than years, and the temptation of numerous laminations of exotic wood exist. Modern strings ensure that breakage is now minimized. All around is evidence of progress, and the work of Hickman and Klopsteg is present in every modern weapon. In reaffirming the longbow and its simplicity, we have consciously regressed to an outdated design, but we must do so in full knowledge of the consequence.

The motto of the British Long-Bow Society is "Keep Faith." To this tenet, we may add, "with the spirit of the past."

Appendix

Bracers

As all of those who have served in the armed forces know, some to their cost, a self-inflicted wound was looked upon with disfavor by authority; shooting oneself in the foot was, at best, a recipe for dishonorable discharge if one was lucky, or something rather more terminal if one was not. There is an enduring myth within the British Army, however, that in olden times, certain self-inflicted damage was allowed as honorable and known in fact as the honorable wound. This was the injury to an archer's arm if the bowstring slapped against it. Since this damage was not intentional and was the result of constant use of the bow for a crucial purpose, it is said to have been looked upon with favor. Whether this myth had substance, no one can say; a bruise on the inner forearm is painful but not incapacitating.

Here we will discuss the bracers, or arm guards, that archers have used to protect themselves from this honorable wound across the years, but we will begin by defining the word itself. The noun "bracer" (or "brace") derives from the Latin *bracchia* (meaning "arm") from whence comes the French *bras* and, by extension, *gardebras*, (alternatively, *wardebras* or occasionally *warbrasse*). Anglicized, the term has become "arm guard." Both the terms "bracer" and "arm guard" are used by archers today. Despite its venerable age, the term "arm guard" has been discarded by certain archaeologists who prefer the description "wrist guard." We will allow them their prejudice.

Mundane in function and desirable, though not essential, the purpose of the bracer is twofold. In neither though does it brace, or offer strengthening support. As an arm guard, it serves to take and absorb the impact of the bowstring when released, either where the bow is low or inadequately strung (i.e., the string is too close to the bow limbs) or where shooting technique is less than perfect. A secondary and important function is to hold loose clothing away from the path of the bowstring.

The use of bracers by archers is evidenced from numerous archaeological remains, and it appears that the need, or perhaps the advisability, to protect his

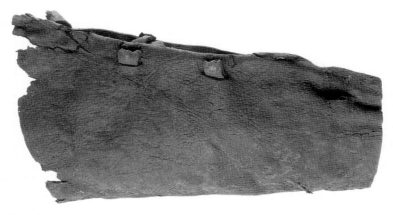

Medieval leather arm guard recovered from the moat of Stogursey Castle, Somerset. Photo courtesy of Taunton Museum, Somerset.

inner forearm with an arm guard was well known to prehistoric man. One such artifact was recovered from a Bronze Age burial excavation close to Stonehenge, and this proved to be of dark gray rock 4 1/4 inches long, 1 1/10 inches wide, and 3/8 inch deep.[1] Countersunk holes were drilled for attachment to fastening thongs or perhaps to a leather sleeve. This was a thoroughly functional item that would be instantly recognizable to a modern archer.

In early historic times, bracers are depicted on illustrations and woodcuts where archers are present, although by no means all are shown thus equipped. An example from the fourteenth century, and representative perhaps of those worn at Crécy during the French campaign of Edward III, appears within the Luttrell Psalter on the well-known marginal drawing of archers practicing at the butts. This is circular in shape with straps and is almost certainly of leather. A replica made for me (which I use) shows it to have been fully effective when used with a longbow. An example similar in shape and early in date has been recovered from the vicinity of Finsbury Fields in London.

Although a bracer is essentially functional in purpose, it is also a very personal item, and where its owner is inclined, it is sometimes decorated. This decoration can take one of several forms; it may be composed of religious icons if it is to be used in warfare or secular and imaginative if for sporting at roving or the butts. Or again, it may define the owner's allegiance to an organization. From early paintings, particularly those representing the martyrdom of Saint Sebastian, come images of formally embossed arm guards linking the owners to a fraternity.

Some, but not all, of those leather bracers recovered from the warship *Mary Rose* are randomly decorated by stamping, and details of these can be found within the archaeological report (part III). They include fleur-de-lys, Tudor roses, a gridiron (symbolic of the martyrdom of Saint Lawrence), and what may be a representation of the "Sunday Christ."[2] In company with these are other more rudimentary items, no-nonsense pieces of roughly cut leather with straps, designed to do a job without the frills of decoration.[3] Although seemingly absent from those recovered from the *Mary Rose*, since none has been identified, there is evidence of an internal stiffening piece glued to the underside of a rectangular bracer of broadly similar date found elsewhere.

Historically enigmatic is the artifact left at Boulton Hall, legend says, by King Henry VI after his defeat at the battle of Hexham. It is a three-quarter sleeve bracer of thick leather, decorated with what some see as leaves of planta genista, symbol of the Plantagenets, within which a rose is centered. Below is the inscription "I H S Helpe" (Jesus Help).

Although the material of which these items are made is largely leather, bracers in horn and ivory also exist. Ivory was a medium favored by Continental archers of earlier years, and a collection of bracers made of this material and gathered together in the nineteenth century by Charles J. Longman (a noted archer and past national champion) was later donated by him to the Pitt Rivers Museum at Oxford. It is believed that they originated from members of a French or Belgian archery society dedicated to Saint Sebastian, since many are etched with decorative and detailed drawings of his martyrdom. A number of them are dated, and these are of the seventeenth century. While ivory may have been the favored material of Continental archers at that time, the English preferred leather. Writing of bracers, Gervase Markham in his treatise, *The Arte of Archerie* (1634), informs us that "these bracers are made for the most part of Spanish leather, the smooth side outwards, and they be the best, sometimes of Spanish leather and the flesh side outward, and they are both good and tolerable, and others are made of gard, stiffe, but smooth Bend-leather, and they be the worst and dangerous."

Although the occasional specimen in ivory[4] may have been made, it would seem that leather for bracers was predominant, and nineteenth-century examples display similarities with Markham's description. Early in the century, men's half-sleeve bracers (4 inches in width) were of dark brown stiff leather with a softer leather lining sewn to the undersurface as protection for the wearer's sleeve. In later years, they were of a more pliable, lighter-colored leather with a piece of thin green material glued in position for a similar protective purpose. Fastening was either by strap and buckle (earlier years) or an elastic strap with ring and hook (later years). Smaller, delicately shaped bracers of stiff leather (2 1/2 inches in width) were available for nineteenth-century ladies, and the undersurfaces of these offered a pad of quilted material as a sleeve protection. During Edwardian times, bracers of soft leather with (generally) three straps and buckles replaced the stiffer half-sleeve examples, and the use of these continued into recent times.

Tabs and Tips

It is a matter of speculation just how the yeoman bowman of Old England protected his fingers from the pressure of the string, and in the absence of recognizable artifacts, we are left with the uncomfortable conclusion that their fingers were hard enough to draw their great war bows without protection. If that were indeed so, then we archers today whose bows are half their draw weight (but for whom a leather tab is a necessary piece of personal furniture) must accord them even more respect.

In later centuries, men used a shooting glove, or so Roger Ascham informs us. A dual-purpose item with a pocket to contain a fine linen cloth and some wax, it would certainly have graced the hand of the sixteenth-century gentleman archer and may perhaps have been in use earlier. Ascham has some detailed comments helpful to his readers.[5] To alleviate chafing, he recommends sewing soft, thick cloth within the string fingers of the glove; and to avoid pinching the nock of the arrow when drawing, he advises either sewing a split goose quill inside the fore and middle fingers of the glove between the material and the leather or attaching a piece of leather to the outside of the glove between these fingers to separate them. Some archers today still use leather separators on their tabs.

Although gloves may have been more widely used in earlier times and are seen occasionally today, it seems likely that if the medieval archer used anything at all, it would have resembled either the two-hole leather tab, once in general use by modern archers, or a three-hole version, similar to the crude juvenile tab recovered from an archaeological excavation in Coventry and described in chapter 7. While the eighteenth-century gentleman archer may have used a glove to protect his carefully manicured fingers from the string, his nineteenth-century successor was largely content with objects called "tips," which were sets of three abbreviated leather glove ends, each having a small leather stop to prevent the string from slipping down the finger pad and—on those made by James Buchanan—knurled brass bolts and nuts to hold them in position. Since they were elegant and did not interfere with clothing, Victorian and early Edwardian ladies habitually used these simple tips, turning only later to the alternative skeleton glove—essentially tips secured to straps that were themselves fastened around the wrist by strap and buckle. In use until the late 1930s, after the Second World War, these gloves were largely replaced by what is today the ubiquitous leather tab, at first cut with two holes, but later made for just the third finger to facilitate the withdrawal of arrows from the target.

Quivers and Pouches

To a quequer Robin went,
A good bolte owthe he toke,
So ney [near] *on the marke he went,*
He fayled not a fothe [foot]

Curious as to the reference in the above verse, which occurs in an early version of the ballad Robin Hood and the Potter, I recollected the belief of a fellow antiquarian that the word "quiver" had been derived as a loan word from the Turco-Mongolian languages of the Huns and Avars who overran Europe in early historic times and in whose language an arrow case is described as a kukur. This colleague drew attention to the early medieval Latin *coccora* and to the medieval German–early English *cohhora* (or *cocer* or *cocor*), thus to the later German *kocher* and its French equivalent, *corquaise*. To the foregoing I can add the early French *couire* and, for good measure, the Gaelic *corcaich*, while in passing, the western English dialect word *kecker* (used to describe a mouth or throat) might also be noticed.[6]

Among numerous archery references, the term "quequer" appears just once within the 36 ballads and extensive notes that comprise Joseph Ritson's *Robin Hood: Poems and Ballads*. Preliminary notes by Ritson suggest that the manuscript ballad as transcribed dated from the time of Henry VII. This may well be true, but the use and spelling of this archaic term presumes an origin when the word was either in common use or was at least understood, thus perhaps predating Ritson's suggested late fifteenth-century usage. So much for etymology. We move now to the more fruitful fields of custom and usage of this oddly named article of personal archery equipment.

For one of the earlier representations of a quiver or arrow case, we may look to the Bayeux Tapestry, for here there are quivers aplenty. Where these are carried, one is suspended from a shoulder, while the others hang around waists; not all archers are equipped with them however. Three arrow cases are separately portrayed, perhaps to indicate reserve stocks. Of the material used in their making, it is impossible to be exact, but portrayal on the tapestry suggests cloth.

It may be fairly presumed that whatever method was used to contain and position sheaves of arrows across the years, three essentials were necessarily fulfilled. They should be capable of quick, easy, and effective replenishment; their vulnerable fletchings should be protected in the confusion of battle; and individual shafts should be readily accessible with the minimum of effort.

There is physical evidence for the carriage of arrows in cloth cases (casses) or bags, separated one from the other by leather spacers; and where this was so, we must assume that each arrow was capable of being drawn and used in an instant. These cloth cases were secured to the archer's person by a girdle, and evidence suggests that they were carried horizontally across the back.[7] Exactly how is unclear, although evidently the spacer needed to have been positioned broadly adjacent to the fulcrum, or point of balance, of the case. Protection of fletchings would be best achieved if they were inside the bag rather than protruding from it, and there is evidence for a particular shape to accommodate these, since a drawing of one such example is known.

Francis Grose, an eighteenth-century antiquarian, records in his notebook after visiting Canterbury that he had seen "an ancient quiver, about the size of a stocking." His freehand drawing shows a bag, perhaps of linen, one end of which is of loose leather with, at its further end, a drawstring to hold the bag closed. At a point between the extremities, there is a leather spacer pierced with holes. Grose's drawing of the leather spacer is strongly reminiscent of the leather discs, each with 24 holes, recovered from the deck of the Tudor warship *Mary Rose*. Since there is evidence for stitching perforations around the circumference of these discs, little imagination is needed to envisage their original appearance and purpose.[8] Where spacers were used, practicality required that arrowheads faced forward, since it is difficult to draw a head through a leather spacer (and impossible if it is barbed). We have an instruction to help us here however, for we are told that, "an archer should first poise his bow on the thumb of the hand with which he holds it when he shoots (to determine the center) drawing an arrow from his quiver in two motions, the reason being that unless he had a very long arm, the arrows would remain jammed in the quiver, from which the feathers would suffer."[9]

Additionally, our anonymous Frenchman tells us that the barbs of arrowheads were fitted in the same plane as the arrow's nock. Thus, since the cock feather is invariably at right angles to the nock, an archer drawing his shaft point first could, by feeling the barbs, do so in such a way that it was ready to be presented to the string with the minimum of adjustment.

Arrow cases and arrow bags feature occasionally in bequests. The 1577 will of John Billingham bequeathed a quiver, an arrow bag, and a sheaf of arrows; while a year later, that of John Smallwood mentioned a sheaf of arrows with barbed heads and an arrow case of straw fitted with a lock and key. Although an arrow case of straw, albeit protected by a lock and key, might seem a touch less substantial than might be thought practical, cases of linen or leather were not uncommon. Since these seem to have come provided with a girdle or a belt, they were presumably intended to be worn for use, begging the question of how this might be achieved.[10]

We think of the quiver today either as a container carried on the person, or as a field device standing beside the archer—a ground quiver. This is the accepted modern definition, but it is one that would have puzzled our eighteenth- and nineteenth-century ancestors, for what we today call the "quiver" was to them the "pouch." It was in the pouch that arrows for immediate use, invariably including one spare, were carried, and early archery treatises are quite explicit about this.[11] A little booklet called *The Archer's Guide, or Instructions for the use of the Long-Bow*, published by A. N. Myers & Co. of London in 1860, gave the following advice to novice archers:

> The quiver is never worn but in roving. In shooting at Target or Butts it is placed a few yards by the side of them, two or three target arrows being sufficient, the rest are kept in reserve to supply the place of those that may meet with an accident, or for any other cause that the shooter may wish to change them.

Earlier, Thomas Waring in his 1814 booklet had mentioned that

> Quivers were formerly made of wood and were succeeded by those of leather, but for the last few years, tin quivers have been preferred by almost every archer as keeping the arrows more secure from the wet and being considerably lighter and through the last reason, not the least, being three-fourths less expense.

F. H. Ayres' little *Handbook of Archery*, published in 1898, is more explicit still.

> The quiver, made of tin (plain or japanned over) is from 24 inches to 28 inches long, with a lid, lock and key. It carries from six to twenty-four arrows, to supply the pouch or to use in roving.

While the anonymous author of another nineteenth-century booklet elaborated further with the surprising information that "The quiver is a tin case somewhat in the shape of that usually represented as forming part of Robin Hood and his Band."

By 1904, however, when Colonel Walrond published his *Archery for Beginners*, the item that Victorians had called a pouch had become more generally known as the quiver, giving rise to today's near universal acceptance of the description. Spare arrows were now largely carried in wooden boxes, typical among which were the Oxford box and the Wiltshire box.[12] This latter had space for 24 arrows, of which 12 were carried in the lid. Additionally, two covered compartments were included for spare strings, tips, shooting gloves, scoring cards, and other essential paraphernalia.

Bow coffins, as they were known in the trade (but better described as traveling Aschams or bow boxes), had for some time incorporated one or two compartments for arrows, together with a lidded space into which gloves or ladies' chatelaines would fit. A sophistication now added was a hinged rack that when stood upright, allowed arrows to be extracted without damage and with the minimum of effort. The ultimate in excellence, however, was the arrow Ascham, a well-crafted miniature version of the earlier bow cupboards, designed to hold 14 shafts in total safety.

Although the modern quiver—be it side, back, bow, or ground—is now in almost universal use, the archaic pouch still makes an occasional appearance as a pocket quiver for coat or trousers, an anachronistic reversion to the nineteenth century when shooting jackets were de rigueur for all gentlemen.

So it is that the quiver-cum-arrow case, transmogrified to arrow pouch, has returned full circle to become, once again, the quiver. And there, subject to the vagaries of custom and fashion, we will leave this most ancient and enigmatic piece of archery furniture.

Arrowheads

The reason for an arrowhead allows of no ambiguity. Essentially functional, whether fashioned of flint shard, bronze or iron, bone, or horn, it is there for a very clear purpose. Early prehistoric lithic heads designed either for hunting or, where circumstances required, warfare were of simple flint shard; only in later times as skills advanced was flint carefully knapped, either to a leaf or a barbed and tanged shape. As technology advanced, first bronze, then iron arrowheads appeared, and it is with their purpose and documentation that we are now concerned.

In an endeavor to bring a semblance of order and to allow for a meaningful listing of functions, it has been the practice of archaeologists and museum curators to identify arrowheads by type and role. For many years, the London Museum Medieval Cataloguing System has identified and categorized early and medieval arrowheads, and the 21 major categories into which heads fall are well known to archer antiquarian and archaeologist alike. Within this typology are heads for penetration of mail and plate armor, their shapes unencumbered to allow smooth entry; heads for cutting into flesh to kill by hemorrhage or by

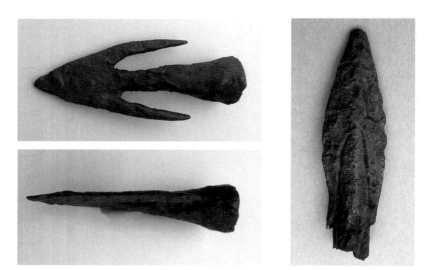

Medieval arrowheads, London Museum Type 16, Jessop's alternative typology M4.
Left upper and lower, plan and side views of a wide-barbed head. Right, plan view of
narrow-barbed head. Photos by Mark Stretton.

striking a vital organ, barbed to make withdrawal difficult; heads with sockets
into which a foreshaft fits; and others with tangs for insertion within the shaft
itself.

While the London Museum catalog arrangements allow for identification of
these heads, it does not classify them by type, and thus it is inadequate where
such a classification is desirable. Enter now a new typology: one devised by
professor Oliver Jessop and published in 1996.[13] This system identifies 28 types
by construction and usage, and it seeks to cover those arrowheads recovered
from archaeological sites within the British Isles and dated between the tenth
and sixteenth centuries.

Jessop used four main categories: T for tanged, M for military, H for hunting, and MP for multipurpose (either military, hunting, or practice). Accepting
these four is done with some reservation, since in my view, there is a case to be
made for a separate and additional category of P for practice (or recreational).
MP9 and MP10 within Professor Jessop's typology are clearly for that purpose
(as indeed is London Museum Type 5) and are paralleled by later eighteenth-
and nineteenth-century examples.[14] To carry the point further, there are sixteenth-century references to "silver spoon" and "rigged" (ridged) piles—used
to confirm full-draw while at pricks or butts—which, although none seemingly
appear in museum collections, are adequately provenanced by their descrip-

tion.[15] Where the definition is MP, therefore, the advantage of this form of typology, although a little blurred at present, is clearly evident where comparison by purpose is desirable.

For everyday usage, it was naturally important in the past to identify heads colloquially within their generic purpose; and although certain of these names are no longer known, a number do survive in documentary form. Today, when archer antiquarians and historians gather, the descriptions (London Museum) Type 16 and Type 7 are readily recognized as, respectively, a hemorrhaging (broad) head and a penetrating head (bodkin point); similarly, our fifteenth-century forebears would have understood a "bykere" or a "dokebyll." That we can no longer do so is of consequence to questing historians and no one else! There may come a time when the term "forker" (Type 6) or "horsehead" (Type 14) are equally mysterious to our descendants.

Said to be one of the most widely recovered heads, the LM Type 16 (Jessop M4) is thought by some to have been the kind with which the Tudor arrows recovered from the *Mary Rose* were armed, and certainly it appears with great regularity upon the shafts of replica arrows of the period. Consumed by curiosity, I decided to conduct a small experiment. I asked a number of colleagues who hand-forged arrowheads in the traditional way to each fashion an example of a Type 16 head, as they understood it, and awaited the results with interest. An analysis of the forthcoming heads is given here, and in the present era of characterless cloning of everything, these eight individual interpretations are of some interest. Each is a practical example of the variation from a standard that might have been expected from arrowhead makers working across the country. Included for comparison are the weights and dimensions of two authentic Type 16 heads dated to the Tudor period.

The average length of the reproduction heads is 2 3/8 inches, the average internal socket diameter is 7/16 inch, and the average internal depth is 1 1/16 inches. A similar comparison of two authentic Type 16 medieval heads shows a corresponding variation of dimension. Averaged, the length is 2 7/16 inches, socket diameter is 3/8 inch, and internal socket depth is 1 7/16.

A seeming variation of socket depth between medieval and modern heads is of some interest. The cones of a sheaf of Tudor arrows appear to vary between 3/4 inch and 7/8 inch, suggesting that short heads, with correspondingly short sockets, were perhaps preferred. Roger Ascham says in *Toxophilus*, "Shorte heads be better than longe because they (the long heads) are always in more jeopardye of breakinge when they are on." It is of note, however, that earlier medieval heads A and B above have longer socket depths. In 1545, Ascham was perhaps reflecting contemporary thought.

Comparison of Modern Forged Type 16 Arrowheads

S°	W	OL	B	Di	De
J. Hartley	280	2 3/8	11/16	3/8	15/16
H. Cole	250	2 1/2	5/8	5/16	15/16
M. Manns	510	3 1/16	13/16	5/16	1 1/2
G. Newall	140	1 1/16	11/16	3/8	1 1/2
M. Stretton	510	2 13/16	1	3/8	1 1/16
S. Stanley	310	3	9/16	3/8	1 1/2
J. Belza	210	2 1/4	7/8	5/16	3/8
M. Reape	210	2 3/16	3/4	5/16	1 1/16
Actual medieval arrowheads:					
A	300	2 1/8	11/16	7/16	1 3/8
B	92.7[†]	2	13/16	7/16	1 1/2

°S=smith; W=weight in grains; OL=overall length in inches; B=breadth in inches; Di=internal diameter of socket in inches; De=internal depth of socket in inches
[†]The head is badly corroded, and this is reflected in the weight.

Examination of head A above by X-ray reveals a pin passing through the socket and into the cone with the presumed intention of securing the head to the shaft. While not unusual in hunting heads (where it was customary to draw an arrow from prey for reuse), the appearance in a head that hitherto has been regarded as being for military purposes (see Jessop M4) seems unusual and suggests that this particular London Museum Type 16 had a dual purpose. Perhaps Jessop's typology requires further amendment.

Among modern smiths there is variation in profile of narrow and wide barbs, depicting personal interpretations. Whether medieval smiths were similarly free or whether their variants of wide or narrow barbs reflected contemporary military thought can only be conjectural. Certainly Ascham, in speaking of early sixteenth-century arrowheads was opposed to barbs of any kind, even the light barbs that were seemingly in use then. "Yea, and I suppose, if the same little barbs which they have were put clean awaye (removed), they should be farre better."

It should be noted that whereas the replicas are forged of mild steel bar, the originals are of wrought iron. Consideration of the source of the raw material from which medieval arrowheads were made is ongoing, but the known importation of Baltic iron bars suggests a trade with those countries. Rather more enigmatic in its origin is the supply by Bristol merchant John Smythe in 1539

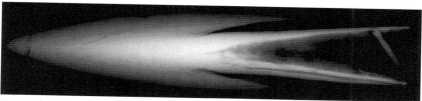

X-ray of a Type 12 arrowhead showing the pin used to secure it to the shaft. This pin had previously gone undetected. Photograph courtesy of Royal Armouries Museum.

to an arrowsmith and recorded in his ledger: "Richard Hickman of Ullerhampton, arrowed maker owith the 20 day of Janyver £6.6s.8d. which is for 1 ton of SS iron to be paide as Midsomer next comyng."

Demand evidently exceeded supply on occasion, however, and draconian measures were necessary. From Swindon's *History of Great Yarmouth*, we have the following:

> The Sheriff of Norfolk in the 42nd year of Edward III's reign (1369) is ordered to provide a certain number of arrows headed with steel for the king's use, and for the heading of these he is directed to seize all the flukes of anchors necessary for that purpose. We gather from this source that the metal from anchor flukes was held in great esteem for the heads of arrows as they were considered to make the best points.[16]

If this was national policy, one may only contemplate the views of those honest sea captains trading from the country's ports.

Glossary

Arbalest   One of a number of alternative descriptions for the crossbow.

Arquebus/harquebus   A sixteenth-century handgun.

Arrow pass   The position on the upper limb of a bow past which the arrow is first drawn and then released. It was often identified on antique longbows by the insertion of a piece of mother of pearl to protect the wood.

Basts or *bosses*   Target mats, usually of straw.

Brazed   Welded with brass. An eighteenth- and nineteenth-century method of fashioning recreational arrowheads and a medieval method of attaching sockets to war heads.

Cast   The velocity that a drawn bow imparts to a released arrow resulting from an efficient conversion of potential to kinetic energy.

Centenars/centeniers   A medieval term for those responsible for the muster and discipline of a unit of 100 men.

Chatelaine   The chain suspended from a woman's belt or sash from which are hung articles appropriate for her activity. A lady archer would have a quiver, scorebook, grease pot, and spare string suspended from her chatelaine.

Chrysalling or *crysaling*   Compression fractures occurring on the belly of a bow limb.

Close season   A period of time when an activity such as hunting is not practiced.

Cranequin   A medieval device for bracing, or spanning, a crossbow lath.

Decentenier   A medieval term for those responsible for the muster and discipline of a unit of ten men.

Deflexed   A condition in which the limbs of an unbraced bow are forward of the handle section.

Falchion   A curved sword, often associated with medieval archers for whom it was a principal side weapon.

Ferrule   A band or cap of metal.

Fishtail splicing   A method of joining two billets of wood to provide the maximum glued area.

Fistmele   A medieval measurement of approximately 6 1/2 inches. The distance

216

between the base of a clenched fist and the tip of an outstretched thumb. The correct length between a bowstring and the center of the bow when braced, or strung.

Footings Harder wood spliced into the foreshaft of an arrow to provide against breakage and to give forward weight. Also called piecings.

Fyrd An Anglo-Saxon levy for the purposes of war. The "great fyrd" was conscripted to fight up to, but not beyond, the shire border; and the "select fyrd" fought at the king's command. Each supported the house carles, bodyguard, or "hearth-troop" of a noble or of the king.

Gaffle A hand-operated device designed to assist the bracing (spanning) of a light crossbow.

Grains An element of Troy weight (one pennyweight equaled 24 grains). Multiples of grains were employed to determine and record the weight of nineteenth-century and earlier arrows, the weight then being converted to that of silver coinage.

Halberdiers Infantry who used the halberd, a pole weapon surmounted by an axe and a spike.

Handle riser Wood or cork affixed to or built into the center section of a longbow to provide thickness at the handle.

Hayward One who in early times had responsibility for the upkeep of "hays," or enclosures, into which the deer were driven for culling.

Herses or *hearses* An early French term for a triangular framework designed to hold candles. Used to describe the deployment of archers in battle.

House carls or *house carles* Also called "huscarls," "house men," or "hearth troop." A body of men bound by loyalty to a person of importance in Anglo-Saxon times.

Hundred court An administrative Anglo-Saxon court dispensing justice within an area of 100 hides. A hide was originally the measure of the acreage of land necessary to support one farming family.

Laager A defensive enclosure formed by wagons.

Livery arrow A basic, or sheaf, arrow. Produced by members belonging to the Worshipful Company of Fletchers, an early livery company.

Numbles The entrails of deer from which derives "numble," or "humble," pie.

Ogival Strictly speaking, the diagonal of a vault, but now taken to describe the combination of shallow (back) and deep (belly) convexity of a longbow's cross section.

Piles Originally the blunt arrowheads permitted to villagers within a hunting forest during medieval times. Presently the head of a recreational arrow.

Purging hole The hole in the upper part of a horn tip through which surplus glue is expelled when the tip is affixed to the bow limb. An archaic practice.

Riband   A ribbon or narrow band of woven material.

Rood   An archaic measurement of either 7 1/2 or 5 1/2 yards. The former defines distances shot at certain formal archery meetings in former times: 120, 90, 60, and 30 yards. The latter defines, among other things, the distance of a cricket pitch (22 yards).

Schiltrons   An early and primarily defensive formation of pikemen particularly associated with Scotland and Scottish armies.

Score   In the context used, a measurement of 20 yards. A convenient method of expressing distances between archery targets, or marks.

Self   Literally, by itself (i.e., with no additions). Used to describe a bow when it is of one piece of wood, although the word is now commonplace for two joined billets.

Sheaf arrow   A livery arrow.

Tang   The end of an arrowhead protruding into the shaft.

Tillering   The act of creating the correct curvature of a bow by bending it and working down small areas of the limbs. From this word comes both artillerer and artillery.

Verderer   An officer with responsibilities for the upkeep of forest law.

Vintinar/vintinier   A medieval term for one responsible for the muster and discipline of a unit of 20 men.

Whipper-in   A modern hunt official with responsibility for the hounds.

Whippiness   The relative elasticity, or spine, of an arrow shaft when bent (measured against a scale).

Whistling arrows   Arrows whose heads are adapted to make a noise when traveling through the air. Used in early times perhaps for warning.

Notes and References for Further Reading

Introduction

1. Mid-Dutch "nocke": The forward upper corner of some sails or the end of yard arm on a sail. *Concise Oxford English Dictionary*, Fowler ed., s.v. "nock."

2. "Cock feather" in this sense means the leading feather, as in the "cock horse," or the leading horse.

3. Obermaier y Wernert 1919. Hernandez-Pacheco 1924. *Paleolithiske Felkunst* (1921–1922), 177ff.

4. J. Bradbury, *The Battle of Hastings* (Stroud, Gloucestershire: Sutton, 1998).

5. Phillipe de Commynes, *The Memoirs of Philip de Commines*, ed. A. R. Scoble (London: 1855).

6. "All males between 15 and 60 shall keep arms, including bows." This is notable for its indication of the minimum age for prospective military service.

7. United Kingdom Public Record Office, Exchequer 101/426/8, no. 66.

Chapter 1

1. Die alt-und mittelsteinzeitliche Funde von Stellmoor, Neumünster. See also Gad Rausing, *The Bow, Some Notes on its Origin and Development* (Manchester: The Simon Archery Foundation, The University of Manchester Museum, 1997). Pages 33–34.

2. Ibid.

3. Paul E. Klopsteg, Clarence N. Hickman, and Forrest Nagler, *Archery, the Technical Side* (City: National Field Archery Association, 1947) and "Constructing the Bow with Rectangular Limb Section," *Sylvan Archer*, (1932).

4. Physicists C. N. Hickman and Paul E. Klopsteg have shown that a flatter shape with a greater width-to-depth ratio is actually more efficient, and this led to the development of the flat-sectioned, low-cambered bow of modern times. In vain have grim-faced traditionalists steeped in bow lore and with respect for the status quo maintained that the high-cambered D section served humans satisfactorily for many thousands of years.

5. J. G. D. Clarke, "Neolithic Bows from Somerset, England, and the Pre-History of Archery in Northern Europe," *Prehistoric Society Proceedings* 29, (1963).

6. Ibid., illustrations facing page 64 and the following (also page 90).

7. Rausing, *The Bow*.

8. Rausing, *The Bow*. The angular bow was made and used in Egypt during the second millennium BC. A simple self-stave was bent, perhaps by indirect heating through

steam, and the distinctive angular shape was created. The profile seemingly had an extended life, since a more sophisticated composite version saw royal service in Assyria a millennium later in the fifth century BC. I have had the opportunity personally to examine the performance of this type of bow, and I can report it to be both pleasant to handle and accurate to shoot.

9. C. J. Longman, Col. W. Walrond, et al., *The Badminton Library: Archery* (London: Longmans Green & Co., 1894).

10. Ibid., page 34.

11. Konrad Spindler, *The Man in the Ice* (London: Weidenfeld & Nicolson, 1994).

12. Saxton Pope, *Hunting with the Bow and Arrow* (New York: G. P. Putnams Sons, 1925). Reprint (City: Wolfe Publishing Co., 1991).

13. Geraldus Cambrensis (Gerald of Wales), *Itinerarium Kambriae*. See G. A. Hansard, *The Book of Archery* (London: Bohn, 1841).

14. Holger Riesch, *Pfeil und Bogen zur Merowingerzeit* (Stuttgart: Karfungel-Verlag, 2002).

15. Lars Jorgensen, Birger Storgaard, et al., *The Spoils of Victory: The North in the Shadow of the Roman Empire* (Copenhagen: National Museum, 2003).

16. Ibid. There is an enigmatic reference in a manifest of weaponry carried aboard the sixteenth-century vessel, *Trinity Smith*, based in Bristol, to a so-far unidentified "bowspere." Perhaps a similar weapon?

17. Edward S. Morse, "Ancient and Modern Methods of Arrow-Release," *Bulletin of the Essex Institute* 17, (Oct.–Dec. 1885).

18. For contrasting views, see Richard Glover, "English Warfare in 1066," *English Historical Review* 17, (1952) and C. Warren Hollister, *Anglo-Saxon Military Institutions* (Oxford: 1962).

Chapter 2

1. Attribution is uncertain but believed to be either Henri de Vegy, Seigneur de la Ferè, or Henri Ferrières.

2. Geoffrey Chaucer, *The Canterbury Tales*. The yeoman rides with the squire as an attendant upon the knight.

3. D. J. Stagg, *A Calendar of New Forest Documents AD 1244–1344* (Winchester: Hants County Council, 1979).

4. John Cummins, *Hound and Hawk* (London: Weidenfeld & Nicolson, 1988).

5. Edward, Duke of York, *The Master of Game*, ed. W. A. Baille-Grohman and F. Baillie-Grohman (London: 1904 and Edinburgh: 1909).

6. Commenced in 1387. Gunnar Tilander, ed., *Deduits de la chasse des Bestes Sauvages et des Oiseaux de praie* (London: Karlshamm Sweden, 1971).

7. Numbles are entrails. *A Geste of Robyn Hode*, vol. 32, first fytte.

8. Gunnar Tilander, "La Venerie de Twiti," (English version) *Cynegetica* 2, (1956).

9. To assail or assault with arrows. *Oxford English Dictionary*, Fowler ed., s.v. "bicker."

10. P. Stone, *Sir Gawain and the Green Knight*. Penguin Classics, A New Translation (London: Penguin Books, 1959).

11. Stagg, *A Calendar of New Forest Documents*.

12. Ibid.

13. Ibid.

14. Ibid.

15. Ibid.

16. Anno 19 H.VII cap. 11

17. H. D. H. Soar [Greybeard, pseud.], "Some Thoughts on Nestroque, An Agincourt Battle Command," *Journal of the Society of Archer Antiquaries* 44, (2001).

18. Virgin wax (i.e., the first year's wax from the hive).

19. Harduin de Fontaines-Guerin, Trésor de Venérie. See John Cummins, *Hound and Hawk* (London: Weidenfeld & Nicolson, 1988).

20. Stephen Knight, ed., *Robin Hood-The Forresters Manuscript* (Cambridge: Brewer, 1998).

21. "Robin Hood and the Foresters," verse 50.

22. "Robin Hood and the Fryer," verses 1 through 4.

Chapter 3

1. J. G. D. Clarke, "The Pre-History of Archery in North Western Europe," *Proceedings of the Prehistoric Society*, (1963).

2. Ibid.

3. Snorri Sturlason, *The Norse King Sagas* (London: Everyman's Library, J. M. Dent, 1930).

4. D. Simon Evans, *A Medieval Prince of Wales, The Life of Gruffydd ap Cynan* (Privately printed, Llanerch Press Enterprises, 1990).

5. Sturlason, *The Norse King Sagas*.

6. C. L. Crow, Maldon and Brunanburgh, *Two Old English Songs of Battle* (London: 1897).

7. Kevin Crossley Holland, *The Exeter Riddle Book*, riddle 23 (London: The Folio Society, 1968).

8. Sturlason, *The Norse King Sagas*.

9. A history of the lighter draw weights of Anglo-Saxon bows may lie with the Old English word for the index finger, or forefinger, which is *scytelfinger*, or "shooting finger." The identification of a single finger suggests the primary, or pinch, draw and release of finger and thumb (see Morse). In later times, when two, then three fingers were employed, the finger was redefined in Middle English as *towcher*, or "touching finger."

10. Lewis Thorpe, *The Bayeux Tapestry and The Norman Invasion* (London: The Folio Society, 1973).

11. C. Morgan and H. Muntz, eds., *Carmen de Hastingae Proelio* (Oxford: 1972). For relevant comment, see J. Bradbury, *The Battle of Hastings* (Stroud, Gloucestershire: Sutton Publishing, 1998).

12. Stephen Morillo, *Warfare under the Anglo-Norman Kings 1066–1135* (Oxford: Boydells, 1994).

13. Ibid.

14. Geraldus Cambrensis (Gerald of Wales), *Itinerarium Kambriae*. See G. A. Hansard, *The Book of Archery* (London: Bohn, 1841).

15. Ibid.

16. *Laws of Henry I, Archaionomia* (Cambridge, 1644). See T. S. R. Hardy, *Longbow* (Cambridge: Patrick Stevens, 1997).

17. Stagg, *A Calendar of New Forest Documents AD 1244–1344*.

18. R. B. Dobson and J. Taylor, *Rymes of Robin Hood* (Stroud, Gloucestershire: Suttons, 1976).

19. Ibid., "A Lytell Geste of Robyn Hode," first fytte.

20. Ibid.

21. One of a number of generic terms for what would be known from the fifteenth century onward as the longbow. From the context, Chaucer is clearly describing a simple weapon and not the complex recurved Turkish bow. The word "turk" is descriptive of the bow and its serious purpose. Other past names were "hand bow" (to distinguish it from the "foot bow," or crossbow), "bend bow" (from its shape when braced), "English bow" (in distinction from either the European bow with its different profile section or the crossbow), "lug" (correctly meaning a bell rope, or pull, which is to say, something requiring a strong pull), "crooked stick" (from the waywardness of the wood's grain), and "longbow" (once more, to distinguish it from the crossbow).

22. Janet E. Gendall, "The Arundel Archive of Arrows and Arrowheads," *Society of Archer Antiquaries Journal* 44, (2001).

Chapter 4

1. A replica crossbow contemporary to the period with a 300-pound draw-weight lath spanned by a gaffle achieved 150 yards in my presence.

2. Morillo, *Warfare under the Anglo-Norman Kings*.

3. M. Strickland, ed., *Anglo-Norman Warfare* (Woodbridge, Suffolk: Boydells, 1994).

4. Sir Charles W. C. Oman, *The Art of War in the Middle Ages*, revised ed. (London: Oxford University Press, 1953).

5. John E. Morris, *The Welsh Wars of Edward I* (London: Oxford Clarendon Press, 1901). Reprint (Privately printed, Llanerch Press, 1994).

6. R. B. Dobson and J. Taylor, *Rymes of Robin Hood*, revised ed. (Stroud, Gloucestershire: Sutton Publishing, 1997). "Robin Hood and the Valiant Knight." Although late in date (1777), the possibility that the anonymous author had tapped a strain of folklore remains, and the theme should not be discounted entirely.

7. William Seymour, *Battles in Britain* (London: Sidgwick & Jackson). Contains a concise account of this battle. See also H. D. H. Soar, *Of Bowmen and Battles* (Tolworth, Surrey: Glade Publishing, 2003).

8. Ibid.

9. Kelly DeVries, *Infantry Warfare in the Early Fourteenth Century* (Woodbridge, Suffolk: Boydell, 1996). Contains an explicit account of this engagement.

10. Clifford J. Rogers, *The Wars of Edward III, Sources and Interpretations* (Woodbridge, Suffolk: Boydell, 1999).

11. Ibid.

12. H. D. H. Soar, "Ordinances of the Bowyers and Fletchers of Bristowe," *Journal of the Society of Archer Antiquaries* 32, (1989).

13. "Indentures of a Bowyers Apprentice of York," *Surtees Society* 120, (1911–1912). Pages 54–55.

14. Barbara Megson, *Such Goodly Company* (London: privately printed by the Worshipful Company of Bowyers). A concise history of the Worshipful Company of Bowyers.

15. J. E. Oxley, *The Fletchers and Longbowstringmakers of London* (London: privately printed by the Worshipful Company of Bowyers). A detailed account of the histories of both companies.

16. Rogers, *The Wars of Edward III*.

Chapter 5

1. See ch. 4, n. 16.

2. Janet E. Gendall, "The Arundel Archive of Arrows and Arrowheads," *Journal of the Society of Archer Antiquaries* 44, (2001).

3. A vintenar controlled 20 men, a centenar, 100.

4. Rogers, *The Wars of Edward III*. King Edward's own account "From Caen through Calais," in Coxe, ed., *The Black Prince* (Edinburgh: Chandos Herald, 1842).

5. DeVries, *Infantry Warfare in the Early Fourteenth Century*. See "The Wars of Edward III: The Crécy Chevauchée."

6. From an inventory of an abbot's ledgers, circa 1460, we have "1 barrel full of osmond bars." Osmond bars were a superior quality of Baltic iron used for arrowheads.

7. A muster document for the parish of Shere in the county of Surrey compiled in 1583 lists ten archers, of whom two were of the "first sort" and five were of the "second sort." Simple mathematics suggests that three were of the third sort. One speculates about their contribution.

8. Henri de Wailly, *Crécy, the Anatomy of a Battle* (Poole, Dorset: Blandford Press, 1981).

9. J. Barry Davies, *The Freemen and Ancient Borough of Llantrisant* (Privately printed, 1989). Chapter 3 contains a brief account, including an alternative interpretation.

10. The reference to "cross-bolts" is unclear and not presently understood. An inventory of archery equipment taken in 1422 includes cross-nocked arrows, providing a similar mystery.

11. Recorded by Geoffrey le Baker, a contemporary chronicler from Oxfordshire.

12. Richard Barber, *Edward, Prince of Wales and Aquitaine* (London: Boydell & Brewer, 1978).

13. Clifford J. Rogers, *War Cruel and Sharp* (Woodbridge, Suffolk: Boydell, 2000). Provides a comprehensive account of this engagement.

14. *Oxford Dictionary* (Complete version). *Oxford Dictionary of Dialect*, Fowler ed., s.v. "byker."

15. Ibid.

16. Arthur Machen, *The Bowmen* (London: Simpkin, Marshall, Hamilton, Kent & Co., Ltd., 1915). This suggests, among other things, a solution to the reported phenomena.

17. Anne Curry, *The Battle of Agincourt, Sources and Interpretations*, (London: Boydell Press, 2000), 95. Brut Version 1478–1479, Lambeth MS.84. "On that Day the Frenchman saw St. George in the air fighting against the Frenchman."

18. Curry, *The Battle of Agincourt*.

19. Oxley, *The Fletchers and Longbowstringmakers of London*. The company's unambiguous motto *Nec habeo: nec careo: nec cuo* (I have not: I lack not: I care not) deserves our casual attention for the stark contrast of its message to the more ostentatious choices of its companion companies of bowyers ("Crécy, Poitiers, and Agincourt") and fletchers ("True and Sure"). The stringers surely knew that without their skill, these proud boasts would have come to nothing. What merit there is in understatement!

20. H. D. H. Soar, "The Bowyers and Fletchers of Bristowe," *Journal of the Society of Archer Antiquaries* 32, (1989).

21. Col. Alfred H. Burne, *The Agincourt War* (London: Eyre and Spottiswood, 1956). Offers a detailed account of the campaign.

22. James Dunlop, "Papers Relative to the Royal Guard of Scottish Archers in France" (Presented to the Maitland Club, Edinburgh, 1835). A source of much information in French and Scots English of this body, its formation, and subsequent problems. The residual strength is said to have been incorporated within the British army.

23. Alan Boardman, *The Battle of Towton* (Stroud, Gloucestershire: W. Sutton, 1994).

24. Veronica Fiorato, *Blood Red Roses—The Archaeology of a Mass Grave from the Battle of Towton AD 1464* (Oxford: Oxbow Books, 2000). Besides a fully detailed osteopathological analysis of over 50 complete and incomplete skeletal remains, this work also contains a historical account of the battle.

Chapter 6

1. There is some dispute concerning the site of this battle. Recent academic research has thrown doubt on the tradition of Ambion Hill in favor of a position closer to the village of Atherstone some miles away. Postulation rests upon monies paid by Henry VII as recompense to parishes in the vicinity for losses to harvest occasioned "by us and our company at our late victorious field." Parishes include those of Atherstone, Witherley, Atterton, Fenny Drayton, and Mancetter.

2. E. F. Jacob, *The Oxford History of England* (Oxford: Clarendon Press, 1997), summarizes the battle. J. R. Lander, *The Wars of the Roses* (Stroud, Gloucestershire: Sutton Publishing, 1996), provides a more detailed account, drawing upon source documents.

3. According to Strutt's *Sports and Pastimes of the People of England*, both "closh" and "kayles" were forms of nine-pin bowling; the first was played with a stick and the second, with a ball. "Half-bowls" required a biased ball and pins. "Hand-in and hand-out" is not described by Strutt and therefore remains a mystery. "Chequer boards" is a form of draughts.

4. Those who excelled with the bow were said to "shoot like Arthur." Posthumously, his name was perpetuated by Prince Arthur's Knights, first a Henrician but later a "reformed" Elizabethan archery society.

5. David Smurthwaite, *Battlefields in Britain* (London: Guild Publishing, 1984). Supplies a topographical summary of the engagement based upon modern ordnance maps. William Seymour, *Battles in Britain* (London: Book Club Associates, 1975). Provides a more detailed account.

6. Ibid.

7. The Mary Rose Archaeological Report, Part Three, (Ordnance and Archery Material) (The Mary Rose Trust, in press).

8. Held privately at Archers Hall, Edinburgh, by the Royal Company of Archers.

9. See n. 7.

10. Cdr. W. F. Paterson, "*Mary Rose*, a Preliminary Report" and "*Mary Rose*, a Second Report," *Journal of the Society of Archer Antiquaries* 23 and 24, (1980–1981).

11. Hardy, *Longbow*.

12. Megson, *Such Goodly Company*. Appendix III: (Sixteenth Century) Bowyers and apprentices.

13. Margaret Rule, *The Mary Rose, the Excavation and Raising of Henry VIII's Flagship*, new ed. (London: Book Club Associates, 1984).

14. S. Knighton and David Loades, *Letters from the Mary Rose* (Stroud, Gloucestershire: Sutton Publishing, 2002).

15. W. F. Paterson, "An Elizabethan Longbow," *Journal of the Society of Archer Antiquaries* 17, (1974).

16. Sir John Smythe, *Certain Discourses Military* (New York: Folger Shakespeare Library, Cornell University Press, 1964).

17. P. L. Pratt and T. S. R. Hardy, "The Arrow Found in Westminster Abbey," *Journal of the Society of Archer Antiquaries* 18, (1975).

18. These will be described in detail within the forthcoming archaeological report of the *Mary Rose* Trust.

19. Taken from a replica of the Cowdray House engraving destroyed by fire.

20. Lindsay Boynton, *Elizabethan Militia* (London: Routledge and Kegan Paul, 1967).

21. Somerset County Record Officer, Taunton, Somerset.

22. Roger Ascham, *Toxophilus, the Schole or Partitions of Shooting* (1544), second book. Reprint (London: Arber, Edward, 1868) and other reprints.

23. See n. 20.

24. See n. 22.

25. Ascham, *Toxophilus*, first book.

26. See n. 20.

27. Compiled by R. S London, 1596. Printed by Richard Johnes at the Rose and Crown, next above St. Andrews Church in Holburne.

28. Richard Robinson, *The Aunciente Order, Societie and Unitie Laudable, of Prince Arthure and his Knightly Armoury of the Round Table* (London: 1583).

> *A rare devise I will set out, to strengthen man and bow,*
> *And when the plain devise thereof the world shall see and know,*
> *The Bow shall come again in fame and win his wonted grace*
> *Look out of hand for my discourse. Till then come, bow in place.*

The reference is enigmatic, but I believe is relevant to Neade's subsequent "invention" of coupled bow and pike. Neade and Churchyard were archers and contemporaries; there is every likelihood that they knew each other and thus would have discussed the bow's decline.

29. "Certain discourses military concerning the forms and effect of divers sorts of weapons and there very important matters military greatly mistaken by divers of our men of war in these days. And chiefly of the musket, the caliver and the long-bow, as also of the great sufficiency, excellency, and wonderful effects of archers, ..." Part of an extensive title.

30. "Certain Discourses written by Humfry Barwicke, Gentleman, with his opinion concerning the severall discourses written by Sir John Smith [sic] and Sir Roger Williams, Knightes and their contraries opinions, touching Muskets and other fierie weapons, and the long-bowe. With other divers points of war by some others afore time mistaken (previously mistaken)."

31. See L. A. Govett, compiler, *The King's Book of Sports* (London: Elliott, Stock, 1870). A history of the declarations of King James I and King Charles I concerning the usage of lawful sports on Sundays.

32. "The Double Armed Man by the new Invention, with several Portraitures proper for the Bow and Pike."

33. From a contemporary account of an incident during the Civil War, August, 1642. "At the entry to the town (Hertford) stood the whole Trained Band in a full Body placed in a war-like equipage. The Court of Guards where he was demanded of the word which was 'Prevention.' Having given this he was then conducted to the second watch, being a Company of Pikes with Bows and Arrows."

34. In a Commission of Array for Leicestershire issued in June 1642, by royal proclamation, bowmen were to be trained to use bows and arrows. They were to be armed with their own, and not other weapons. Thomas Carlyle alludes to the commission in volume 1 of *Cromwell's Letters and Speeches*, 1846 (page 153). In 1643, Cromwell's men were concerned to learn of the king's intention to set up a store in Oxford "onley for Bowes and Arrows which they intend to make use of against oure Horse, and that all the Bowyers, Fletchers and Arrowhead makers that they can possibly get they imploy and set to work for that purpose."

35. Charles E. Whitelaw, *Scottish Arms Makers* (Edinburgh: Arms and Armour Press, 1977).

36. David Stevenson, *Highland Warrior—Alasdair MacColla and the Civil Wars* (Edinburgh: Saltire Press, 1994). Contains explicit accounts of this battle, with others engaged by MacColla and Montrose against Covenanter forces and others during the 1640s.

Chapter 7

1. Fifth fytte, verses 282–285.

2. Holt, J. C. Robin Hood. (London: Thames & Hudson, 1982.)

3. Thomas Roberts, *The English Bowman* (London: Printed for the author, 1802; reprint Shumway, York: Penn, 1973). Section II, chapter 10.

4. A social game with practical overtones. Shooting to clear an overhead obstacle would be of value in a wooded environment for both hunting and personal protection. To my

knowledge, it is not described anywhere else in either academic or vernacular terms. It has a near parallel in "shooting beneath the screen," an early French practice. See also *L'art d'archerie.*

5. Church Wardens Accounts, Croscombe Parish, Somerset, England.

6. Joseph Strutt, *Sports and Pastimes of the English People* (London: Thomas Tegg, 1838). Book II, chapter 1, sections 10 and 14.

7. "May use and exercise the shotyng of their Long-Bows, Cros-bowes and their Hand-gonnes, at Almaner (all manner) of Markys, and Buttys, and at the Game of the POPY-MAYE (sic), and other Game or Games." HVIII. 29

8. Cordier, De Bertier, and Guglielmini, *Le Tir a l'Arc* (Paris: Librairie Hatchette, 1900). Chapter 3, section 2.

9. Letter Book N. ff. 169b-170 (1521) City of London Guildhall.

10. Roberts, *The English Bowman.*

11. Henri Stein, *Archers d'Autrefois, Archers d'Aujourd'hui* (Paris: Longuet, 1925). Appendix 7 *The Archer's Register,* 1903. Part 5 contains an English translation.

12. Ascham, *Toxophilus.*

13. Anno 15 H8 Cap:7

14. Richard Robinson, *The Auncient Order, Societie and Unitie Laudable of Prince Arthure and his Knightly Armoury of the Round Table* (London: 1583). "Third Assertion, English Historical."

15. Bath Archaeological Trust: 4 Circus, Bath BA1 2EW North East Somerset. Monograph, Acton Court.

16. H. D. H. Soar, "Tudor Longbows, a Comparative Study," *Journal of the Society of Archer Antiquaries* 34, (1991).

17. See n. 10.

18. Soar, "The Bowyers and Fletchers of Bristowe."

19. Coventry Museum, Godiva City Exhibition. Accession no. 1949/227/204, seq. 0590, film 96 20/04/94.

20. Richard Robinson, *Learned and True Assertion of the Original Life, Acts and Death, of the most Noble, Valiant and Renowned Prince Arthur, King of Great Britaine* (London: 1582).

21. See n. 13.

22. Alan Sutton, **Stow:** *A Survey of London* (1598), revised first ed., facsimile (Dover: N.H., 1603). In modern facsimile 1994.

23. Sir William Wood, *The Bowman's Glory, or Archery Revived* (1682), facsimile ed. (London: SR Publishers, 1969). "Then last of his Train (the Earl of Buckley) came the Baron STIRROP, whose costly Stake will be in memory after he is dead, now standing at Mile-end."

24. In June 1583 the Privy Council directed the Lord Mayor of London to improve observance of the laws governing archery. The September procession of archers and gathering in Hoxton Fields may well have stemmed from this directive.

25. It is difficult to be exact about the amounts in modern terms. Within my memory, 5 shillings were equivalent to $1 in the 1930s. The first prize may therefore have amount-

ed to something under $11. Late sixteenth-century wages were not overgenerous, how-ever, and depending upon the contestant and his circumstances, 53 shillings and 4 pence may have represented a full year's pay. It is no great surprise then that "thirty hundred" would-be winners competed.

Chapter 8

1. Capt. G. A. Raikes, *History of the Honourable Artillery Company*, vol. I (London: Bentley, 1878).

2. E. B and J. J., *An Alphabetical Table of the Names of Everie Marke within the same Fields with their true distances both by the Map and dimensuration by the Line* (London: RF, 1601).

3. See n. 1.

4. Joseph Ritson, *Robin Hood, Poems, Songs and Ballads* (1795). Reprinted (London: Nimmo, 1832).

5. Ascham, *Toxophilus*.

6. Anon., *The Ancient Honour of the City of London Restored and Recovered* (London: Guildhall, 1663).

7. Richard Seymour, *The Compleat Gamester* (London: 1721). Chapter 3. The accuracy of this statement must remain in doubt. Encroachment had by then seriously reduced the land available for the purpose. I understand that the comment cannot be verified from records.

8. Partridge, James, *Ayme for Finsburie Archers* (London: 1628).

9. Wood, *The Bowmans Glory*.

10. Robert Shotterel and Thomas Durfey, subtitled "An Heroic Poem, being a description of the use and Noble Vertues of the Long-Bow, in our last Age, so famous for the many great and admired Victories won by the English and other Warlike Nations over most of the World. Exhorting all brave Spirits to the banishment of Vice by the use of so Noble and Healthful an Exercise."

11. Ben Hird, *The Antient Scorton Silver Arrow, the story of the oldest sporting event in Britain* (sic) (London: The Society of Archer Antiquarians, 1972).

12. James Balfour Paul, *History of the Royal Company of Archers* (Edinburgh: Blackwood, 1825 [or 1875?]). John Hay Beith, *The Royal Company of Archers 1676–1951* (Edinburgh: Blackwood, 1951).

13. H. D. H. Soar, "Seventeenth Century Archery," *Journal of the Society of Archer Antiquaries* 35, (1992).

14. A. G. Credland, "The Longbow in the 16th and 17th Centuries," *Journal of the Society of Archer Antiquaries* 32, (1989).

15. H. D. H. Soar, "Uriah Streater, Apprentice Fletcher," *Journal of the Society of Archer Antiquaries* 42, (1999).

16. Neil Beeby, ed., *Records and Reminiscences of Archery & Archery Medals, Aberdeen Grammar School 1664–1699* (Edinburgh: privately printed, 1906). Reprint, 2002.

17. Eli Hargrove, *Anecdotes of Archery 1792* (London: Facsimile Tabard Press, 1970).

18. *British Archer Magazine* (April–May edition, 1964). Page 241.

19. Archery practice was still nominally required by statute law, and other Cheshire villages paid at least lip service to its continuation. Sevenoaks and Newton-by-Dewsbury kept their archery butts in repair well into the eighteenth century. Those at Sevenoaks were repaired as late as 1727 when an account "for fitling (repairing) shuting butts 6 pence" was presented for payment. Those at Newton were kept in trim even longer until 1754. Laws requiring this practice were not repealed until the 1860s.

20. Longman and Walrond, *Archery*.

21. Christopher Hassall, *Songs from Bow-Meetings of the Society of the Royal British Bowmen 1819–1822* (Taunton, Somerset: privately printed, 1997).

22. See n. 12.

23. Richard Oswald Mason, *Pro Aris et Focis* (for hearth and home) 1798 (London: Facsimile Tabard Press, 1970). Subtitled "Consideration of the Reasons that exist for reviving the use of the Long-Bow with the Pike. In aid of the Measures brought forward by His Majesty's Ministers for the Defence of the Country."

Chapter 9

1. Thomas Waring, *A Treatise on Archery, or the Art of Shooting with the Long Bow* (London: privately printed, 1830). "When an archer has shot, he must turn to his left and go behind the person he is shooting with, who then in his turn comes forward and shoots his Arrow, which having done, he turns to the left, and the first Archer comes forward again and shoots his second arrow, and so in rotation." Grand National Archery Meeting Rules: 1844 York. "All Archers previously to shooting shall stand on the left behind the Target; each Archer shooting shall advance not exceeding a bow length in front of the Target, and after shooting his three arrows, shall return to the right and behind the Target." These arrangements contrast curiously. While in 1814, archers moved counterclockwise when they had shot, 30 years later, this had been reversed. One cannot but think that the later system was the more natural.

2. Ibid., rule 12. "Gentlemen must not draw their arrows from the Target until the Marker shall have called to the Gentleman to declare his Hits and shall have marked the same."

3. George Agar Hansard (Gwent Bowman), *Book of Archery being the Complete History and Practice of the Art* (London: Bohn, 1841). Section 1, Juvenile Bowmen.

4. Records of the Woodmen of Arden from 1785 to 1885 (Private circulation, 1885). "October 10th 1788, the Silver Arrow given by the Countess of Aylesford was (first) shot for at 9 score yards, and in 3 Ends was won by Mr. W. Dilke."

5. Roberts was also unimpressed by the performance of a bow marked "Robin Hood." Curiously, the author recently acquired a bow thus marked, having contemporary (1802) associations with Forest Hall, Meriden. It is entirely possible that this is the bow to which Roberts penciled note refers.

6. The inscription reads, "PRIZE BOW given by Dr. Nathaniel Spens upon the 26th May 1810. The Anniversary of his 60th year as an Archer. Won By Mr. James Millar Advocate." Miller had been elected to the Royal Company of Archers on July 7, 1800.

7. Paul, *The History of the Royal Company of Archers*. Peter Muir began his employment in 1828 and served for 50 years. He was national champion in 1845, 1847, and 1863.

8. *The United Bowmen of Philadelphia 1828–1953* (Philadelphia: privately printed, 1953). Commemorating the 125th anniversary. Also *The United Bowmen of Philadelphia 1828–1978* (Philadelphia: privately printed, 1978). Commemorating the 150th anniversary.

9. A poster advertising this event is preserved in the Guildhall Library. Accession no. GR.1.3.5.

10. *The Archer's Register*, (1864). Page 56, list of 146 existing societies in England and Wales; page 125, list of 22 Irish societies; page 136, list of 9 Scottish societies.

11. A woman's bow; the back is of hickory and the belly is of greenheart. The stringing horn is faced forward and embodies a purging hole, reflecting practice by Waring the Younger.

12. In business between 1841 and 1844 (John) and 1845 and 1846 (David). They jointly owned the Abbey Green Tavern in St. John's Wood, London, with its associated archery ground.

13. In 1918, this firm advertised the provision of "accessories for racquets, tennis, croquet, archery, or any game, sport or recreation in addition to the manufacture of bicycles, velocipedes, motor cycles, and motor cars."

14. Longman and Walrond, *Archery*.

15. *The Archer's Register*, (1865). Costing 10s. 10d. (post free). The advertisement claimed "a few hours suffice to carry Reconnoiterer to almost the remotest Post Town in the Kingdom."

16. Printed by the Montpelier Library, Cheltenham, 1859. See W. Butt, Ford on Archery (London: Longmans, 1887).

17. In one of his *Scribner's* articles, Maurice mentions a curious experience that happened while he and Will were practicing one day. A tramp approached them and, after watching them for a while, said, "Archery is a noble sport." This was readily agreed, and the man continued sadly, "On Brighton sands I have seen good shooting, and I have shot there myself." Intrigued, the brothers set their bows down, and at the stranger's polite request, they allowed him a shot. At 40 yards, he drew up, and his first arrow centered in the gold; then after politely thanking the brothers, he went on his way. Now, Brighton (in England) is the place where Horace Alfred Ford, 12 times English champion, honed his skill. How intriguing it would be if this tramp, who claimed to be a gentleman, had perhaps met, or even shot with, the great man.

18. Patented in 1879 by Messrs. W. H. Wright and G. L. Thorne. The associated arrow was itself unusual, having a metal rod inserted at its foot to "improve balance" and having hair cloth "wings" fitted in place of fletchings.

Chapter 10

1. James Duff, *Bows and Arrows* (New York: Macmillan, 1927). "Jimmy" Duff, of Edinburgh, served an apprenticeship in Scotland under the guidance of William Fergie Senior and "Dick" Thompson of the Thompson family, bowyers to the Woodmen of Arden. Afterward, he served as bow maker to James Buchanan before emigrating to the United States where he was to establish a thriving business.

2. *The Archer's Register* (1904–1905). Provides a full account of the event.

3. Albert, le Comte De Bertier, V. Cordier, and A. Gugliemini, *Le Tir a l'Arc* (Paris: Librairie Hachette, 1900). Chapter 11. Also *The Archer's Register* (1904–1905). Offers an account in English.

4. *The Archer's Register* (1908–1909). Provides a full account of the archery competition.

5. A cursory study of the introductory edition of *Archery News* reveals that without exception, women archers outnumbered men by ten to one. Archery had become an activity dominated by women.

6. H. D. H. Soar, "John Spreat, a Bath Bowyer," *Journal of the Society of Archer Antiquaries* 36, (1993).

7. Mrs. J. Dunton was awarded a prize of £17 for achieving third gross hits (95, with 403 scored) at the 1856 championship event. In 1857, she achieved best gold at 50 yards and was awarded £5.

8. Robert Rhode, *History of the Federation Internationale de Tir a l'Arc* (Minneapolis: VanWold Stevens, 1931).

9. Arrows with blunt tips were chalked on their ends to identify hits on the target face. This practice was also employed in Japanese indoor archery to avoid damaging delicate walls.

10. Dr. Robert Potter Elmer, *Target Archery* (New York: Knoff, 1946). Chapter 4.

11. P. Klopsteg, C. Hickman, and F. Nagler, *Archery the Technical Side* (United States National Field Archery Association, 1947). Contains all articles originally published within these sources.

12. W. Searle, *The Duoflex Bow* (Durham: privately printed, 2003). Exemplifies the construction of both duoflex and moduflex bows.

13. Ascham, *Toxophilus*.

14. *The Archer's Register* (1881). In memoriam, James Spedding, page 186.

15. Arthur W. Lambert, *Modern Archery* (New York: Barnes & Co. 1929). Chapter 30, "Sighting Devices."

16. Ibid.

17. Dave and Cia Craft, *Teaching of Archery* (New York: Barnes & Co. 1936). The survey was conducted during 1935. While advising that novices should be acquainted with the purpose of the bow sight, the Crafts added, a little curiously, "even though in many cases they would be unable to afford them."

18. Robert Rhodes, *Archery Champions* (Minneapolis: VanWold Stevens, 1963).

19. The firm advertised these in 1912 as "A Long-Felt Want, ALDRED'S PATENT UNBREAKABLE ALUMINIUM NOCKS. A proved success. As used by Olympic Gold Medalist 1908, and the Championess 1911, and 1912." Added, perhaps as an afterthought, "IN NO WAY DAMAGES THE STRINGS." This possibly in answer to rival bowyer Thompson who had dismissed them as "string cutters."

20. *British Archer Magazine*, (April–May edition, 1951). Page 17.

21. The Deer Act of 1963. "An Act to provide close seasons for deer, to prohibit the killing and taking of deer by certain devices and at certain times. 31st July 1963" Article 3 1 Subject to Sections 10 and 11 of this Act, if any person . . . (c) uses for the purpose

of injuring or killing or taking any deer . . . (ii) any arrow, spear or similar missile. He shall be guilty of an offense. NB. Sections 10, and 11 exclude from the Act the taking or killing of deer on private land, providing the owner has agreed in writing. The act did not apply in Scotland or Northern Ireland.

22. Export may have accounted for much of hunting tackle business. In January 1930, a private letter from James Izzard (then manager of F. H. Ayres, Ltd., Archery Department) mentions, "I have many Clients who hunt only with Bow and Arrow in all parts of the World. I have pictures from Stockholm and California. . . . and from Poland this week, a request to send three more Hunting Bows, up to 65 lbs."

Appendix

1. J. G. Evans, "Stonehenge: A Beaker Age Burial," *Wiltshire Archaeological and Natural History Magazine* 78, (1984). Pages 17–19.

2. The gridiron is the symbol of the Worshipful Company of Girdlers, a London livery company that merged with the Wiredrawers Company during the sixteenth century. "Sunday Christ" is a piece of Christian symbolism that shows Christ attacked by the tools of his trade. A dire warning to artisans and others against working on a holy day. It is understood to have been particularly conspicuous in England's south-west and suggests the possible origin of its wearer.

3. An excellent example has been recovered from the moat previously surrounding Stogursey Castle in Somerset in 1983, and this may be viewed in Taunton Museum. A full sleeve of unidentified leather (perhaps calf), plain and without visible ornament, it was held in position by four straps passed through an incision on the upper outside edge and perhaps secured by simple foldover knots. Length is 8 inches; width is 10 inches tapering to 7 inches.

4. An example of an ivory bracer can be seen at Southend Museum, Essex. Accession no. 636-8. Another (MR81A0815) will be described within the *Mary Rose* Trust Archaeological Report, part 3.

5. Ascham, *Toxophilus*, second book.

6. H. D. H. Soar, "More Notes on Quivers," *Journal of the Society of Archer Antiquaries* 40, (1999). Curiously, the ancient Cornish word for a quiver is "goon." A Concordance of archery references within the early Robin Hood poems and ballads shows there to be just one reference to a quiver (quequer).

7. A. G. Credland, "Arrow Spacers—A Note on Sixteenth Century Archery," *Archery International Magazine* 2, no. 9, (1982).

8. Dr. Margaret Rule, *The Mary Rose* (London: Book Club Associates, 1982). Pages 176–179. These will be placed in context within the *Mary Rose* Trust Archaeological Report, Part 3, in course of publication.

9. Henri Stein, *Archers d'Autrefois: Archers d'Aujourd'hui* (Paris: Longuet, 1925). Appendix 7 Neuvième Chapitre. For English translation, see *The Archer's Register*, (1903). Pages 264–274.

10. In August of 1540, Sir John Smith, a wealthy Bristol shipowner, purchased "ten sheaves of arrowes with casses and girdles." Bristol fletchers at that time included John Williams and John Badnall.

11. Traditionally a pair of arrows consisted of three. At some unknown period, the third arrow came to be shot and modern practice emerged.

12. "Oxford" to commemorate the venue of GNA meetings, "Wiltshire" in recognition of the then highly regarded Society of Wiltshire Archers (now a tennis club). Sewn within the shooting coats worn by the Woodmen of Arden and the Royal Company of Archers on formal occasions or latterly carried in a shooting jacket pocket. It was *infra dig* for any Victorian or Edwardian gentleman to be seen in his braces.

13. *Medieval Archaeology* 40, (1996).

14. The recovery of one of these heads from a Free Grammar School strongly suggests recreational practice.

15. Roger Ascham. "They (the arrowhead makers) made a certaine kinde of heades, which men call Hie Rigged, Creased, or Shouldred heades, or Silver-spoon heades. These heades be good both to kepe a length withall, and also to perche (cut through) a winde withall."

16. To place the circumstance in historical context, 1369 saw the grand *chevauchée* of John of Gaunt who, having landed at Calais, marched with little or no opposition to Harfleur and back.

Index

Bourgthéroulde (1124) 59, 60, 68
Crécy (1346) 80-82
Evesham (1265) 64, 65
Falkirk (1298) 66, 67
Flodden (1513) 99
Gate Fulford (1066) 43
Gerberoy (1079) 46
Halidon Hill (1333) 70
Hastings (1066) 44, 45, 58
Maldon, (991) 42
Mulroy (1688) 117
Pinkie Cleugh (1547) 100
Poitiers (1356) 86, 87
Stamford Bridge (1066) 43
Stirling Bridge (1297) 65, 66
Tippermuir (1644) 117
Towton (1461) 94, 96
Verneuil (1424) 93, 94
battle axe, Saxon 45
Bayeux Tapestry 44, 45, 208
belly wedge, Scottish 143, 154, 156
bicker'd, bickering 26, 90, 104
Black Train, archers of 108, 132
bow making
    American 182, 184
    17th c. 143
    18th c. Scottish 154, 165
    19th c. procedures 172, 174
bow & pike, exercise 157
bowmen (see archers)
bows
    and arrows, carrying forbidden 49
    Anglo-Saxon 58
    birding 18, 30
    boga (foga) 42, 42
    bough 14, 53, 71
    broad-backed 127
    carriage, hinged 144, 146
    cast of 161
    chrysalling (damage to) 165
    compound 203
    crooked stick, poetic term ix, 54
    crossbow (arbalest) 29, 45, 59, 80
    deflexed 161
    dimensions of 55, 100, 124, 174
    draw weight of 71, 89, 101, 167, 169
    duoflexed 8, 194
    ears, nonworking 194
    eastern composite 47
    English 18
    flat 194, 198
    hand 28, 40, 45, 58, 71, 92

jointed, 164
juvenile 178
medieval 77
piked, or shortened 104
recreational 18, 138, 167-170
recurved 8, 199
reflexed 77
self 7, 11, 14, 165
steel 170, 190-192, 198, 199
stick 4, 5, 8
strength of 51, 111
tensile and compressive properties 193
Turkish 18, 54
versus gun 109
war 15, 18, 39, 44, 47, 99
war, last use of 117
war, replica 102
warlike weapon, revival as 134, 157
Welsh 49
with pike 112, 113, 157
yumi 162
Bowstringmakers, Company of 92, 93
bowstrings x, 15, 19, 27, 72, 93, 116, 136,
    192
bow woods
    bamboo 162, 184, 202
    beefwood-backed hickory 172
    boxwood 19
    ebony 152
    elm 4, 11, 49
    fustic 164
    greenheart 169
    lancewood 152, 164, 177
    lemonwood, backed 167, 172
    pine 3, 11
    ruby 152, 162, 171
    ruby wood, backed hickory, 172
    wych elm/wych hazel 49, 102
    yew ix, 5, 6, 11, 12, 19, 54, 172
bowyercraft, bowyery 72, 73
bowyers & fletchers separated 74
Bowyers, London Co. of 72, 168, 169
bowyers of Bristol (Bristowe) 127
bowyery, Scottish 116
bowyery, penalties for poor work 72
bowyery, 17th c. 143
bracers 9, 104, 192, 204-207
bracing height 19
Buchanan dips 12
butts 71, 118, 120, 126, 128, 141, 186

Calais, aborted capture of 78, 80, 85

Acknowledgments

To acknowledge the encouragement I have received from so many antiquarian and other archery colleagues by name would require a list beyond the realistic limit of space. It has been the kind comments I have received for my first book *Of Bowmen and Battles* that have provided the catalyst for this second, an attempt at a history of that most charismatic of weapons, the English longbow.

Above all, recognition is due to the late Richard Galloway, bow maker extraordinaire, whose skill created a particular "crooked stick," the inspiration for the title of this book. My thanks to Bruce H. Franklin, my publisher, who met my pedantry with equanimity; to Christine Liddie, my editor, who prepared my manuscript; and to Veronica-Mae, whose patience kept me on course. Thanks to Tony Lockwood who responded to my requests for photography with fortitude; to Wolfgang Bartl for his imaginative drawings; to Mark Stretton for his help with arrowheads; and Jan Gendall for her encouragement. Much appreciated was the cooperation of David Starley of the Royal Armouries and Martin Wright of the Salisbury and South Wiltshire Museum. Also acknowledged is the Society of Archer Antiquaries.